本书受两个基金赞助：

教育部人文社会科学规划基金项目"学术英语写作任务认知负荷分层设置研究" 编号：23YJA740034

上海对外经贸大学优秀出版基金

王春岩 著

# 任务型学术英语写作认知负荷的调节策略研究

EAP

上海三联书店

# 目　录

## 第三部分　认知负荷理论下的课程设置

# Table of Contents

**Part III　Cognitive theory guided curriculum**

# 序 言

　　我国大学英语教学从通用英语转向学术英语开始于2013年，发起者为上海市的高等院校。在高等教育国际化背景下，这些院校希望培养大学生具备国际期刊学术发表的能力。学术英语教学改革很快影响了国内其他地区的高校，并在2020年教育部颁布的大学英语教学指南中得到了肯定。受国际主流学术英语教学中"任务型"教学模式的影响，基于"研究任务"的学术英语写作教学模式具有广泛的影响地位。该模式下，学习者自主探索研究性课题，完成研究性报告写作。但是教师和学习者很快发现，学术英语实施中，以探索性学习为主的教学模式难度非常大。学术英语写作任务从外语语言能力、专业知识、学术研究能力方面均对学习者形成了挑战。在缺乏专业知识和英语阅读能力的背景下，大学生学习阅读理解英文学术文献，描述专业相关问题，设计实施研究方案，获得研究结论，用英文表达整个研究成果的能力不足。很多高校完全退出了学术英语教学，或者仅保留了研究生阶段的学术英语教学。《任务型学术英语写作认知负荷的调节策略研究》正是基于这一背景，深入分析学术英语写作中学习者认知负荷优化和调节问题，并提出了基于认知负荷理论的分层任务设置原则。

　　过去几十年的教育研究中，认知负荷理论（Cognitive Load Theory, CLT）具有很强的影响力，被广泛用于评估学习环境或解释教学投入和产出效果。认知负荷理论由澳大利亚心理学家 John Sweller 提出。在随后的研究中，得益于 Paas、Rumelhart 等学者的共同努力，理论得到了深入发展和广泛应用。在 1988 年的一篇开创性论文中，Sweller 全面介绍了这一理论。该理论基于人类认知结构，对教学进行设计和量化评估。通过利用目前对工作记忆和长期记忆之间关系的知识，认知负荷理论能够设计产生一些更合理的，甚至是会与直觉相悖的教学程序。

　　本书基于认知负荷理论分析任务型学术英语写作课程的合理设置，旨在为学术英语写作教学提供理论支持和实践指导。作者通过对学术英语写作过程中认知负荷的影响因素进行系统研究，揭示了学术英语写作任务的复杂性如何影响学习者的认知资源分配，以及如何通过教学设计减轻认知负荷，从而提高学术英语写作课程的效率和质量。

　　本书共分为三个部分，第一部分为认知负荷理论的介绍及测量。共有三章，分别介绍认知负荷理论，写作中的认知负荷理论，以及任务型学术写作中认知负荷的测量。作者介绍了认知负荷理论的起源、发展和应用，设计了任务型学术英语写作认知负荷量表，并对量表的可靠性进行了验证。

　　第二部分为任务型学术英语写作认知负荷的影响因素分析，共有九章，分别分析学习者的专业知识、语言能力、动机情感、学习策略，教学环境中教师支持、同伴合作和技术手段，以及写作体裁因素对任务型学术英语写作认知负荷的影响。这部分是研究的主体，也是第三部分提出课程设计方案的基础。

第三部分为认知负荷理论指导下的层级教学设计方案。通过控制认知负荷的影响因素，如写作任务的复杂度（从体裁、步骤、学术资源、时间等方面），教学支持的方式（讲座、小组辅导、写作反馈、团队合作培训、技术工具使用能力培训等方面），逐渐提高学习者的写作能力，最终达到学习者能够写作完整的研究性英文学术报告的目标。

作者来自上海市首批进入学术英语教学试点单位的高等院校，从事学术英语教学十年。作者认为，通过认知负荷层级教学设计，合理安排任务难度，调整教学环境中的支持策略，可以有效降低学习者（本科学生）在任务型学术英语写作过程中感知的认知负荷。同时研究也探讨了学习者的先前知识、动机和情感等因素如何交叉影响认知负荷，以及如何通过改变这些因素来调节认知负荷。

本书适合广大英语学习者、教育工作者以及对认知负荷理论感兴趣的研究者阅读。对于学习者而言，书中提供的调节策略有助于减少任务的负荷，提高学术英语写作能力；对于学术英语写作课程设计者，书中的教学建议有助于改进教学设计，提升教学质量；对于研究者，书中的研究成果提供了新的研究视角和数据支持。在全球化和信息化的今天，学术英语写作能力的提升对于个人发展和国际学术交流具有重要意义。本书不仅为学术英语写作的教学和学习提供了宝贵的参考，也为认知负荷理论的应用研究开辟了新的领域。随着教育技术的不断进步和教学方法的不断创新，学术英语写作教学将更加高效，学习者的写作能力将得到更大的提升。

本书中第七章"积极情绪对认知负荷的影响"由作者与李国华老师合作完成；第十一章"AI工具的使用对认知负荷的影响"由作者与张子祎女士合作完成。感谢上海对外经贸大学对图书出版的赞助，教学团队对新型教学模式的支持。期待通过学术英语写作的认知负荷的研究，能够开启教师和研究者更宽广的视野和深度的探索。

# 内容概述

　　《任务型学术英语写作认知负荷的调节策略研究》用认知负荷的理论分析研究学术英语教学中遇到的学习者认知负荷过高的问题。全书从理论介绍入手，分别进行了项目式学术英语写作（PBAW）认知负荷测量和验证，认知负荷影响因素的分析，之后根据以上影响因素，提出了认知负荷理论指导下，分层设计课程复杂度的框架，并给出认知负荷理论框架下的课程设置原则。全书主要内容如下：

## 第一章　认知负荷理论

　　认知负荷理论借助人类认知结构设计教学程序。该理论假设知识可分为两类：一是生物学意义上的主要知识，即人类在长期进化过程中所获得的知识；二是生物学意义上的次要知识，它与主要知识不同，是教学的主要内容。在处理次要知识时，人类认知需要一个大的信息存储库，通过从其他信息库获取信息并进行加工。在给定时间内，大脑只能处理有限的次要知识。

　　认知负荷分为内在、外在和相关三种类型。内在认知负荷由学习任务的复杂性和学习者的先前知识决定，可通过孤立元素效应、预训练原则等降低；外在认知负荷通常由学习材料的教学设计引起，可通过优化课程设计如模态原则、减少冗余效果等方式降低；相关认知负荷涉及学习者积极参与学习的活动，促进学习加工并产生积极学习情绪。

以上各种效应中对 PBAW 教学有启发意义的有：孤立元素效应，教学中可提前训练任务中可以分离的部分能力，尤其分离英语阅读、专业知识和研究方法，避免三重挑战所产生的交叉效应。冗余效应，提示教学中只提供必要的信息支持，防止无用信息增加外在认知负荷；参考样本效应，提示同伴写作在写作知识和写作动机两方面的支持作用；专家反转效应，提示教学者调整 AI 等技术手段对不同学习者的使用效果，减少无关信息的干扰。这些效应在最后一章的课程设置原则中会再次提及。

认知负荷的测量方法有主观测量、双重任务测量和生理测量等。PBAW 中主流的测量方法为主观感知认知负荷测量。目前研究表明，整体感知认知负荷的测量方法不能满足研究和教学的需要，教育研究者应设计可以同时测量内在、外在和相关负荷的测量方法，并在任务执行过程中及时多次测量。分项认知负荷测量与阶段性跟踪测量是 PBAW 任务认知负荷研究需要的测量方法。

## 第二章　学术英语写作任务的认知负荷

本章探讨第二语言（L2）学术写作中的项目式学习（PBL）的认知负荷，这种教学方法将学生置于学习中心，要求学生通过团队合作来研究问题并撰写学术报告。本章首先回顾了 Hayes 和 Flower

提出的经典写作模型，该模型分析了写作过程中计划、转写和审查等子过程。写作模型有助于读者理解写作作为一种多维任务所需的认知加工过程。

接着，文章分析了基于项目研究的学术英语写作（PBAW）的复杂性（参图 1）。PBAW 的复杂性体现在三个方面：一是复杂的写作过程。与传统语言课程相比，PBAW 教学不注重学术词汇和学科知识讲解。学生在学习过程中需自主选择研究问题、查阅文献等，对很多大学生学习者，该模式带来了理解学术文章的困难。PBAW 过程分为信息搜集、产生思想和表达思想三个阶段。在信息搜集阶段，学生可能遇到资料选择和理解困难；在产生思想阶段，学习者可能遇到分析推理困难；在表达思想阶段，学生可能缺乏学科特定的语言和语篇表达能力。除了写作过程的复杂性之外，PBAW 的复杂性来源于读写综合的任务对阅读能力的严格要求。PBAW 属于读写紧密结合的综合任务。综合写作任务要求作者理解相关文本、结合文本内容表达思想。该过程中阅读与写作紧密结合，阅读可在多个层面影响写作，第二语言学生若阅读能力不足，会在写作过程中面临诸多问题。此外，学术英语写作中对知识的构建或者产生新知

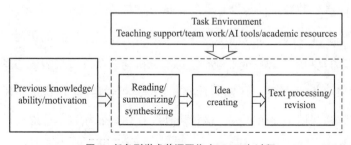

**图 1　任务型学术英语写作（PBAW）过程**

识的能力要求远大于其他体裁。

最后文章分析了项目式教学方式中普遍存在的认知负荷过高的问题。关于教学指导在学生学习中的作用，争论一直存在。项目研究模式，或者探索模式的教学倡导者主张最小化指导，让学生独立发现信息。但有实证研究表明，最小化指导不如系统的教学支持有效。学习者工作记忆的容量和时间限制常被最小化指导方法忽视，该批评指向基于建构主义的探究式教学模式。新手学习者在有限工作记忆下解决问题的困难常被忽视。本章为理解和改进学术写作教学提供了理论基础，强调了认知负荷管理在提升 PBAW 教学效果中的重要性。

## 第三章　任务型学术英语写作认知负荷量表的开发与验证

任务型学术英语写作过程伴随大量的认知活动。本章报告了英语作为外语的任务型学术写作认知负荷量表的开发和验证过程。研究者首先在学生中做调研（使用了学习者日志），产生了认知负荷测量的问卷题目，之后研究者在不同学习者中，两次对量表的结构和效度进行了探索和验证。研究 1 用来探索量表的结构，研究 2 用来验证量表的稳定性与外在效度。量表的最终版本包含 16 个题目，评估三个维度的认知负荷：阅读阶段的负荷、产生思想的负荷和文本写作的负荷。探索性和验证性因子分析均表明，该量表的心理测量结果可靠而稳定。认知负荷测量结果与学习者的知识储备（阅读、话题知识）显著相关。该量表使写作研究者和教师能够科学地理解 PBAW 学习者感知的认知负荷，从而可以采取有针对性的干预策略。任务型学术英语写作认知负荷量表（PBAW_CLS）如下：

表1　PBAW_CLS量表的探索性因子分析结果

| Factor & Item | Factor Loading | | | |
|---|---|---|---|---|
| | 1 | 2 | 3 | a |
| Reading Cognitive Load | | | | 0.829 |
| 1. Understanding terminologies in English academic literature | 0.863 | | | |
| 2. Fast reading and judging the value of the literature in English | 0.766 | | | |
| 3. Fast reading and finding specific information in the literature in English | 0.621 | | | |
| 4. Detailed reading and understanding of the literature in English | 0.605 | | | |
| 5. Taking notes in your own language while reading English academic literature | 0.598 | | | |
| Planning Cognitive Load | | | | 0.765 |
| 1. Finding the topic worth of study | | 0.838 | | |
| 2. Finding the academic literature related to the topic | | 0.702 | | |
| 3. Clarifying the scope of knowledge involved in the topic | | 0.653 | | |
| 4. Designing research methods | | 0.647 | | |
| 5. Obtaining data | | 0.598 | | |
| 6. Analyzing data | | 0.572 | | |
| Writing Cognitive Load | | | | 0.727 |
| 1. Using appropriate academic language | | | 0.820 | |
| 2. Selecting the content of literature review | | | 0.754 | |
| 3. Comparing and synthesizing multiple articles | | | 0.754 | |
| 4. Writing in your own language | | | 0.690 | |
| 5. Writing in proper structure | | | 0.516 | |
| a Cronbach's alpha | | | | |

## 第四章　学术英语写作认知负荷的影响因素假设

学习者主观感受的认知负荷可能与任务本身的复杂度、学习者的知识储备、认知能力、情感动机，以及教学环境有关。如果能够明确影响学习者主观感知认知负荷的因素，教学中就可以设计方案对认知负荷进行调节。在明确认知负荷测量方法的基础上，观察相关因素与学习者感知到的认知负荷的关联性，可以确定认知负荷的影响因素，进而对认知负荷进行调节。

在 PBAW 环境中，内在负荷由学习任务中涉及要素的复杂性及要素之间的交互性水平产生，与任务本身的复杂度相关，难以通过教学设计改变。影响 PBAW 写作任务内在认知负荷的因素包括写作类型（体裁）和内容的复杂性。由于认知负荷是主观感知的指标，学习者的知识储备、情感动机和思维特征等可能影响感知的负荷。外在负荷由任务信息呈现方式和学习活动环境产生，与教学设计相关。对于 PBAW 任务，影响外在负荷的学习环境包括教学支持、同伴合作，技术工具（AI）等。当学习者建构新知识或者存储信息时会产生相关负荷。以上分析产生影响 PBAW 认知负荷的六种可能因素：1. 写作体裁；2. 学习者的储备知识和能力；3. 学习者的学习动机和情绪；4. 学习者使用的读写策略；5. 批判思维；6. 技术手段（如：AI）。但这些因素是否真实影响 PBAW 学习过程中的认知负荷，需要用实验观察。图 2 为任务型学术英语写作认知负荷影响因素关系图。

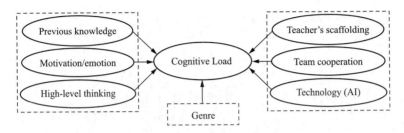

图 2　影响 PBAW 认知负荷的影响因素假设

## 第五章　学习者阅读能力对认知负荷的影响

　　阅读能力在基于研究的写作任务中起着至关重要的作用，因为阅读是知识的来源。任务型学术报告写作是读写综合写作任务的一种，阅读理解能力对这类任务至关重要。因为读写相互依存，若不先理解原文材料，综合写作任务就无法完成。阅读还能调节写作过程中学习策略的有效性。如果学生的阅读能力处于一定语言能力水平之下，在进行二语阅读时学生会难以与二语文本产生有效互动。只有达到一定语言能力，学生才能在学术任务中表现良好，达不到阅读能力的学生在语言输入和输出任务中都会遇到困难。有研究提出阅读能力阈值可作为学生开始 PBAW 课程学习的门槛，但是具体的阅读能力要求尚无定论。

　　研究者对上海一所商科院校的学术英语写作课程进行了研究。研究发现，随着学习者英语阅读能力的提高，感知到的写作任务的认知负荷逐渐降低。但当阅读能力达到大学英语 4 级（CET4）测试中，阅读成绩 210 附近时，阅读水平的提高不再引起认知负荷的下降。认知负荷在这里趋于平稳（见图 3）。研究表明，当学习者

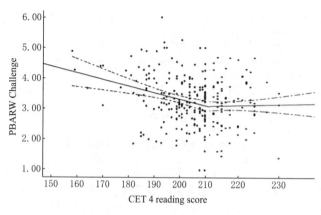

**图 3    英语阅读能力预测认知负荷的分段线性回归图**

的阅读能力到达 CET4 级 210 分，相当于欧洲语言参考框架的 B2
高端水平时，学习者感知到的认知负荷基本与阅读能力无关。此
时，学习者可以完成英文阅读，掌握学科知识，进行分析写作。从
而这个阅读水平可以认为是学习者进入任务型学术英语写作的基础
水平。对于阅读水平不足以应对 PBAW 写作任务的学习者，研究
者建议可以设计与专业相关的阅读训练，提高专业词汇、阅读速
度、摘要写作能力。这样的训练可以避免用第二语言学习专业知识
带来的交叉效应，从而减少认知负荷。本研究的价值在于为学习者
选择课程提供前行语言能力评估，也为课程设计者提供教学内容
参考。

## 第六章    先前知识对认知负荷的影响

认知负荷理论是理解学习过程中认知资源分配的关键理论。它
将认知负荷分为外在、内在和相关三类，其中内在认知负荷受任务

复杂性及学习者前行知识的影响。元素交互性是内在认知负荷的关键因素。一般而言，先前储备知识有助于学习者降低元素交互性，进而降低认知负荷。然而在某些情境下，这种关系可能变化。例如，当研究的问题涉及复杂系统时，专业知识储备较少的学习者可能低估问题复杂性，报告较低内在负荷；而专业知识较多的学习者可能因引入更多交互元素而引发更多的认知负荷。

　　本章中报告的研究证实了这一发现。我们对 227 名大学学习者在 PBAW 写作的过程中感知的认知负荷进行观察，研究发现知识储备与认知负荷并非线性相关。虽然话题知识最少的参与者所感知的认知负荷最高，但话题知识最多的参与者感知到的认知负荷并不是最低的，他们感知的认知负荷显著高于知识水平较低的研究者。这一结果表明，认知负荷理论关于内在负荷和先前知识的关系假设

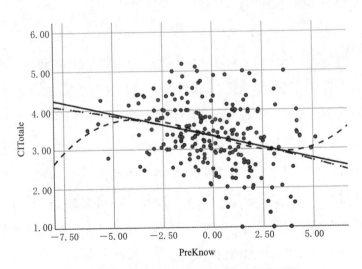

**图 4　学习者的知识储备与 PBAW 认知负荷关系图**
**（ PreKnow 知识储备 ; CITotale 认知负荷 ）**

在大多数情况下存在，但两者的关系应该细化分析，因为知识与负荷之间的关系有时被逆转。教学中应尽量考虑任务设计时的不同解决方法，避免不必要的和过于复杂的解决方案。图4为学习者储备知识与认知负荷的关系图。

## 第七章　积极情绪对认知负荷的影响

动机和情感是可能降低 PBAW 认知负荷的心理因素。写作乐趣与认知负荷的关系复杂：根据情感研究，消极情绪会消耗工作记忆资源并导致高认知负荷，而积极情绪如写作乐趣则可预防消极情绪反应，减少认知负荷。从神经心理学的多巴胺假说来看，写作乐趣可提高大脑多巴胺水平，进而提升学习者的努力投入，减少认知负荷对写作的负面影响。但也可能因引发额外认知负担而加剧认知负荷对写作的负面影响。

本研究招募了 417 名学生，调查了他们的写作乐趣、进行学术写作时感知到的认知负荷以及写作能力。通过研究感知到的认知负荷在写作乐趣和写作成就之间的中介效应，我们发现：（1）写作乐趣直接正面影响写作能力；（2）写作乐趣有助于减轻认知负荷对写作表现的负面影响。这一发现显示了在学术写作课程中提高写作乐趣的重要性。在教学中，PBAW 教师应该采取策略提高学习者的写作愉悦感，比如，教师可以把写作的选题权利交给学习者，把小组成员的组织权利交给学习者，鼓励学习者的进步，增加写作效能感，对学习者提供更多的积极反馈。

## 第八章　教学支持对认知负荷的影响

本章探讨教师在项目式学术英语写作（PBAW）课程中的支持作用对学生认知负荷和学习努力程度的影响。基于建构主义的 PBL 课程倡导最小化指导，对缺乏必要知识储备的新手学习者来说，任务的难度可能导致无效学习。本章讨论了教师支持、学习动机与认知负荷的关系。在 PBAW 课程中，尽管学习者有较大探索空间，但如果缺乏动机和投入，优化认知负荷的效果有限。动机对于学生应对复杂学习任务至关重要。任务的重要性、有用性、自我效能等会影响学习努力程度，而教师提供的支持也会影响学习者对学习任务的认知。教师的外部指导可以提供知识构建所需的执行指导，促进学习动机，降低不必要的认知负荷。

研究以 227 名参加学术写作课程的学生为对象进行调查。课程采用项目式教学法，在上海对外经贸大学展开，学生在一学期内完成研究提案写作等任务。研究使用问卷调查收集数据，测量工具包括教师支持量表、学习努力程度量表和认知负荷量表，并运用结构方程模型进行分析。研究结果显示，教师支持通过提高学习者的努力程度，间接减少学习者感知的认知负荷。但研究未发现教师支持对降低认知负荷有直接作用。

本章的案例表明，PBAW 课程中教师支持可以影响学习者的努力程度，继而影响认知负荷。研究指出了 PBL 课程的不足，强调了根据认知负荷理论设计 PBAW 课程的可行性。实践中教师应提供必要的支持，如提供更多写作反馈、组织更多的小组辅导，提供个性化帮助, 讲授写作知识等。对于本科生新手来说, 在高度复杂的 PBAW 任务中, 教师指导尤其重要。表 2 为 PBAW 课程中教师给予支持的示例。在不同的教学目标与学习对象中, 教学支持内容需要调整。但总体而言, 教学支持通过学习者的投入会减少学习者感知的认知负荷。

表 2　PBAW 课程中的教师支持方式

| Meeting time | Theme | Scaffolding |
|---|---|---|
| 1st meeting | Locating reliable academic information | Teacher gives lecture and students search online |
| 2nd meeting | Taking notes, summarizing, and synthesizing | Teacher shows writing procedure and samples |
| 3rd meeting | Writing a research proposal | Teacher shows samples and lectures on genre and language support |
| 4th meeting | Collecting and analyzing data | Teacher lectures on research method, students choose research method |
| Group conference with teacher | | |
| 5th meeting | Writing the introduction part | Teacher lectures on genre and language support |
| 6th meeting | Writing the body part | |
| 7th meeting | Writing the conclusion part | |
| 8th meeting | Revising | Revise based on the feedback from the teacher and classmates |

## 第九章　自主学习策略对认知负荷的影响

过去几十年中, 自我调控策略和认知负荷一直是最有影响力的两个概念。作为学习者的主体行为特征, 自我调控学习策略的应用可能对认知负荷产生影响。本文旨在将这两个概念联系起来, 阐释自我调控学习策略与认知负荷的关联性。PBAW 学习环境要求学习者自我调控其学习过程。学习者需要设定目标和计划，使用写作策略并监控他们的学习进度。然而自我调控策略是否可以降低认知负荷并促进写作成绩，依赖于学习者的认知资源是否充足。在学术写作任务中，认知资源包括学习者的学术阅读能力、专业知识、研究能力等。在认知资源不足的情况下自我调控可能导致认知负荷的增加。本文分析了内在、外在和相关认知负荷与自我调控策略的关系，并用两个实验研究展现了自我调控学习策略、学习者的资源和认知负荷的关系。

在研究一中，274 名学生参与调查。研究者将学生按阅读能力分为高、低两组。通过分段多元回归分析，研究发现，高阅读能力组中自我调控学习策略与认知负荷显著相关，且学习策略能负向预测认知负荷（策略使用越多，认知负荷越低）；但是，低阅读能力组中只有阅读能力能预测认知负荷，自我调控学习策略对其无影响。在研究二中，165 名学生参与了调查。高阅读能力组中阅读能力和读写策略都能预测写作表现，低阅读能力组只有阅读能力能预测写作表现。低阅读能力学生难以有效使用学习策略影响写作表现，而高阅读能力学生在运用策略方面更有能力（参图 5）。

研究表明，PBAW 课程在设定写作任务和教学写作策略时，需要考虑学习者的认知资源是否充分，只有在认知资源充分的情况下，学习策略才可能发挥效用。认知负荷、学习者认知资源与学习策略之间的关系图如下。在相对于学习资源而言，过于简单或者复杂的任务中，自我调控策略的使用或者浪费资源，或者增加负荷。

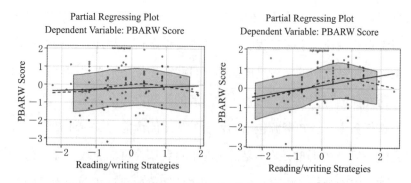

图 5　不同阅读能力学习者的自我调控策略对写作成绩的预测图

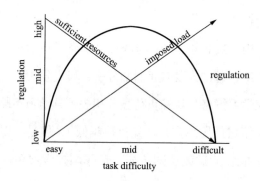

图 6　认知负荷、认知资源与自我调控策略关系图 (source: Seufert, 2018)

## 第十章　小组合作对认知负荷的影响

PBAW 常使用小组合作学习，通过与同班同学合作，加深对研究性课题的理解。本章关注 PBAW 课程的学习者形成小组学习的过程与相关认知负荷水平之间的关系。具体而言，研究分析了小组合作对内在学习动机与相关负荷之间关系的影响。研究提出两个假设：一、小组合作与相关认知负荷正相关；二、小组合作调节内在动机与相关认知负荷的关系。研究通过问卷调查收集数据。测量指标包括小组合作策略、相关认知负荷和内在动机。双变量相关性分析显示，小组合作与相关认知负荷、内在动机与相关认知负荷均呈显著正相关，且内在动机与小组合作也显著正相关。线性回归分析表明，小组合作和内在动机对相关认知负荷有较强的预测力。方差分析和交互效应检验进一步证实了小组合作对内在动机与相关认知负荷关系的调节作用。

结果表明，小组合作能调节内在学习动机与相关认知负荷之间的关系：虽然内在学习动机在所有的学生中均可以预测相关认知负荷，小组合作水平更高的学生获得了更多的相关负荷，也就是说产生了更多有效的学习（参图7）。这项研究显示了小组合作在促进学习者学习上的细分作用。研究鼓励学习者充分参与小组的合作，进行有效的学习。最后，文章给出了提高学生团队合作技能的实用建议，包括确定团队领导、了解成员优势、确保良好沟通、及时处理问题、直接给予反馈、明确问题等，以避免冲突共同解决问题。

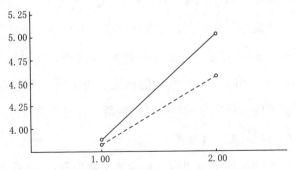

图7 小组合作对内在动机与相关认知负荷的调节作用
（斜率大者为小组合作多的学习者）

## 第十一章　AI 工具的使用对认知负荷的影响

学习环境对学习者的认知负荷会产生影响。生成式人工智能（AI）工具的出现对学术英语写作的冲击是颠覆性的。AI 工具的开发者与语言教师认为，对二语写作者而言，AI 工具可以降低他们遇到的认知负荷，提高写作的效率。但我们在研究生班级进行的研究表明并非如此。

本章报告了一项 AI 工具使用与写作认知负荷关系的研究。研究者调查了 AI 对 PBAW 中不同外语水平学习者的认知负荷产生的影响。研究数据来自作者与同事为研究生开设的写作课程。课程采用 PBAW 模式，允许学习者使用 Quillbot、Kimi 和 小绿鲸 等 AI 工具，教师鼓励使用 AI 工具，但要求学生不能用其生成的内容替代自己的工作。共有 327 名研究生参与问卷调查，8 名学生参与了后续的半结构化访谈。结果显示，AI 使用中出现了"专家反转效应"：不同外语水平的学习者在 AI 使用后，效果有差异：对于英语水平较低的学习者，AI 使用与认知负荷无显著关系，但 AI 使用与写作自我效能感呈正相关，主要在阅读文献和学习研究方法方面提高了学习者的效能感。对于高英语水平的研究生，AI 使用与认知负荷呈显著正相关，与自我效能感无显著关系。研究还发现 AI 工具没有显著降低研究生的写作认知负荷，且未能提高他们在语言使用方面的自我效能感（见图 8）。

这项研究表明教师与研究人员应理解如何利用 AI 技术提高学术写作的能力，降低写作过程中的认知负荷。AI 技术人员和教育

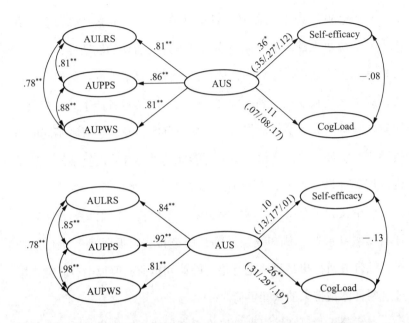

**图8 不同英语水平的学习者使用 AI 对认知负荷与写作效能感的影响**
（上图：低水平学习者；下图：高水平学习者）

者需要合作设计专门用于写作的 AI 工具，减少无用信息增加学习者外在认知负荷。教师应根据学生二语水平，调整 AI 工具的使用方式。语言水平低的学生可将其作为支持手段，但语言水平高的学生应使用 AI 完成更复杂任务，并学习与 AI 有效互动的能力。教师还应规范 AI 使用范围，避免学习者过多使用 AI，从而阻碍语言能力发展的可能性。

## 第十二章　写作任务类型对认知负荷的影响

认知负荷理论的研究者针对口语和写作任务的复杂性做了广泛的研究，这些研究为教学中安排口语或者写作任务的顺序给出参考。Robinson 考虑了任务复杂性的认知因素、环境因素和学习者因素对口语表现的影响，但该模型针对口语活动的复杂性，因此在写作活动中不适用。本章写作体裁作为任务复杂性变量的研究。这类研究大多比较议论文和记叙文写作任务对学习者产生的认知负荷影响。这些研究表明体裁作为任务变量确实引发了学习者不同的语言使用。比如：议论文比记叙文更能促使学习者使用复杂的句法结构。但是体裁之间的复杂性比较少在其他类型的任务中进行过讨论。议论文和研究报告是两种常见的学术体裁，议论文需要逻辑推理、反驳和说服，认知复杂性高；研究报告需要处理一手信息资料、综合分析得出结果，也有很高的认知负荷，但很少有研究观察过这两种体裁带来的认知负荷。

本章分析了研究性报告与议论文产生的认知负荷差异。参与者分别为来自研究性报告写作课程的 240 名本科生以及来自议论文写作课程的 177 名本科生。参与者均为商科院校非英语专业学生。这些课程旨在培养学生的学术写作技能，帮助他们提高学术写作中的读者意识、语篇结构和学术语言能力。这两个班级的学习者分别在一个学期中完成自选题目的写作，写作长度为 2000 字。学习者自己收集有价值的文献信息，完成观点性的议论文写作，或者是研究性的报告写作。在一个学期学习之后，教师使用问卷测量学生对写作任务认知负荷的感知。研究结果表明，两种体裁都对学习者产生很高的认知负荷，但比起议论文写作，报告写作任务产生的认知负荷更高，因为报告写作需要更多的子步骤（收集分析一手数据）和新知识（统计分析）。议论文依靠二手研究资料，相对步骤少，且为学习者熟悉的体裁。步骤少与经验知识多结合，降低了学习者感知的认知负荷。

本章中的研究案例证明体裁与认知负荷之间存在紧密联系。研究表明教学中教师需要了解学生对不同体裁的写作知识和学习需求，帮助学习者在 PBAW 课程中选择适合的写作任务类型。此外，二语写作教学往往侧重于提高学习者的议论文写作技能，而对其他体裁的关注相对较少。建立基于任务复杂度评估的 PBAW 任务类型，将使二语学习者更有效地发展写作能力。比如，如果在报告写作中希望减少内在认知负荷，可以考虑减少写作步骤，通过直接提供样本数据，省略收集信息和分析信息的步骤，把能力培养范围集中在狭义的学术写作概念下。

## 第十三章 任务型学术英语写作课程的认知负荷层级设置

基于前面章节认知负荷影响因素的分析，PBAW 课程设计可以利用认知负荷理论，从三个方面调节课程的复杂性（见图9）：首先是学习者因素。学习者的二语阅读/写作能力、项目有关专业知识和学术研究知识，以及学习者对研究性学习的动机是否足够积极是调节认知负荷的主观层面；其次是任务本身的复杂性：研究项目中概念的复杂性、问题和解决方案所涉及的认知过程的复杂性、数据获取和分析步骤的多少、写作时间和写作长短是影响认知负荷的客观层面；最后是任务执行的环境因素：教师的支持、学习小组的支持、数据的可用性以及技术手段（如人工智能工具）的可获得性是影响认知负荷的环境因素。基于认知负荷理论的课程设计应将这

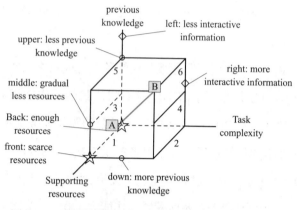

图9　基于认知负荷理论的 PBAW 课程层级设置

三方面的要素整合到不同复杂度层级的 PBAW 课程中，从低复杂性学习任务和高教学支持开始，辅助不同能力的学习者，一直到自主完成高复杂性任务。本章给出基于认知负荷理论的课程设置指导原则。这 8 个课程设置原则分别是：1）确定课程任务所需的前行知识和能力；2）确定课程任务复杂度的层级；3）了解学习者写作能力的发展；4）确定支持水平的高低；5）训练合作学习能力；6）监控认知负荷；7）明确教师的重要性；8）控制学术资源。

# 第一部分
## 认知负荷理论与测量

# Part I
## Cognitive load theory and measurement

# 第一章　认知负荷理论
## Chapter 1　Cognitive load theory

**本章内容概要 Abstract of the chapter**

　　本章介绍认知负荷的基本理论，内容包括认知负荷的定义，人类认知结构简述，认知负荷的种类，认知负荷的测量。认知负荷理论借助人类认知结构设计新颖的教学程序。该理论假设知识可分为两类：一是生物学意义上的主要知识，即人类在长期进化过程中所获得的知识；二是生物学意义上的次要知识，它与主要知识不同，是教学的主要内容。在处理次要知识时，需要一个大的信息存储库，通过从其他信息库获取信息，进行加工之后存储。在给定时间内，大脑只能处理有限的次要知识。

　　认知负荷分为内在、外在和相关三种类型。内在认知负荷由学习任务的复杂性和学习者的知识储备决定。内在认知负荷很难发生变化，但可以通过孤立元素效应、预训练效应等降低；外在认知负荷通常由学习材料的教学设计引起，可通过优化课程设计如模态原则、减少冗余效果等方式降低；相关认知负荷涉及学习者参与学习的活动，能促进学习加工并产生积极学习情绪。

　　认知负荷的测量方法有主观测量、双重任务测量和生理测量等。主观测量基于个人对认知过程的内省报告，虽广泛使用但存在可靠性问题；双重任务测量要求学习者同时执行两项任务，通过观察次要任务的表现来推断认知负荷，但有干扰学习和无法确定负荷类型等缺点；生理测量基于生理变量反映认知活动变化，如测量心率变异性、瞳孔反应等。测量认知负荷是评价教学效率，探索个性化训练的前提。

本章涉及的理论知识将引领全书的实证研究和教学设计。

## 1. Introduction

In the educational research field, Cognitive Load Theory (CLT) has been the most influential and controversial one in the past 30 years. It is widely used to assess learning environments or explain empirical results of educational related research. Cognitive Load Theory, proposed by Australian psychologist John Sweller (1988), has been deeply developed and widely applied in subsequent research. The theory is based on the understanding of human cognition, using human cognitive structure to produce experimental teaching effects. Although CLT is not the only theory that uses human cognition to generate teaching programs, it is a pity that teaching designs based on human cognitive structure are rare. By leveraging our knowledge of the relationship between working memory and long-term memory, CLT can produce some teaching programs that seem counterintuitive to some people.

## 2. Definitions of cognitive load

The amount of load placed on working memory by an instructional task is a critical factor in effective learning and affects resource/attention allocation. Since it is the load on working memory during problem solving, thinking, and reasoning (including perception, memory, language, etc.), working memory load is often used interchangeably with cognitive load (see Sweller et al., 1998; Ayres, 2006). Some researchers, such as Ayres (2006), prefer the term "mental workload". The term "mental load" is also used (Bonnardel & Piolat, 2003), but more often it is included within the concept of cognitive load (Paas & van Merriënboer, 1994).

Cognitive load primarily describes the load on learners from the input aspects of a task, that is, the demands or requirements of the tasks. It is conceptualized within the framework of information processing, which integrates mental processes (including cognitive and emotional aspects) and representations (knowledge). However, differences also exist in the definition of cognitive load. The main difference lies in the fact that some scholars define cognitive load based on the interaction between task requirements and human capabilities or resources (e.g., Rubio et al., 2004), while others view task requirements as an independent, external variable that learners have to cope with more or less efficiently (e.g., Cooper, 1998; Ayres, 2006).

## 3. Human cognitive structure

Cognitive Load Theory (CLT) is based on the theory of human cognitive structure (Sweller, 1988, 2010a), as well as Geary's (2007,

2008) theory of knowledge classification. CLT divides knowledge into primary and secondary knowledge. It posits that humans have evolved to automatically acquire certain specific types of knowledge, referred to as primary knowledge, while they have only recently needed to acquire other types of knowledge, called secondary knowledge, and thus have not yet evolved the ability to automatically acquire this information. It is this kind of knowledge that is difficult to obtain from a biological perspective and is the subject of learning and teaching.

### 3.1 Evolution of human knowledge

Knowledge and skills can be categorized into countless categories. However, the vast majority of classification schemes have failed to connect with teaching, and a single teaching design may simultaneously promote the learning of various types of knowledge. In contrast, Geary (2007, 2008) divides knowledge into biologically primary and secondary knowledge, which is directly related to teaching programs.

- Primary Knowledge

In the process of a young child learning to speak and listen to their native language, the child typically receives significant assistance from parents and those around them. Adults may repeat key words, speak with a clear and slow pace, and use simple vocabulary and grammar; this way of speaking is often referred to as "baby talk." However, children are not directly taught how to listen and speak. In fact, apart from professional speech therapists, most people may not understand how to teach children their native language. For instance, without explicit guidance, children can master complex movements related to speech, such as the coordination of the tongue, lips, breathing, and voice. For most of us, learning to speak our native language comes naturally just by being part of society, even though it is a complex task that does not require explicit teaching.

Learning to listen and speak is a biologically primary skill (Geary, 2007, 2008). These skills are naturally acquired through countless generations of evolution. We do not need external incentives to master these language skills; we can easily, effortlessly, and unconsciously acquire them without teaching. We automatically mimic the accents of those around us, rather than just learning our parents' accents, because we have evolved to learn to speak alongside our peers. Many skills are biologically automatically acquired, essential knowledge needed for survival. We learn the basic rules of social existence and learn to recognize faces as easily as we learn our native language. This learning does not require external incentives. External incentive factors are irrelevant because we have evolved to acquire these skills without explicit guidance.

• Secondary Knowledge

The nature and acquisition of biologically secondary knowledge are completely different from those of primary skills. Humans may have evolved to the stage of acquiring secondary skills, but only in a general sense, not to the stage of having an automatic modular storage for these abilities. Biologically secondary knowledge encompasses the information that we must acquire within a space that has certain cultural and social characteristics in order to apply it within society. While listening and speaking provide biologically primary knowledge, reading and writing provide biologically secondary knowledge, and from the characteristics of reading and writing, we can analyze some features of secondary knowledge.

For example, most of us will simply learn to listen and speak as a result of living in a normal, listening/speaking society. In contrast, merely living in a reading/writing society is not sufficient for most people to learn to read and write. It is only in certain societies where modern education has emerged that reading and writing have become nearly universal skills. A minority of people in some cultures could read and write, but this was not enough to enable most people to become literate situation that persisted for thousands of years. People will learn to listen and speak without explicit teaching; but they rarely learn to read and write without specific teaching.

The difference between listening/speaking and reading/writing is evolutionary. We have evolved to learn to listen and speak. We can learn to read and write, but we have not specifically evolved for reading and writing. The evolved perceptual, motor, and cognitive skills we use for reading and writing did not evolve specifically for those activities. These skills evolved for other reasons, but we can harness them to learn to read and write. The different evolutionary histories of speaking/listening and reading/writing have both cognitive and educational consequences.

- The implication of the distinction between biologically primary and secondary knowledge

Regarding cognitive consequences, although we have an internal drive to learn to listen and speak, and we learn relatively effortlessly and unconsciously without external encouragement or explicit teaching, the same effortless acquisition is not evident in learning to read and write. We may not have the motivation to learn to read and write, thus learning to read and write may require a long period of substantial conscious effort. A significant portion of people in a reading/writing culture may never learn to read and write.

The educational consequences of learning to read and write are clear compared to learning to speak and listen. If a society wishes for the majority of its people to read and write, it must organize itself through its education system to ensure that the majority of its members learn to read and write. We do not need an education system and programs to teach people to listen and speak. Schools and other educational and training institutions have been established to deal with biologically secondary knowledge such as reading and writing. Almost every subject taught by educational and training institutions can be classified as containing biologically secondary knowledge.

## 3.2  The acquisition and organization of secondary knowledge

The way the human cognitive system is organized to acquire, retain, and disseminate biologically secondary information is directly relevant to instructional design. For instance, if human cognition is better suited to discovering secondary information rather than receiving it, then instruction should be organized to encourage discovery. On the other hand, if our cognitive system is better at acquiring information from others than discovering it, then instructional systems should emphasize presentation over discovery (Kirschner, Sweller & Clark, 2006; Klahr & Nigam, 2004). Moreover, if we acquire primary information in a very different way from secondary information, the distinction between the two becomes important. Therefore, how we handle information, especially secondary information, is crucial for instructional design.

There are many approaches to understanding how the human cognitive system processes information, with the most common being the study of components like working memory or long-term memory. However, there is an alternative, complementary approach: humans are part of nature, and nature processes information. Evolution by natural selection, for example, can be considered a natural information processing theory.

Evolution by natural selection creates new information, stores it for future use, and spreads it across space and time, acting as a natural information processing system. The human cognitive system, arising from biological evolution, shares similar characteristics with this system. When dealing with secondary information, it also creates, stores, and disseminates new information. The characteristics of natural information processing systems can be described by five basic principles:

- Information Store principle

Our human cognitive system needs a lot of information to navigate our complex world, and that's where our long-term memory comes in. Long-term memory is important for how we think and learn, but sometimes it's overlooked, especially in education. People sometimes think of it as just a bunch of random facts, but it is more important than that. It is the key to all our thinking. For example, becoming a chess master takes a long time—like ten years or more. During that time, they play and study a lot, learning patterns of the game and what moves work best in each situation. They do not have to figure out their moves from scratch every time; they just draw on their huge store of knowledge in long-term memory. This idea applies to more than just chess. Experts in any field—math, reading, whatever—have a big store of knowledge that helps them remember and solve problems. They can recognize situations and know the best moves to make. It means that being good at something is not about having some special problem-solving trick. It is about having a lot of knowledge stored in long-term memory. And that is what education should be about—helping students build up their knowledge in specific areas. Teaching general thinking skills might be a good idea, but first, we need to figure out what those skills are.

- Borrowing and Reorganizing principle

Natural information processing system require a sighificant anount of information to function effectively. In evolution, this information is passed down through reproduction, with asexual reproduction copying genomes exactly, and sexual reproduction reorganizing them. Our long-term memory works more like sexual reproduction, where we borrow information from others but reorganize it based on what we already know. We get information from other people by imitating, listening, reading, and looking at visuals. But instead of copying it exactly, we store it in our own unique way by combining it with our existing knowledge. This is how we build schemas, or knowledge structures, which are crucial for learning and are the focus of cognitive load theory. The theory suggests that we learn best when information is presented in a way that helps us build these schemas. Constructivist teaching methods emphasize generating information, but humans rarely create novel information on their own. We usually prefer to get information from others, and only when it's not available do we generate it ourselves. There's no solid evidence that teaching students to construct knowledge leads to better learning outcomes. In fact, direct instruction often leads to better learning, especially when it comes to building schemas.

- The Narrow Limits of Change principle

The narrow limits of change principle states that random generation and testing should only deal with a very small number of elements at a time due to the exponential increase in possible combinations as the number of elements increases. This principle is crucial for natural information processing systems when dealing with novel information from the external environment.

In evolution, the epigenetic system manages the interaction between the genetic system and the environment, facilitating genetic alterations in response to environmental signals. However, mutations are relatively rare and must be small and incremental, as large changes are likely to be maladaptive.

Similarly, human working memory has limitations in capacity and duration when dealing with novel information. It can store about seven items for up to 20 seconds and can only process about three to four items at a time. These limitations are crucial for instructional design, as procedures that overload working memory can hinder learning by preventing information from being fully processed and transferred to long-term memory. Cognitive load theory emphasizes the importance of considering these limitations in teaching methods to facilitate effective learning.

- Environmental Organizing and Linking principle

This principal deals with handling large amounts of organized information. The environmental organizing and linking principle explain how natural information processing systems use environmental signals to organize information and determine appropriate actions. The epigenetic system in biology and working memory in humans serve this role, linking environmental cues to the information store. Working memory uses environmental cues to select relevant information from long-term memory. When dealing with familiar information, working memory's capacity and duration limits disappear, and it can process large amounts of organized information cued by environmental signals. This is in contrast to its limited capacity when handling novel information.

Instructional design should consider these principles, aiming to increase biologically secondary knowledge in long-term memory, thereby expanding our capabilities. Cognitive load theory utilizes this framework to develop effective instructional procedures. Together, these principles show how information can be created, stored, disseminated, and used by natural information processing systems, which is essential for designing effective learning experiences.

## 4. Categories of cognitive load

Sweller et al. (1998) classified cognitive load into three types: intrinsic cognitive load, extrinsic cognitive load, and germane cognitive load. Intrinsic cognitive load originates from the interrelatedness of elements within a learning task, while extrinsic cognitive load consists of additional burdens caused by improper instructional design, unrelated to the task itself. Germane cognitive load refers to the efforts that facilitate the learning process.

## 4.1 Intrinsic cognitive load

Intrinsic cognitive load is produced by the inherent complexity of a learning task, influenced by two main factors: the interactivity of task elements and the learner's prior knowledge. Interactivity involves the number of knowledge elements that learners must process simultaneously in working memory (Chandler & Sweller, 1996). Low interactivity tasks allow learners to process knowledge elements one at a time due to their minimal interdependence, whereas high interactivity tasks include highly interconnected knowledge elements requiring simultaneous processing (Sweller, 2010b). For instance, in language learning, if learners only need to write words rather than construct sentences with correct grammar, the cognitive load is relatively low. However, if they write complex vocabulary and use correct grammar simultaneously, the cognitive load is relatively high. This is also the theoretical basis for measuring learners' language proficiency in linguistics by the complexity of their language use. Learners' prior knowledge is crucial for processing new information, as they must relate new information to existing knowledge structures in their minds (Gerjets et al., 2004), making the information processing more comprehensive and structured, reducing the need to process irrelevant elements in working memory. Chess players can memorize many chess patterns, remembering board layouts in a modular way instead of recalculating the possibilities each time, which is a typical example of reducing cognitive load. Similarly, fixed idioms in Chinese are a strategy to save cognitive resources, reducing the intrinsic cognitive load in organizing language through established word combinations.

The intrinsic cognitive load of a learning task depends on several key factors: the number of elements contained in the knowledge, the interactivity between these elements, and the learner's prior knowledge. To reduce intrinsic cognitive load, the following principles can be applied:

• The Isolated Elements Effect

Assume that what students are required to learn has a high level of element interactivity due to intrinsic cognitive load. It may be so high that the number of elements that must be processed exceeds the capacity of working memory. In this case, understanding and learning cannot proceed until levels of expertise are attained that permit interacting elements to be incorporated into schemas and treated as single elements using the environmental organizing and linking principle. It may be preferable to initially present the interacting elements in isolated form so that they can be processed even though they cannot be fully understood. Each element can be presented without reference to the other interacting elements. Once learned, the material can be presented again, but on this occasion in fully interacting rather than isolated form so that students can learn the interactions. Pollock, Chandler, and Sweller (2002) presented students with very complex information in isolated elements form thus reducing the intrinsic cognitive load followed by a presentation of the same information with the links between elements indicated. Another group was presented with the fully interacting material twice. The students who were presented with the elements in isolated form first performed better on subsequent test problems, providing an example of the isolated elements effect.

• Pretraining Principle

Mayer (2005) recommends providing learners with relevant information before formal learning to reduce intrinsic cognitive load. However, it is often difficult to significantly reduce intrinsic load without changing learning objectives. This is because, without changing the task itself, the complexity of information is hard to reduce. When learners need to understand a complex problem, they must grasp all related concepts and their structures. Therefore, only by changing the task itself, such as by adding certain information or removing some requirements, can intrinsic cognitive load be truly affected. Analyzing the task situation of second language writing, students using open AI's generative language tools in writing are actually provided with relevant content information while simultaneously reducing the requirements for effective language use. In such a writing environment, the intrinsic cognitive load of the writing task is reduced, but the use of open AI changes the nature of training and evaluating language and thought in the writing task.

## 4.2 Extrinsic cognitive load

Instructional design usually focuses more on how to present necessary information rather than the learning content itself, that is, it focuses more on changing extrinsic cognitive load. Extrinsic cognitive load is usually caused by the instructional design of learning materials, such as when learners have to invest mental resources in task-irrelevant processes like searching for information. By optimizing course design, such as making new vocabulary more visual or linking new and old information through associations in foreign language learning, extrinsic cognitive load can be reduced. This means that designers of learning materials can effectively control extrinsic cognitive load through design. To reduce extrinsic cognitive load, researchers have proposed various beneficial instructional design principles. For example:

- Modality Principle

This principle suggests that presenting text auditorily when combined with images is more effective than presenting it visually, as it makes better use of the different systems of working memory.

- Redundancy effect

This effect arises from the extraneous cognitive load imposed by processing unnecessary elements, like attempting to connect a self-explanatory diagram with redundant text. The effort to relate such elements can lead to unnecessary cognitive strain, such as machinery operation and simultaneous verbal presentation in multiple formats, with numerous examples and reviews available in the literature.

- Worked Example Effect

The worked example effect is a well-known principle in cognitive load theory, indicating that students often learn more effectively from studying worked examples rather than solving problems on their own. The effect has been widely replicated since its introduction by Sweller and Cooper (1985), initially in subjects like math and science but also in ill-defined areas such as language-based curricula or design issues. The worked example effect is closely tied to the principles of cognitive architecture, allowing for the accumulation of schemas through the information store principle and the borrowing and reorganizing principle, rather than the slower process of problem-solving via the randomness as genesis principle.

- The Split-Attention Effect

If the information is structured in a way that requires additional search, like in geometry examples with separate diagrams and text, it can lead to unnecessary cognitive load. This happens because learners must split their attention between the diagram and text, searching for connections. The split-attention effect is relevant to all instructional materials, not just worked examples, and should be considered when designing instruction with text, diagrams, or other sources. The aim is to physically integrate materials to prevent mental integration by learners. However, the effect only applies when integration is necessary for understanding; redundancy does not trigger the split-attention effect.

- The Element Interactivity Effect

All cognitive load effects rely on the information that is being processed imposing a heavy, intrinsic cognitive load. If element interactivity due to intrinsic cognitive load is low, any element interactivity due to extraneous cognitive load may have few instructional consequences. It may be possible to process the interacting elements due to extraneous cognitive load without exceeding working memory capacity. If so, cognitive load effects will not be obtained when element interactivity due to intrinsic cognitive load is low. Information can be processed in working memory and transferred to the long-term store even under the presence of elements imposing an extraneous cognitive load. Neither the split-attention nor the redundancy effects are likely to be obtained using intrinsically low element interactivity information (Sweller & Chandler, 1994).

- The expertise reversal effect

The expertise reversal effect occurs when a teaching method that works well for novices becomes less effective as learners gain expertise, and may even become counterproductive. This effect is closely related to the redundancy effect, where information that is helpful for novices can become redundant and interfere with learning for more knowledgeable learners. For instance, in the worked example effect, studying examples is beneficial for novices as it reduces the cognitive load associated with problem-solving. However, as learners become more proficient, they may need less guidance and can solve problems more effectively on their own, making the worked examples redundant. The effect suggests a shift in instructional approach based on the learner's level of expertise. The adaptive approach should ensure that while instructional materials remain optimally challenging, the instruction method should avoid excessive cognitive load for novices and redundancy for more advanced learners.

By adhering to these principles, instructional design can effectively reduce extrinsic cognitive load, thereby improving learning efficiency. Cognitive load theory provides an optimization framework for instructional design, especially in reducing extrinsic cognitive load. With carefully designed teaching activities and multimedia materials, including the use of advanced technologies such as artificial intelligence (AI), teachers can avoid poor design, free up more learning resources, and allow learners to engage in effective learning activities.

### 4.3 Germane cognitive load

Germane cognitive load involves a series of activities that learners must engage in, which not only enhance the learning process but also stimulate positive learning emotions (Paas et al., 1993). For example, effective reading strategies such as taking notes while reading, using mnemonic techniques, or explaining the content to others can increase germane cognitive load. A higher germane load indicates that learners are actively participating in the learning process and investing their cognitive resources in effective learning activities. Van Gog et al., (2006) described effective design principles aimed at promoting the generation of germane cognitive load. For example, in reading training, teachers can ask students to write titles for text paragraphs, find examples of topic sentences, or summarize the theme in their own words. These activities not only help generate germane cognitive load but are highly dependent on intrinsic cognitive load. Learners can only invest cognitive resources in these germane learning activities when the extrinsic load does not exceed their working memory capacity.

In theory, intrinsic, extrinsic, and germane cognitive loads are three independent and clearly defined types of loads. However, in practice, there are close connections between intrinsic, extrinsic, and germane cognitive loads (Sweller, 2010b). Especially germane cognitive load is inseparable from intrinsic and extrinsic, and some studies have even proposed that the concept of germane cognitive load should be abandoned, retaining only the intrinsic and extrinsic cognitive loads of learning tasks (Sweller, 2010b). Understanding the interaction between these three types of loads is crucial for designing effective teaching strategies. In this way, teachers can ensure that learners can use their cognitive resources more effectively when facing complex learning tasks, thus achieving more efficient learning outcomes. It is necessary to clarify the three types of cognitive load theoretically, which also helps to understand all loads in the learning situation. This study involves all three aspects of cognitive load. However, so far, there is no tool that can differentiate these three types of loads in a differentiated way.

## 5. Cognitive Load Measurement

As cognitive load theory developed, it became clear that the measurement of cognitive load was crucial for evaluating instructional strategies and learning outcomes (Sweller, 1988). The measurement of cognitive load has been approached from various angles, including subjective ratings, performance tasks, and more recently, physiological measures such as heart rate variability and pupillary response (Paas, Tuovinen, Tabbers, & Van Gerven, 2005). Each method offers unique insights but also presents challenges in terms of reliability and validity.

### 5.1 Subjective measures

Subjective measurements are based on the assumption that individuals can introspect their cognitive processes and report the extent of mental effort they have expended. Despite potential doubts about the reliability of self-ratings, it has been demonstrated that people are indeed capable of numerically indicating their perceived mental burden. The most popular scale for measuring cognitive load was developed by Paas (1992), which was designed based on the scale constructed by Bratfisch et al. (1972) for measuring perceived task difficulty. Paas's scale consists of a single item, where participants are asked to rate their perceived cognitive load on a 9-point Likert scale, with 1 indicating very low mental effort for the learning task and 9 indicating very high mental effort. This measurement method has been widely replicated, with scholars largely adopting similar rating methods. The typical measurement language includes phrases such as: "I invested... amount of effort" or "The effort I put in was...". The scale is typically designed as a 5 to 9-point Likert scale. Research has shown that reliable measurements can be obtained with unidimensional scales (e.g., Paas & van Merriënboer, 1993). It has been demonstrated that such scales are sensitive to relatively small differences in cognitive load and that they are valid, reliable, and non-intrusive.

While single-item scales are concise and clear, from a psychometric perspective, there is no way to separate true variance from measurement error. van Gog and Paas (2008) discussed the issues with scale items in detail. They criticized the use of different wordings and inconsistent scale ranges. Additionally, research by van Gog et al. (2006) demonstrated that introspective ratings are not very reliable, with overall retrospective load measurements typically higher than the average of multiple measurements taken during the learning process. More importantly, single-item measurements cannot distinguish between the various sources of load assumed in CLT. In fact, the sources of cognitive load are inferred from the combination of task performance and mental effort: if learning outcomes are poor and effort is high, cognitive load may be the result of poor instructional design, that is, the outcome of high extraneous load. It may also be due to high task difficulty, that is, the result of high intrinsic load. However, inferring the source of cognitive load from outcomes is extremely unscientific and may lead to circular reasoning.

## 5.2 Dual-task measures

Cognitive load measurement using the dual-task paradigm requires learners to perform two tasks simultaneously. It is assumed that as the primary task, which is the learning task, becomes more demanding, the performance on the secondary task will decline. There are two possible ways to conduct dual-task measurements: on the one hand, while performing the learning task, the accuracy and reaction time of the observation task can be measured (e.g., Brünken et al., 2003); on the other hand, during the learning process, a second task must be performed concurrently (e.g., Park & Brünken, 2011), and the increase in the load of the first task is measured through the performance impairment of the secondary task. The advantage of dual-task load measurement is its objectivity and that it reflects the entire learning process, allowing for the collection of rich data. However, the most obvious disadvantage is the invasiveness of these techniques; such measurements disrupt the learning process and add to the cognitive load themselves. In addition, learners with high working memory capacity may not be affected by the secondary task as much as those with low working memory capacity. Another disadvantage is that, as mentioned earlier for subjective ratings, this type of measurement also cannot determine the specific type of load being measured.

## 5.3  Physiological measures

Physiological measurement techniques are based on the assumption that changes in cognitive function can be reflected by physiological variables. These techniques include measuring heart activity (e.g., heart rate variability), brain activity (e.g., task-evoked brain potentials), and eye activity (e.g., pupillary dilation and blink rate). Psychophysiological measurements are best suited for visualizing the detailed trends and patterns of load, including the learner's instantaneous, peak, average, and accumulated load. A study by Paas and van Merriënboer (1993) demonstrated a physiological measurement method used within the cognitive load framework. They measured heart rate variability to estimate the level of cognitive load and found this measurement method to be intrusive to learners, resulting in invalid measurements and insensitive to subtle fluctuations in cognitive load. Unlike heart rate variability and other physiological measurements, the cognitive pupillary response appears to be a highly sensitive tool for tracking fluctuating levels of cognitive load. Beatty and Lucero-Wagoner (2000) identified three useful task-evoked pupillary responses (TEPRs): mean pupil dilation, peak dilation, and latency to the peak. These TEPRs typically intensify as a function of cognitive load. In a study by Van Gerven, Paas, van Merriënboer, and Schmidt (2004), these TEPRs were measured as a function of different levels of cognitive load in both young and older participants. They found that mean pupil dilation is a useful TEPR for measuring cognitive load.

## 5.4 Measurement of three CLs

As all the above measurements gain the overall CLs including intrinsic, extrinsic and germane CLs mixed. Jimmie Leppink (Leppink et al., 2013) emphasize the necessity of accurately measuring the three loads respectively to enhance our understanding of learning outcomes and instructional effectiveness. They introduce a ten-item instrument designed to measure the three types of cognitive load, grounded in CLT.

The study employs both subjective and objective measures to assess cognitive load. Subjective measures include self-reported questionnaires that ask participants to rate their perceived mental effort and load. Objective measures involve physiological indicators such as heart rate variability, offering a non-intrusive way to gauge cognitive load. The findings from the study indicate that the ten-item instrument successfully differentiates between the three types of cognitive load. The results also suggest that subjective measures of mental effort correspond with objective heart rate measures, providing preliminary evidence for the convergent validity of these measures.

The authors suggest that the three-factor model of cognitive load provides a robust framework for understanding the dynamics of learning. They propose that instructional designers can use this model to develop interventions that minimize extraneous load, optimize germane load, and tailor instruction to match learners' prior knowledge to enhance learning outcomes.

The above are four of the most commonly used methods for evaluating cognitive load. Clearly, the measurement of cognitive load is of general theoretical interest to cognitive psychologists and has practical implications for instruction, especially regarding how to teach and learn complex tasks. The measurement of cognitive load provides the possibility of assessing the effects of instructional interventions. In the experiments of Van Gerven, Paas, van Merriënboer, and Schmidt (2004), and Pollock, Chandler, and Sweller (2002), differences in intrinsic cognitive load were directly reflected in the learners' performance outcomes. In complex learning tasks, the use of worked examples and incremental instructional methods showed better performance than not using examples and non-incremental instructional approaches. Studies on the split-attention effect and modality effect have also demonstrated differences in cognitive load on learners. In addition, learners' knowledge and age differences have a significant impact on cognitive load during learning. Finally, in an experiment by van Merriënboer (1990), methods were found to increase germane load. Therefore, although there are some exceptions, most empirical results support the main hypothesis of CLT: the differences in effectiveness between teaching or learning strategies are mainly determined by the differences in cognitive load on the brain.

In China, a small number of studies have begun to apply cognitive load theory to instruct learners. For instance, Han Juan's (2010) research explored the impact of the free goal effect and the worked example effect on the academic achievements of students with different academic levels in various subjects. The study suggested that the free goal effect is more suitable for application in Chinese composition, while the worked example effect is more appropriate for mathematics teaching. He Junxia's (2011) research combined the worked example effect from cognitive load theory with transfer theory, arguing that this approach not only reduces students' cognitive load but also enhances their transfer capabilities. The study emphasized that instructional design must ensure that students can master complex skills and transfer learning activities, placing great importance on the transfer of cognitive and metacognitive abilities. This view aligns with the perspective of learning strategies, which encompasses both cognitive and metacognitive capabilities of students.

The implication of measuring cognitive load is that it allows us to calculate the relative mental efficiency of instructional conditions (Paas & van Merriënboer, 1993). They combined measurements of mental effort with performance on the learning task, dividing the former by the latter to obtain a ratio of mental effort to performance, known as mental efficiency. If a learner's performance under specific instructional conditions is higher than what is expected based on their invested mental effort, or if their invested effort is lower than the general level expected based on their performance, their learning behavior is considered more effective. This measurement method plays a very important quantitative role in evaluating the effectiveness of teaching and learning.

The measurement of cognitive load also has research value in exploring the possibility of personalized training for intelligent interactive learning systems. Since individual differences resulting from the interaction between tasks and learner characteristics are important determinants of the level of cognitive load, it can be assumed that optimized efficiency can only be ultimately achieved when the assigned learning tasks suit the learner's needs and capabilities. One possible way to achieve this goal is to monitor the learning process and use the cognitive state of the learner to select appropriate learning tasks.

## 6. Summary of the chapter

This chapter introduces the theoretical background of Cognitive Load Theory (CLT). Cognitive load refers to the amount of load on working memory during problem-solving and thinking. It uses human cognitive structure to produce experimental teaching effects and is widely used to assess learning environments and explain educational research results.

CLT is based on human cognitive structure and Geary's theory of knowledge classification. It divides knowledge into primary and secondary knowledge. Primary knowledge is automatically acquired through evolution, while secondary knowledge must be acquired within a cultural and social context and is the subject of learning and teaching.

Sweller et al. classified cognitive load into intrinsic, extrinsic, and germane cognitive load. Intrinsic cognitive load comes from the complexity of a learning task and is influenced by task interactivity and learner prior knowledge. Extrinsic cognitive load is caused by instructional design and can be reduced by optimizing course design. Germane cognitive load involves activities that enhance learning and is dependent on intrinsic and extrinsic cognitive load.

Measurement of cognitive load is crucial for evaluating instructional strategies and learning outcomes. Methods include subjective ratings, dual-task measures, and physiological measures. However, each method has its challenges. Measuring cognitive load allows us to calculate mental efficiency and has research value in making teaching effects quantifiable by scientifically observing the change of cognitive loads in teaching environment.

## 7. References

Ayres, P. (2006). Using subjective measures to detect variations of intrinsic cognitive load within problems. Learning and Instruction, 16, 389–400.

Ayres, P., & Sweller, J. (2005). The split-attention principle in multimedia learning. In R. E. Mayer (Ed.), *The Cambridge Handbook of Multimedia Learning* (pp. 135–146). Cambridge University Press.

Baddeley, A. D. (2003). Working memory: Looking back and looking forward. *Nature Reviews Neuroscience*, 4, 829–839.

Beatty, I. D., & Lucero-Wagoner, B. (2000). *The additive benefits of visual and auditory presentation modes in reducing cognitive load.* Journal of Educational Psychology.

Bonnardel, N., & Piolat, A. (2003). Design activities: How to analyze cognitive effort associated to cognitive treatments? *Cognitive Technology*, 8(1), 6–15.

Booth, S., & Marton, F. (1997). *Learning and Awareness*. Lawrence Erlbaum Associates.

Bratfisch, O., Borg, G., and Dornic, S. (1972). *Perceived Item-difficulty in Three Tests of Intellectual Performance Capacity*. Report No. 29. Stockholm: Institute of Applied Psychology.

Brünken, R., Plass, J. L., & Leutner, D. (2003). Direct measurement of cognitive load in multimedia learning. Educational Psychology, 38(1), 53–61.

Chandler, P., & Sweller, J. (1996). Cognitive load while learning to use a computer program. Applied Cognitive Psychology, 10(2), 151–170.

Cooper, G. (1998). Research into Cognitive Load Theory and Instructional Design at UNSW. Retrieved from http://education.arts.unsw.edu.au/CLT_NET_Aug_97.HTML.

Geary, D. C. (2007). Cognitive Load Theory. In J. M. Spector, M. D. Merrill, J. J. G. van Merrienboer, & M. P. Driscoll (Eds.), Handbook of research on educational communications and technology (3rd ed., pp. 389–400). Lawrence Erlbaum Associates.

Geary, D. C. (2008). Evolution of the human brain: Learning, development, and instruction. In J. C. Kaufman & R. J. Sternberg (Eds.), Cambridge handbook of intelligence (pp. 248–264). Cambridge University Press.

Gerjets, P., Scheiter, K., & Catrambone, R. (2004). Designing instructional examples to reduce intrinsic cognitive load: Molar versus modular presentation of solution procedures. Instructional Science, 32(1–2), 33–58.

Han, J. (2010). Cognitive load and learning from computer-based instructions. In J. M. Spector, M. D. Merrill, J. J. G. van Merrienboer, & M. P. Driscoll (Eds.), Handbook of research on educational communications and technology (3rd ed., pp. 389–400). Lawrence Erlbaum Associates.

He, J. (2011). Cognitive load and second language acquisition. Language Teaching Research, 15(4), 435–452.

Kalyuga, S. (2011). Cognitive load theory: How many types of load does it really need? Educational Psychology Review, 23(1), 1–19.

Leppink, J., Paas, F. G. W. C., van der Vleuten, C. P. M., van Gog, T., & van Merriënboer, J. J. G. (2013). Development of an instrument for measuring different types of cognitive load. Behavior Research Methods, 45(3), 1058–1072.

Klahr, D., & Nigam, M. (2004). The equivalence of learning paths in early science instruction: Effects of direct instruction and discovery learning. *Psychological science, 15*(10), 661–667.

Leppink, J., Paas, F. G. W. C., van Gog, T., van der Vleuten, C. P. M., & van Merriënboer, J. J. G. (2014). Effects of pairs of problems and examples on task performance and different types of cognitive load. Learning and Instruction, 30, 32–42.

Kirschner, P., Sweller, J., & Clark, R. E. (2006). Why unguided learning does not work: An analysis of the failure of discovery learning, problem-based learning, experiential learning and inquiry-based learning. *Educational Psychologist, 41*(2), 75–86.

Marton, F., & Booth, S. (1997). Learning and Awareness. Lawrence Erlbaum Associates.

Mayer, R. E. (2001). Multimedia Learning. Cambridge University Press.

Mayer, R. E. (2005). Cognitive theory and the design of multimedia instruction: An overview. In R. E. Mayer (Ed.), The Cambridge handbook of multimedia learning (pp. 31–48). Cambridge University Press.

Paas, F. G. W. C. (1992). Training strategies for attaining transfer of problem-solving skill in statistics: A cognitive-load approach. Journal of Educational Psychology, 84(4), 429–434.

Paas, F. & van Merriënboer, J. J. G. (1993). The efficiency of instructional conditions for proportional reasoning tasks. Journal of Educational Psychology, 85(4), 655–668.

Paas, F., Tuovinen, J. E., Van Merrienboer, J. J., & Aubteen Darabi, A. (2005). A motivational perspective on the relation between mental effort and performance: Optimizing learner involvement in instruction. *Educational technology research and development, 53,* 25–34.

Paas, F. G. W. C., van Gog, T., & Sweller, J. (2010). Cognitive load theory: New conceptualizations, specifications, and integrated research perspectives. Educational Psychology Review, 22(1), 115–121.

Park, Y., & Brünken, R. (2011). Cognitive Load Theory: New directions for future research. Educational Technology Research and Development, 59(2), 175–186.

Pollock, E., Chandler, P., & Sweller, J. (2002). Assimilating complex information. Learning and Instruction, 12, 61–86.

Rubio, S., Díaz, E., Martín, J., & Puente, J. M. (2004). Evaluation of Subjective Mental Workload: A comparison of SWAT, NASA_TLX, and Workload Profile Methods. Applied Psychology: An International Review, 53(1), 61–86.

Sweller, J. (1988). Cognitive load during problem solving: Effects on learning. Cognitive Science, 12(2), 257–285.

Sweller, J. (1994). Cognitive load theory, learning difficulty, and instructional design. Learning and Instruction, 4(4), 295–312.

Sweller, J., & Chandler, P. (1994). Why some material is difficult to learn. Cognitive Instruction, 12(3), 185–233.

Sweller, J., & Cooper, G. A. (1985). The use of worked examples as a substitute for problem solving in learning algebra. *Cognition and instruction*, *2*(1), 59–89.

Sweller, J., van Merriënboer, J. J. G., & Paas, F. G. W. C. (1998). Cognitive architecture and instructional design. Educational Psychology Review, 10(3), 251–296.

Sweller, J. (2010a). Cognitive load theory: Recent theoretical advances. In J. L. Plass, R. Moreno, & R. Brünken (Eds.), Cognitive Load Theory (pp. 29–47). Cambridge University Press.

Sweller, J. (2010b). Element interactivity and intrinsic, extraneous, and germane cognitive load. Educational Psychology Review, 22(2), 123–138.

van Gerven, P. W. M., Paas, F. G. W. C., van Merriënboer, J. J. G., & Schmidt, H. G. (2004). Memory load and the cognitive pupillary response in aging. Psychophysiology, 41(2), 167–174.

van Gog, T., & Paas, F. G. W. C. (2008). Instructional efficiency: Revisiting the original construct in educational research. Educational Psychology, 43(1–2), 16–26.

Van Gog, T., Paas, F., & Van Merriënboer, J. J. (2006). Effects of process-oriented worked examples on troubleshooting transfer performance. *Learning and Instruction, 16*(2), 154–164.

van Merriënboer, J. J. G. (1990). Strategies for programming instruction in high school: Program completion vs. program generation. Journal of Educational Computing Research, 6(2–3), 265–285.

# 第二章 学术英语写作任务的认知负荷

## Chapter 2 Cognitive load of project-based academic writing task

**本章内容概要 Abstract of the chapter**

本章探讨第二语言（L2）学术写作中的项目式学习（PBL）的认知负荷，这是一种将学生置于学习中心，要求他们通过团队合作来研究问题并撰写学术报告的教学方法。本章首先回顾了 Hayes 和 Flower 提出的经典写作模型，该模型分析了写作过程中计划、转写和审查等子过程。写作模型有助于读者理解写作作为一种多维任务所需的认知加工过程。

接着，文章分析了基于项目研究的学术英语写作（PBAW）的复杂性。PBAW 的复杂性体现在三个方面：一是复杂的写作过程。与传统语言课程相比，PBAW 教学不注重学术词汇和学科知识讲解。学生在学习过程中需自主选择研究问题、查阅文献等，对自主学习能力不强的学习者，该模式带来了理解学术文章的困难。PBAW 过程分为信息搜集、产生思想和表达思想三个阶段。在信息搜集阶段，学生可能遇到资料选择和理解困难；在产生思想阶段，学习者可能遇到分析推理困难；在表达思想阶段，学生可能缺乏学科特定的语言和语篇表达能力。除了写作过程的复杂性之外，PBAW 的复杂性来源于读写综合的任务对阅读能力的严格要求。PBAW 属于读写紧密结合的综合任务。综合写作任务要求作者理解相关文本、结合文本内容表达思想。该过程中阅读与写作紧密结合，阅读可在多个层面影响写作，二语学生若阅读能力不足，会在写作过程中面临诸多问题。此外，学术英语写作中对知识的构建或者产生新知识的能力要求远大于其他体裁。

## 1. Introduction

Investigations in English first language (L1) writing and English as a second language (L2) writing have centered on the portrayal of the writing process and its cognitive dimensions. The 1980s ushered in the perspective of writing as both a sociocultural and cognitive endeavor, known as the social-context approach. Writing, as a multidisciplinary field, saw extensive research in the 1990s that encompassed writing within its various contextual settings. Scholars in the realm of second language writing have examined L2 writing processes as referenced in the works of Silva (1993), Cumming (1989), Zamel (1983), and Wang & Wen (2002). While the L1 writing process encompasses planning and idea generation, selecting appropriate vocabulary for transferring thoughts onto paper, and revising or editing the text, L2 writing involves all of these elements, with distinct differences. This research underscores the necessity for an L2 writing model that accounts for the intricacies of the L2 writing process. The chapter focuses on cognitive load of second language (L2) academic writing carried out based on research project teaching method. Both L1 and L2 writing theories with respect to project or task-based writing tasks will be reviewed.

## 2. Project Based Academic Writing (PBAW)

PBL is learner-centered, and it involves students learning cognitively and interactively in a group. As a PBL teaching model in writing courses, project-based writing (PBW) is a type of project-based and process-oriented writing that is frequently used to solve problems in various disciplines. It requires students to form groups, work together to discover a problem they are interested in, formulate a project that they will research, and finally compose academic reports or arguments laying out solutions. Throughout the writing process, teachers provide scaffolding by introducing searching skills, research methods and writing knowledge to support students.

The process of PBW requires the ability to use discipline-specific norms (including vocabulary, sentence patterns, discourse structures and styles within the field) (Capraro, 2013); metacognitive competence (Robinson 2005); an understanding of research methods, research procedures, value judgment and demonstration methods (Hyland, 2014). For example, postgraduate academic English competencies include the following aspects: language and discourse skills such as understanding the problems frequently encountered in the course and mastering the commonly used terms in the discipline; academic cognition and metacognitive abilities such as understanding the purpose of reading and writing, and critical analysis of text; subject research skills such as subject specific knowledge building, and the practical skills related to the discipline, such as how to find and sort out the literature (Sun & Wang, 2020).

## 3. Cognitive load of PBAW

### 3.1 Writing Theories

Writing theories of cognitive field studied why writing quality differs as a consequence of writing process. Hayes and Flower (1980) first proposed their process-based model (See Figure 1 for reference). Their model was divided into three major components: (1) the task environment, (2) the writer's long-term memory, and (3) the writing processes. They believed writing ability is related to how well a writer can use resources in long-term memory in the writing process to accomplish the task (Flower & Hayes 1981). In this seminal model, the writing processes include three operational processes: *planning*, *translating*, and *reviewing*, which take place recursively and generate the written text under the control of a control process—monitor. In the planning process, three sub-processes are involved: generating ideas, organizing information, and setting goals. Writers generate mental representation of the knowledge about writing a topic by combining information on the task with the knowledge from their long-term memory, and then organize their ideas and set procedural and substantive goals in the form of a writing plan. The translating process runs under the control of the writing plan in which writers transform the mental representation into written language on the page or screen. During the process of reviewing, writers read the text they have produced, evaluate the appropriateness of the written text in terms of the linguistic, semantic and pragmatic particularities according to the goal they set, and revise it if necessary.

All these operational composing processes occur in the context of the writer's long-term memory and the task environment. The long-term memory holds knowledge the writer stores, including the general text topic (knowledge of topic), the communicative act (knowledge of

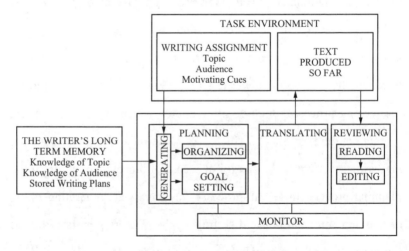

**Figure 1    The Hayes-Flower model (Hayes & Flower, 1980)**

audience), and linguistic knowledge about specific text plans (writing plans stored). The writer's task environment involves all of the exterior factors, including the rhetorical problem, the topic, audience, and situation prompting the writer to write, and the constraints brought on the writer by the text produced so far. In order to carry out the task successfully, the mature writer should set up their goal by considering the readers, the intended effect of the text on them, the creation of meaning, and the way to put the ideas through the text coherently. Flower and Hayes' writing model establishes the interaction of context and cognition in performing a particular writing task. Writing is thought of as a contextually constrained cognitive activity so students need to develop strategic knowledge and the ability to transform information to meet rhetorically constrained purposes (Grabe & Kaplan, 1996).

Recognizing that there is more than one processing model in text writing because of the differences between the writers in their writing abilities, Bereiter and Scardamalia (1987) propose a developmental view with two main writing processing models (knowledge-telling model vs. knowledge-transforming model) that suggests reasons for the differences between skilled and less-skilled writers. Less skilled writers operate at the level of *knowledge-telling*, including three components: the mental representation of assignment, two types of knowledge in Long Term Memory (content knowledge and discourse knowledge), and the writing process (knowledge telling process). They produce a text depends on the processes of retrieving ideas from long term memory with regard to topical and genre cues, and immediately write without reorganizing the conceptual content or the linguistic form of the text. Their primary goal of writing is to generate content during composing. They tend to be inflexible in planning and revising, and seldom revise beyond the word level. There is a very local control of the writing activity. In general, they are overly concerned with mechanics like spelling, punctuation, and grammar in the process of writing because these are not yet automatic for them, just to bypass the high-level aspects of text production activities. So less-skilled writers follow "a streamlined set of procedures" (Grabe & Kaplan, 1996: 119) described in the *knowledge-telling* model. It is economical for them, but it "can only provide some local coherence between two idea units" (Alamargot & Chanquoy, 2001: 8). Relatively uncomplicated writing tasks such as writing about personal experiences can be within their reach, but they will feel much less manageable when writing tasks demand more complex processing in abstract or logical organization.

When task complexity increases, more skilled writers are involved in *knowledge-transforming*, which includes readjustments of the text conceptual content according to the goal-setting and the text produced so far. They may have multiple processing, which is revealed through writing tasks that vary in processing complexity. The main difference between the two models is that the knowledge-transforming model involves more reflective problem-solving system and goal-setting. The different components in the knowledge transforming are functioning interactively to make the problem-solving system effective in the writing process. The "problem analysis and goal setting" component makes skilled writers set the goals according to assignment cues and means to achieve them through the composing process. According to Bereiter, Burtis, and Scardamalia (1988), the development of writing expertise needs to be considered as a progressive change form knowledge telling to knowledge transforming, via intermediate strategies (in Alamargot & Chanquoy, 2001: 6). Although problems arise in explaining how or when writers move from one stage to the other, the two-process developmental writing model promotes the understanding of differences in the writing performance of different writers. Just as the Flower and Hayes writing process model, the two-process writing model is also the most influential model serving as theoretical basis for using the process approach in writing research and instruction.

Given that the working memory is limited in capacity and duration, the capacity to manage simultaneously different types of processing is a vital problem of language production (Glynn, *et al.*, 1982). Therefore, 1990s witnessed a shift in research focus on an in-depth study of working memory and long-term memory and their role in writing processes, as much effort was devoted to developing new writing models along this direction.

Hayes (2012) focused on developing more detailed sub-processes in his task schema model, where the emphasis was on the central role of working memory in the activity of text writing (See Figure 2 for reference). The task environmental dimension comprises the writer's social and physical environment that concerns the external factors of writing. The individual dimension describes all the cognitive processes of writing in relation to working memory, with knowledge stored in long-term memory and equally with the writer's motivation and affect. Two main categories are distinguished: *fundamental cognitive processes*, a reorganization of the original writing processes, including reflection (original planning), text production (original translating, which has been elaborated considerably in the 2001 Chenoweth & Hayes' model) and text interpretation (original revision), and *resources stored either in working or long-term memory*, all under the control of a revision-specific task schema. In this schema, critical reading plays a more important role in the writing process, through which a writer will discover a problem, thereby selecting an appropriate resource stored in his long-term memory and activate it in his working memory. Hayes identified several functions of reading during writing: reading source texts, task definition, and text revision. It demonstrates that the same cognitive activity as reading can fulfill different functions depending on the context of the process (Rijlaarsdam & van den Bergh, 2006). Working memory is the interface where the cognitive processes and the knowledge stored in long term memory are matched under the influence of motivation and affects (Alamargot & Chanquoy, 2001). Writers who can utilize their working memory capacities more effectively generally have stronger reading skills and a better understanding of the writing topic, thus producing higher quality texts.

In general, depending on the tasks involved, the capacity of working memory is affected by these simultaneously operating processes in writing, especially the central executive of working memory which is activated during most of the activities (Becker, 2007). With more knowledge of the topic and developed skills, skilled writers have better overall memory capacity as they write. Less-skilled writers or L2 writers often have some difficulties in linguistic processing because some

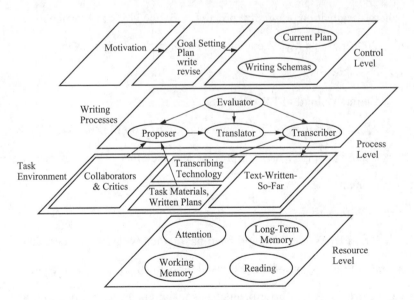

**Figure 2　Hayes's writing model (2012)**

types of these activities do not operate automatically and demand more phonological loop capacity and controlled attention of central executive capacities to devote to written formulation.

In the context of second language (L2) learning, when learners write in their L2, it can lead to even higher cognitive overload due to more element interactivity, increasing working memory demand and intrinsic cognitive load. Waddill and Marquardt (2011) differentiate between "controlled" and "automatic" knowledge retrieval; L1 writing is automatic, while L2 writing requires controlled retrieval, which is effortful and capacity-limited. Ransdell et al., (2002) note that excessive focus on knowledge retrieval can leave students with insufficient resources for higher-level writing tasks. This struggle can disrupt schema acquisition, a mindful process as defined by van Merriënboer et al., (2006), especially when learners frequently switch between L1 and L2.

## 3.2  Cognitive load of PBAW tasks

Here I want to address two causes of complexity for PBAW tasks: one is complex writing process and the other is the high reading requirement.

- PBAW process

The PBAW teaching approach has gained widespread acceptance against the backdrop of this extensive implementation of EAP courses. Literature indicates how project-based language teaching provides meaningful contexts for authentic language use in much the same way as task-based language teaching (Aghayani & Hajmohammadi, 2019; Artini et al., 2018; Ellis, 2003; Guo et al., 2020; Yang & Han, 2012). These meaningful and authentic interactions aid in acquiring language and are also supportive of areas such as improving student motivation (Egbert, 2003) and student autonomy for learning (Allen & Hecht, 2004). Many case studies have reported how projects can be successfully integrated in a broad range of English as a second language (ESL) and English as a foreign language (EFL) classroom context (Poonpon, 2011; Thang et al., 2014).

Formidable challenges encountered by learners, however, were observed by PBARW practitioners who implement PBARW teaching tasks. PBARW teaching does not place great importance on elaborating academic vocabulary or disciplinary knowledge compared with traditional language courses. In the project learning approach, students are at the center of the learning process, continually encountering, exploring, and overcoming problems (Grant, 2017). They independently choose research questions, consult academic literature, design research methods, collect data, and complete written reports. Teachers provide the necessary support for the course. The detachment from traditional language teaching practice, coupled with insufficient teaching time, has led to formidable challenges. In particular, the challenge of understanding authentic English academic articles unsuitable to their reading comprehension level has detrimental consequences for students' learning (Gong, 2016; Sun & Gong, 2017; Wang et al., 2015).

Researchers have extensively explored the cognitive challenges or difficulties faced by L2 students in the composition process (Cumming et al., 2016; Evans & Morrison, 2010; Hyland, 2016; Morrison & Evans, 2018). Following the cognitive writing process theory (Flower & Hayes, 1981; Hayes, 2012; Teng & Zhang, 2016), the PBARW process can be divided into three stages: information seeking and interpretation, idea creation before writing, and text processing. See Figure 3 for details.

Information seeking/interpreting is the initial stage of a PBARW task. During this process, students may encounter difficulties when they search for related literature to link with their own work (Berman & Cheng, 2001; Hellekjær, 2009; Mattus, 2007). For EAP learners, seeking and interpreting conceptually complex sources of information has been observed to be challenging (Hirvela, 2004; Neumann et al., 2019). Learners' limited knowledge of disciplinary terminology and general academic vocabulary may prevent them from comprehending disciplinary textbooks and journals quickly and fully (Uchihara & Harada, 2018). Moreover, the challenges at this stage are more formidable for undergraduates because understanding complex theories and research methods used by prestigious scholars is cognitively taxing even at the postgraduate level (Hyland, 2016).

Idea creation is the second stage of a PBARW task. It involves multiple small tasks, such as critical evaluation of prior knowledge, raising research questions, and proposing solutions. Idea creation in an academic writing task is much more complex than that in writing about daily life or personal experiences (Myles, 2002). For L2 students, the process is more cognitively challenging, considering the fact that they simultaneously engage in two difficult tasks: both constructing disciplinary knowledge and understanding texts in a foreign language with unfamiliar expressions (Bereiter & Scardamalia, 2014).

Text processing is the third writing stage that is both linguistically and structurally demanding (Rahmat, 2019). The development of text processing skills is an essential part of a writing course but it is difficult even for many first language (L1) students (Horning, 2009). In this process, the ability to use discipline-specific vocabulary, sentence patterns, textual structures, and styles within the field is essential (Nagy & Townsend, 2012), but students are often found lacking in these abilities and overly reliant on copying source notes without proper citation

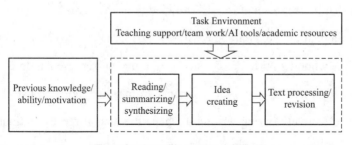

Figure 3　the writing process of PBAW

(Neumann et al., 2019). Students have also reported difficulties with expressing complex ideas in a second language and challenges in developing confidence and a convincing academic voice (Hyland, 2016).

• High reading requirement

Academic report writing is a part of reading/writing integrated writing tasks (Grabe & Zhang, 2013). Reading comprehension ability is of vital importance for the implementation of these integrated tasks (Delaney, 2008; Hirvela, 2004; Neumann et al., 2019; Park, 2016; Payant et al., 2019). An integrated task requires writers to comprehend source texts, synthesize source ideas, and express those ideas using appropriate stylistic conventions (Delaney, 2008; Knoch & Sitajalabhorn, 2013). As reading and writing draw on the same knowledge and cognitive systems and influence each other, an integrated writing task cannot be performed well if students do not first comprehend the source materials (Delaney, 2008; Hirvela, 2004; Neumann et al., 2019; Park, 2016; Payant et al., 2019).

Reading benefits writing through understanding topic knowledge and shaping representation of knowledge at the semantic, syntactic, and pragmatic levels (Grabe & Stoller, 2013; Hayes, 2012). Proficient readers who are skilled at constructing a mental representation of the text and selecting important elements from it are likely to use these skills effectively during writing to shape the mental representations of the texts they compose and select relevant content (Spivey, 1990). Poor

L2 reading skills, limited vocabulary knowledge, and inadequate reading experience may pose challenges in the integrated writing process (Grabe & Zhang, 2013). Empirically, insufficient reading ability has been found to cause problems in locating and structuring the ideas of source texts and processing texts with expressions of low quality (Plakans, 2009). In China, EAP practitioners have reported that learners with inadequate reading abilities have difficulty finding relevant information and understanding important academic concepts (Sun & Gong, 2017; Wang et al., 2015).

Reading can also affect writing by moderating the effectiveness of learning strategies used, such as the effectiveness of self-regulation strategies (e.g. attention control), socioemotional traits (e.g. motivation), and the effectiveness of activating mental presentation of topic knowledge in the writing process (Y. Cai & Kunnan, 2019b; Kim, 2020a, 2020b). The constraining role that reading ability plays on these strategies and knowledge is particularly germane to beginner writers. For more advanced writers, language proficiency is not likely to be as great a constraint, and these writing strategies and knowledge may make a greater contribution to writing (Kim, 2020b).

## 4. Problem of PBL from cognitive load perspective

Debate over the role of instructional guidance in teaching has persisted for decades. Some argue for minimal guidance, allowing learners to discover information independently, such as PBL (Bruner, 1961; Papert, 1980; Steffe & Gale, 1995). Instructional programs with minimal guidance assume: 1) students learn best by solving real-world problems independently, and 2) knowledge acquisition is optimized through discipline-specific experiences, mirroring the field's methods and epistemology (Kirschner, 1992). Empirical research over the past 50 years clearly shows that minimal guidance in instruction is less effective than tailored support for cognitive processing. This leads to recommendations that are difficult for educators to apply, as they may not foster effective learning.

Working memory is where conscious processing happens, but it has limitations in capacity and duration, especially with novel information. Minimal guidance approaches often overlook the impact of working memory limits on learning new information, which is a key challenge in constructivist and inquiry-based teaching methods. Advocates of such methods need to address how they can work within the known constraints of working memory. Inquiry-based learning, which involves problem-solving with limited guidance, can be cognitively demanding and may not enhance long-term memory storage, as working memory is occupied with the search process rather than learning.

The challenges faced by novice learners when using limited working memory for problem-solving are often overlooked, leading to instructional approaches that don't align with cognitive research.

Despite early advocacy for discovery learning, our current understanding of cognitive architecture calls for more guided instructional theories, which have been supported by systematic research (e.g., Anderson, 1996; Glaser, 1987). These theories should guide effective instructional design. From the problems related to PBL revealed above, how to adjust teaching method and lower high CL in academic writing course is worth studying.

## 5. Summary

This chapter explores project-based academic writing tasks (PBAWT) within the context of second language (L2) writing in English. In the course, CL can be adjusted by including training in group collaboration skills, structuring learning tasks from simple to complex, and the role of tutors in facilitating learning.

The chapter also reviews cognitive models of writing, acknowledges the complexity of writing as a multidimensional task requiring significant mental effort and engagement, and addresses the challenges faced by L2 writers, including less skilled writers who operate at the knowledge-telling level.

Furthermore, the complexity of PBAWT is discussed, highlighting the dual challenges of the writing process and the complex reading requirements. The writing process involves information seeking, idea creation, and text processing, with each stage presenting unique cognitive demands. The reading requirement involves comprehending source texts, synthesizing ideas, and expressing them using appropriate stylistic conventions, which can be challenging for L2 writers with limited reading abilities. Considering the complex writing process and high cognitive load accompanying PBAWT, it is important to understand how to measure the CL of the task, and the influential factors for affecting CL of the task, so that the higher CL related to PBAW tasks can be adjusted.

## 6. References

Aghayani, B., & Hajmohammadi, E. (2019). Project-based learning: Promoting EFL learners writing skills. *LLT Journal: A Journal on Language and Language Teaching*, 22, 78–85.

Allen, N. J., & Hecht, T. D. (2004). The "romance of teams": Toward an understanding of its psychological underpinnings and implications. *Journal of Occupational and Organizational Psychology*, 77, 439–461.

Anderson, J. R. (1996). ACT: A simple theory of complex cognition. *American Psychologist*, 51, 355–365.

Artini, L. P., Ratminings, N. M., & Padmadewi, N. N. (2018). Project based learning in EFL classes: Material development and impact of implementation. *Dutch Journal of Applied Linguistics*, 7, 26–44.

Becker, A. A Review of Writing Model Research Based on Cognitive Processes. Retrieved 2007-01-30 from http://wac.colostate.edu/

books/horning_revision/chapter3.pdf.

Berman, R., & Cheng, L. (2001). English academic language skills: Perceived difficulties by undergraduate and graduate students, and their academic achievement. *Canadian Journal of Applied Linguistics*, 4, 25–40.

Bereiter, C., & Scardamalia, M. (1987). *The Psychology of Written Composition*. Hillsdale, NJ: Lawrence Erlbaum Associates.

Bruner, J. S. (1961). The art of discovery. *Harvard Educational Review*, 31, 21–32.

Capraro, R. M., Capraro, M. M., & Morgan, J. (Eds.). (2013). *Project-based learning: An integrated science, technology, engineering, and mathematics (STEM) approach* (2nd ed.). Rotterdam: Sense.

Cumming, A. (1989). Writing expertise and second language proficiency. *Language Learning* 39: 81–141.

Cumming, A. (2016). Students' writing from sources for academic purposes: A synthesis of recent research. *Journal of English for Academic Purposes*, 23, 47–58.

Delaney, Y. A. (2008). Investigating the reading-to-write construct. *Journal of English for Academic Purposes*, 7(3), 140–150.

Egbert, J. (2003). A study of flow theory in the foreign language classroom. *The Modern Language Journal*, 87, 49–518.

Ellis, R. (2003). *Task-based language learning and teaching*. Oxford University Press. Available at: https://www.google.com.sg/

books/edition/Task_based_Language_Learning_and_Teachin/
coO0bxnBeRgC?hl=zh-CN&gbpv=1 (accessed November 2023).

Flower, L., & Hayes, J. R. (1981). A cognitive process theory of writing. *College Composition and Communication*, 32, 365–387.

Glaser, R. (1987). Further notes toward a psychology of instruction. In R. Glaser (Ed.), *Advances in instructional psychology* (Vol. 3, pp. 1–39). Hillsdale, NJ: Lawrence Erlbaum Associates, Inc.

Glynn, S. M., Britton, B. K., Muth, K. D., & Dogan, N. (1982). Writing and revising persuasive documents: cognitive demands. Journal of Educational Psychology, 74(4), 422–430.

Grabe, W., & Zhang, C. (2013). Reading and Writing Together: A critical component of English for academic purposes teaching and learning. *TESOL Journal*, 4(1), 9–24. https://doi.org/10.1002/tesj.65.

Grant, S. (2017). Implementing project-based language teaching in an Asian context: A university EAP writing course case study from Macau. *Asian-Pacific Journal of Second and Foreign Language Education*, 2–4.

Grabe, W., & Stoller, F. L. (2013). *Teaching and researching: Reading*. Routledge.

Hellekjær, G. O. (2009). Academic English reading proficiency at the university level: A Norwegian case study. *Reading in a Foreign Language*, 21, 198–222.

Hirvela, A. (2004). *Connecting reading & writing in second language writing instruction*. University of Michigan Press ELT.

Hyland, F. (2016). Challenges faced by second language doctoral student writers in Hong Kong and their writing strategies. *Australian Review of Applied Linguistics*, 39, 158–180.

Kim, Y. G. (2020a). Hierarchical and dynamic relations of language and cognitive skills to reading comprehension: Testing the direct and indirect effects model of reading (DIER). *Journal of Educational Psychology,* 112, 667–684. https://doi.org/10.1037/edu0000416.

Kim, Y. G. (2020b). Structural relations of language and cognitive skills, and topic knowledge to written composition: A test of the direct and indirect effects model of writing. *British Journal of Educational Psychology*, 90, 910–932. https://doi.org/10.1111/bjep.12301.

Kirschner, P. A. (1992). Epistemology, practical work and academic skills in science education. *Science and Education*, 1, 273–299.

Knoch, U., & Sitajalabhorn, W. (1913). A closer look at integrated writing tasks: Towards a more focused definition for assessment purposes. *Assessing Writing*, 18(4), 300–308. https://doi.org/10.1016/j.asw.13.09.003.

Neumann, H., Leu, S., & McDonough, K. (2019). L2 writers' use of outside sources and the related challenges. *Journal of English for Academic Purposes*, 38, 106–120. https://doi.org/10.1016/j.jeap.2019.06.001.

Papert, S. (1980). *Mindstorms: Children, computers, and powerful ideas.* Basic Books.

Park, J. (2016). Integrating reading and writing through extensive reading. *ELT Journal*, 70, 287–295. https://doi.org/10.1093/elt/ccw006.

Plakans, L. (2009). The role of reading strategies in integrated L2 writing tasks. *Journal of English for Academic Purposes*, 8(4), 252–266. https://doi.org/10.1016/j.jeap.2009.05.001.

Rahmat, N. H. (2019). Problems with rhetorical problems among academic writers. *American Journal of Social Sciences and Humanities*, 4, 506–515.

Robinson, P. (2005). Cognitive complexity and task sequencing: Studies in a componential framework for second language task design. *International Review of Applied Linguistics in Language Teaching*, 43 (1), 1–32. https://doi.org/10.1515/iral.2005.43.1.1.

Ransdell, S., Lavelle, B., & Levy, C. M. (2002). The effects of training a good working memory strategy on L1 and L2 writing. In S. Ransdell & M.-L. Barbier (Eds.). New directions in for research in L2 writing (pp.133–144). The Netherlands: Kluwer.

Silva, T. (1993). Toward an understanding of the distinct nature of of L2 writing: The ESL research and its implication. TESOL Quarterly, 27, 657–677.

Spivey, N. N. (1990). Transforming texts: Constructive processes in reading and writing. *Written Communication*, 7, 256–287. https://doi.org/10.1177/0741088390007003002.

Sun, T., & Wang, C. (2020). College students' writing self-efficacy and writing self-regulated learning strategies in learning English as a foreign language. *System*, 90, 1–17. https://doi.org/10.1016/j.system.2020.102221.

Sun, X. J., & Gong, R. (2017). Investigating student perceptions toward a project-based EAP writing course in a blended learning environment. *China ESP Study* (Zhong guo ESP Yan jiu), 8, 87–95.

Waddill, P. J., & Marquardt, M. P. (2011). A comparison of automatic and controlled processing in writing. *Journal of Writing Research*, 3 (1), 1–18.

Wang, W. Y., & Wen, Q. F. (2002). L1 use in the L2 composing process: An exploratory study of 16 Chinese EFL writers. *Journal of Second Language Writing*, 11: 225–246.

Yang, L. P., & Han, G. (2012). An empirical study on the teaching of academic writing in college English based on project-based learning model. *Foreign Language World* (Waiyu Jie), 5, 8–16.

Zamel, V. (1983). The composing processes of advanced ESL students: Six case studies. *TESOL Quarterly*, 17, 165–187.

# 第三章　任务型学术英语写作认知负荷量表的开发与验证

## Chapter 3　Measurement of PBAW cognitive load: scale development and validation

**本章内容概要 Abstract of the chapter**

　　任务型学术英语写作过程伴随大量的认知活动。本章报告了英语作为外语的任务型学术写作认知负荷量表的开发和验证过程。研究者首先在学生中做调研（使用了学习者日志），产生了认知负荷测量的问卷项目，之后研究者在不同学习者中，两次对量表的结构和效度进行了探索和验证。研究1用来探索量表的结构，研究2用来验证量表的稳定性与外在效度。量表的最终版本包含16个项目，评估三个维度的认知负荷：阅读阶段的负荷、产生思想的负荷和文本写作的负荷。探索性和验证性因子分析均表明，该量表的心理测量结果可靠而稳定。认知负荷测量结果与学习者的知识储备（阅读、话题知识）显著相关。该量表使写作研究者和教师能够科学地理解PBAW学习者感知的认知负荷，从而可以采取有针对性的干预策略。

## 1. Introduction

　　Determined by the interaction between tasks and learners, cognitive load in second language writing (SLW) is often described as a "black box". An accessible writing cognitive load measurement tool would have important implications for both teaching and learning writing, as well as PBL more broadly. However, there is a lack of such measurement scales in the literature. Accordingly, we developed the Project-based Academic Writing Cognitive Load Scale (PBAW_CLS), based upon cognitive load theory, the cognitive models of writing, and PBAW learners' reports of cognitive load experiences. We wanted to use the scale to measure cognitive load of all projected-based academic writing genres in academic contexts, such as research-based argumentation, research proposal and research-based report. Practicing writing teachers who use the scale may gain improved understanding of their students' cognitive resources distribution and accordingly optimize intervention strategies to improve students' writing process management. PBAW learners can use the scale to self-diagnose their cognitive load in writing and achieve self-regulated learning. Finally, the scale makes it possible to measure learners' writing cognitive load directly and ensures the validity of independent variable in writing task complexity research.

## 2. Literature Review

### 2.1 Writing Cognitive Load

As discussed in the previous chapters, writing is a complex cognitive activity that involves several subprocesses, such as planning, translating, and reviewing or monitoring, as outlined by Flower & Hayes (1981) and Kellogg (1996). Planning involves setting goals and organizing ideas, translating is the conversion of ideas into written form, and reviewing or monitoring is the evaluation and revision of the text. Hayes (2012) expanded this writing model to include transcribing, which encompasses spelling and orthography. These subprocesses compete for limited working memory, leading to cognitive overload, especially for L2 writers whose language proficiency constraints require more cognitive resources.

L2 writers often struggle more with planning and revision compared to L1 writers, as noted by Silva (1993), and spend a significant amount of time on formulation and revision, as observed by Roca de Larios et al. (2008) and Hall (1990). Despite the differences in cognitive load, the writing process for L2 writers mirrors that of L1 writers, involving the same subprocesses.

While there is general agreement on the subprocesses of writing, there are variations in how they are labeled and understood across different cognitive models. For instance, monitoring in Kellogg's model is similar to reviewing in Flower and Hayes' model, but Hayes' (2012) model views planning and reviewing as holistic writing activities. To provide a comprehensive view, our study defines writing cognitive load as the cognitive difficulties or challenges placed on learners during planning, translating, transcribing, and monitoring within the writing task.

## 2.2  Writing Cognitive Load Measurement

Cognitive load can be assessed through three main metrics: mental load, which is task-based and shaped by the complexity of the task rather than personal traits; mental effort, which is centered on the learner and is thought to mirror the reallocation of cognitive resources during task execution (Paas & Van Merriënboer, 1994); and task performance, which serves as an indirect measure of cognitive load by correlating with it. Focusing on mental effort as the key metric, self-assessments of cognitive load typically use a single-item scale from Paas (1992). Participants are tasked with rating their mental effort on a scale from 1 to 9 after completing a task, with 1 being minimal and 9 being maximal effort. Additionally, they might rate the task's difficulty on the same scale, but it's important to note that perceived difficulty and mental effort are separate concepts and do not have a direct, linear link. A task perceived as very hard does not automatically mean more mental effort will be exerted; in fact, it could deter effort (Van Gog & Paas, 2008). Thus, perceived difficulty alone is not a reliable indicator of the cognitive effort invested. In this study, mental difficulty was selected as the primary index to measure the cognitive load, with a focus on the complexity of research-based academic writing tasks.

Following Robinson's (2001) triadic framework, task complexity is often adjusted across various dimensions such as planning, the number of elements involved, the demands of reasoning, and the reliance on prior knowledge. However, studies like those by Johnson et al. (2012), Kuiken & Vedder (2008), Ruiz-Funes (2015), and He & Shi (2012) have yielded inconsistent and sometimes conflicting results regarding the impact of these manipulations on language performance. Johnson (2017) noted the inconclusiveness of these findings. Some researchers (e.g., Révész, 2014) attributed these divergent findings to the inadequacy of current research practices in the measurement of the independent factors and the causal processes. Cognitive load resulted from the manipulated task often failed to be measured and was merely assumed in most cases. To resolve the controversy, researchers must validate the assumption of cognitive task complexity (Sasayama, 2016), i.e., provide separate evidence that the task manipulation has indeed led to the desired changes in cognitive load, and that these changes have actually triggered the predicted causal processes (Révész, 2014; Révész et al., 2016).

Therefore, assessing the cognitive load that arises from various task adjustments has become a crucial matter. An increasing number of research efforts are recognizing the limitations in current methodologies and are starting to scrutinize if the task adjustments made according to the triadic framework truly bring about the desired shifts in cognitive load among learners. Certain studies have incorporated the examination of the writing process to gather evidence (for instance, Tabari, 2021), while the majority have been gauging cognitive load by means of self-assessments, expert evaluations, task duration, concurrent task performance, or a mix of these techniques. Self-ratings used in most studies were adapted and extended from Robinson's (2001) questionnaire, and used a 9-point scale (e.g., Révész et al., 2017), a 5-point scale (e.g., Golparvar & Rashidi, 2021), a 6-point scale (e.g., Zalbidea, 2017) or a 4-point scale (e.g., Choong, 2014) to assess participants' perceptions of overall mental effort, task difficulty or both to validate the task complexity.

In these studies, all self-ratings focused on learners' overall impressions of cognitive load when completing the entire task. A limited number of investigations inquired about the specific challenges learners encountered (e.g., Choong, 2014) or the mental effort they dedicated to sub-tasks, such as planning (e.g., Révész et al., 2017). To enhance the validation of task complexity, some researchers have integrated self-ratings with expert assessments, task duration, or dual-task approaches. In Rahimi and Zhang's (2018) research, both educators and students evaluated task complexity. In Choong's (2014) study, participants were required to report not only their perceived difficulty but also the time they spent on the task. Lee (2020) merged subjective self-ratings with expert evaluations and task duration. Both learners and experts completed a 9-point Likert scale to gauge overall perceived task difficulty and mental effort; learners also provided information on their stress levels and estimated the time spent in the pre-task phase and the time pressure experienced during task completion. Moreover,

Xu et al. (2023) used a multi-faceted approach, combining self-ratings, expert judgment, and dual-task methodology to confirm the effectiveness of the task complexity manipulations.

Considering the necessity of differentiating between mental effort and perceived difficulty mentioned above in this section, some researchers gauged both (e.g., Xu et al., 2023). Nevertheless, the mental effort scale employed in these studies was usually single-item and aimed to tap the overall amount of mental effort learners invested, while less consideration has been given to the mental effort distribution in writing processes. Furthermore, cognitive load is largely task-dependent; argumentative tasks are assumed to be more cognitively demanding than narrative tasks (Ruiz-Funes, 2015; Yoon, 2021), but there is a paucity of instrument designed for measuring learners' cognitive load in specific writing genres. To fill this gap, and considering the academic importance of project-based report writing for learners, the present study uses perceived difficuty as the measurement index and attempts to develop and validate a scale for measuring PBAW learners' cognitive load (PBAW_CLS).

## 3. Method

Given the popularity of project-based academic writing and limited research on students' perceived cognitive load in the writing process, it is necessary to examine the extent of cognitive load in their learning process. In order to fill this gap, we aimed to develop and validate an instrument, the Project-based Academic Writing Cognitive Load Scale (PBAW_CLS). In study 1, the PBAW_CLS was administered to a sample of university students (n=317) and the data were subjected to exploratory factor analyses (EFA) to elicit the underlying factors of the cognitive load. In study 2, the fine-grained PBAW was administered to another sample of students from the same universities (n=361). Confirmatory factory analyses (CFA) through structural equation modeling (SEM) were conducted to check the reliability, construct validity, and discriminant validity. The predictive validity was assessed through correlations between cognitive load, previous knowledge (reading ability, topic knowledge) and writing performance. We hope that our effort of developing and validating the PBAW_CLS would enhance our understanding of cognitive load in PBL, thus enriching the growing body of research on L2 writing and second language acquisition. With the information, we also expect to offer pedagogical implications for teaching L2 students to adjust CLs, in the hope of fostering their effective and proactive learning.

## 4. Study 1 and 2

### 4.1 Study 1: Instrument Development and Initial Validation

In Study 1, we aimed to develop and modify the PBAW_CLS and

then check the content validity, face validity, reliability, and construct validity.

- Participants and Procedures

A total sample of 317 university students were voluntarily recruited from a business university in Shanghai, China. All participants were second-year students from three majors: International Trade (34%, n=108); International Investment (28%, n=88); Management (38%, n=121). Of these, participants' ages ranged from 18 to 23 (M=19.78, SD=1.37), with 57% males (n=180) and 43% females (n=136). At the time of the study, all participants had been enrolled in an academic writing course, which was administered to non-English major students with 90 min each week (an average of 20–30 students in each class). The course was designed to improve undergraduates' academic writing proficiency and help them increase problem-solving ability. The teaching syllabus for the writing course was designed in accordance with the requirement of the National College English Teaching Syllabus with a focus on academic writing skills.

- Course Setting

PBAW tasks lasted for a semester, separated into eight sections. The course was provided exclusively for about 800 students with the best English proficiency. During the eight sections, students worked in groups, read authentic academic literatures, chose research questions, collected data, and wrote academic reports in English. At the end of the semester, every student was required to write and submit a report of more than 2,500 words. During the learning process, four EAP teachers provided necessary scaffolding. Among the four teachers, two were associate professors with more than 10 years of teaching experience, and the other two were young teachers with doctorates in education. Students' writing was accessed across 5 dimensions covering the ability to clarify writing focus, develop academic ideas, organize content, and write with academic style and language conventions (Good et al., 2012).

During the eight sections, two writing teachers lectured on reading/ writing strategies and genre knowledge to students distributed across six classes. Students were divided into small groups. They chose writing topics freely with group members, but each student read and wrote individually. The first four sections were used for students to locate academic information, read academic papers critically, and write research proposals. Teachers lectured on related reading/writing strategies and organized group conferences to provide scaffolding for the different learning needs. Sections five to seven were allocated for writing reports. Teachers, with the help of teaching assistants, lectured on genre knowledge pertaining to academic reports and gave brief feedback on unfinished drafts. Section eight was for peer review and revision. In addition to regular teaching, a mock academic conference was organized at the end of the semester. Refer to Table 1 for detailed reading/writing strategies taught in the course.

Table 1    Reading/writing strategies taught in the PBARW course

| Meeting time | Reading/Writing Strategies |
| --- | --- |
| 1st meeting | Locating reliable academic information |
| 2nd meeting | Taking notes, summarizing, and synthesizing |
| 3rd meeting | Writing a research proposal |
| 4th meeting | Collecting and analyzing data |
| 5th meeting | Writing the introduction part |
| 6th meeting | Writing the body part |
| 7th meeting | Writing the conclusion part |
| 8th meeting | Revising |

- Procedure

At the end of the semester, all participants were invited to complete an integrated self-report questionnaire, which was intended for gathering their demographic information and their perceived use of motivational regulation strategies in classroom settings. Given that they were undergraduate students with over 9 years of English learning experience, we adopted the English version questionnaire written in plain English. All participants were briefed on the purpose of the study and informed of their rights to withdraw from the research at any time during or after data collection. On average, participants spent approximately 15 min to complete the whole questionnaire.

Items in the PBAW_CLS were prepared according to social cognitive writing theory (Flower & Hayes, 1981; Hayes, 2012), and academic writing challenges elaborated in the literature (Grabe & Zhang, 2013; Hyland 2007, 2016). The challenges possibly created in three sub-stages of writing activities were included in the questionnaire: information seeking/interpreting activities before writing, idea creation, and text processing activities. The original items came from learning journals from 20 students learning the course (See appendix for more information). For content validity, 2 experts who possessed expertise in applied linguistics, or academic writing were invited to scrutinize the initial pools, evaluating the theoretical rationale, the consistency of construct and items, and wordings of questions. For face validity, we interviewed 8 students who had taken part in the project-based writing course through telephone. They were asked to evaluate the readability and the clarity of the questionnaire. After addressing the questions raised by the experts and students, the revised questionnaire was formally used to measure the challenges of PBAW activity. Participants were asked to indicate the extent to which they thought the statement was consistent with their perceptions of challenges in the learning process.

Sample items of the cognitive load include the load of reading before writing (e.g., Understanding terminologies in English academic literature is difficult or not.); planning before writing (e.g., Clarifying the scope of knowledge involved in the topic is difficult or not); idea translating (e.g., Using appropriate academic language is difficult or not). An initial list of 19 items was generated. After addressing their questions (e.g., ambiguous wording and inconsistent questions with the construct), we removed eight items, resulting in 20 items in total. The final questionnaire was a 6-point

Likert scale rating from 1 (1 means the task is not difficult at all) to 6 (6 means the task is very difficult). Participants were asked to choose one number that most properly suits the challenges they felt when doing the sub-tasks in the project-based academic writing course.

- Results

Descriptive Statistics and Test of Univariate Normality

Descriptive analysis showed that the mean scores of all items ranged between 3.98 and 5.45, with the standard deviations from 0.76 to 1.68. The values for skewness and kurtosis of all items were within the cut-off values of |3.0| and |8.0|, respectively (Kline 2011), suggesting the univariate normality for factor analysis. Before conducting the EFA, two missing values were deleted listwise, meaning the whole cases were excluded from the analysis. Given that the total proportion of missing values was less than 1% (Enders 2010), the deletion would not result in a substantial decrease in the total cases.

Exploratory Factor Analyses (EFA)

Although the design of the questionnaire was theory-driven, we initially applied EFA to explore the underlying structure of project-based academic writing cognitive load given the exploratory nature of this study. A principal axis factoring (PAF) analysis was performed on the scores of 20 items via promax rotation with Kaiser Normalization, allowing for intercorrelations among factors (DeVellis 2012). The Kaiser's eigenvalues-greaterthan-one (K1) rule, the scree plot, and parallel analysis were adopted as criteria to retain the number of factors. All the extraction methods supported a three-factor solution, accounting for 69% of the total variance. The factor loadings of all items were over the minimal level of ±0.30 for a sample size of at least 300 cases (Field 2009). Further assessment resulted in the elimination of two items low loadings and one items complex loading. Table 1 shows the final results of EFA of the PBAW_CLS scale.

From the item clustering around each factor, the three different cognitive loads were labeled as Academic Reading Load (Factor 1), Idea Creating Load (Factor 2), Text Processing Load (Factor 3). The Cronbach's alpha of the subscales were all above the 0.70 threshold value based on the sample size, corroborating the internal consistency reliability (DeVellis 2012) (see Table 2).

**Table 2　Results of EFA and reliabilities of the PBAW_CLS scale**

| Factor & Item | Factor Loading | | | |
|---|---|---|---|---|
| | 1 | 2 | 3 | a |
| Reading Cognitive Load | | | | 0.829 |
| 1. Understanding terminologies in English academic literature | 0.863 | | | |
| 2. Fast reading and judging the value of the literature in English | 0.766 | | | |
| 3. Fast reading and finding specific information in the literature in English | 0.621 | | | |
| 4. Detailed reading and understanding of the literature in English | 0.605 | | | |
| 5. Taking notes in your own language while reading English academic literature | 0.598 | | | |

continue

| Factor & Item | Factor Loading | | | |
|---|---|---|---|---|
| | 1 | 2 | 3 | a |
| Planning Cognitive Load | | | | 0.765 |
| 1. Finding the topic worth of study | | 0.838 | | |
| 2. Finding the academic literature related to the topic | | 0.702 | | |
| 3. Clarifying the scope of knowledge involved in the topic | | 0.653 | | |
| 4. Designing research methods | | 0.647 | | |
| 5. Obtaining data | | 0.598 | | |
| 6. Analyzing data | | 0.572 | | |
| Writing Cognitive Load | | | | 0.727 |
| 1. Using appropriate academic language | | | 0.820 | |
| 2. Selecting the content of literature review | | | 0.754 | |
| 3. Comparing and synthesizing multiple articles | | | 0.754 | |
| 4. Writing in your own language | | | 0.690 | |
| 5. Writing in proper structure | | | 0.516 | |

a Cronbach's alpha.

## 4.2  Study 2: Factorial Validation

The second study aimed to cross-validate the structure generated in the EFA stage with another sample in terms of the construct validity and discriminant validity using CFA. Predictive validity was assessed based on the correlations between cognitive load and students' previous knowledge.

Participants and Procedures

• Participants

There were 361 second-year university students aged between 18 and 23 (M=19.89, SD=0.97) with 58% males (n=211) and 42% females (n=150) from the same university as those in the first study. These participants were from three different majors: International Business (n=127, 35%); Accounting (n=103, 29%); and Management (n=131, 36%). They were invited to complete the refined version of the PBAW_ CLS (English version) with the same procedure as conducted in the EFA period. At the time of the study, all participants were enrolled in the same writing course as earlier discussed in Study 1. By the end of the semester, we collected students' reading and writing scores of College English Text (Band-4) and self-reported topic knowledge. Then the students' reading and writing scores, self-reported topic knowledge were correlated with their reported cognitive load to check the predictive validity of the instrument.

- CET Band 4 Scores

We used the reading and writing score of the College English Test (CET) band 4 as a measure of English reading and writing ability and previous knowledge that influence cognitive load when doing project-based academic writing. The CET 4 is a standardized English proficiency test designed to assess whether university students meet the requirements of the college English course set by the National College English Syllabus for Non-English Majors. The participants took the CET 4 exam on June 21, 2020, two months before they took the PBAW course. In the reading section, students were required to read one article of about 1, 200 words and two articles of about 500 words to test their speed reading and reading for detail skills. In the writing section students were asked to write an essay of about 220 words showing their attitudes to using PPTs by teachers.

- Topic knowledge

Topical knowledge was measured using 5 questions adapted from Khabbazbashi (2016). These questions measure the familiarity of the learners with the topic knowledge that they write on in the PBAW course. Table 3 shows the 5 items. It was designed with a six-point Likert scale ranging from 1 (not at all true of me) to 6 (very true of me). The values of internal reliability for the instrument were 0.89.

**Table 3    Topic knowledge Measurement**

| Prompt: Please choose one number that most properly describes the knowledge that you have on the topics written on in the academic writing course: 1 means it is not at all true of you; 6 means it is very true of you. | | | | | | |
|---|---|---|---|---|---|---|
| 1.  This topic is familiar to me. | 1 | 2 | 3 | 4 | 5 | 6 |
| 2.  I have thorough knowledge about this topic. | 1 | 2 | 3 | 4 | 5 | 6 |
| 3.  It was easy for me to produce enough ideas for this topic. | 1 | 2 | 3 | 4 | 5 | 6 |
| 4.  If I were to talk about this topic in my first language, I would have more ideas to talk about. | 1 | 2 | 3 | 4 | 5 | 6 |
| 5.  I had appropriate words to express my ideas about this topic. | 1 | 2 | 3 | 4 | 5 | 6 |

- Data Analysis

The second round of data was subjected to CFA using the maximum likelihood (ML) estimation. Given the sensitivity of CFA to missing values and outliers, five cases were eliminated due to the systematic response bias (two cases) and missing values (three cases).

The final sample size of 359 met the desired cases-to-variables ratio (10:1) analysis for CFA (Field 2009). Several omnibus fit statistical analyses were employed to evaluate the model fit. Three absolute fit indices were consulted, including the ratio of $\chi^2$ to its degree of freedom; the standardized root mean square residual (SRMR), and the root mean square error of approximation (RMSEA) with values less than 0.08 and 0.06, respectively, as acceptable fit (Hu and Bentler, 1999). Two incremental fit indices, TLI and CFI, were also examined with a recommended cut-off value equal to or more than 0.95 (Hu and Bentler 1999). This indicates the requirement of normality for CFA was satisfied.

• Results

Confirmatory Factor Analyses (CFA) CFA results show that all goodness-of-fit indices revealed an overall acceptable model fit ($\chi^2$=2.78; df=689.75; p<0.001; TLI=0.93; CFI=0.94; RMSEA=0.058 [0.053, 0.060]; SRMR=0.045), although TLI was still below the acceptable threshold value of 0.95. Given the minimum item requirement for each factor and the sensitivity of TLI to misspecification and sample size (Fan & Sivo, 2007), no elimination of indicators was further conducted. So it was accepted with good model fit, as depicted in Figure 1.

In this congeneric model, each factor only loaded on the one of the factors as designed to measure, factor covariances were free to be estimated, and measurement errors were assumed to be uncorrelated. All 16-item parameter estimates were statistically significant at p<0.001 and

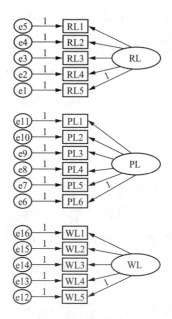

**Figure 1    Three-factor model. RL reading cognitive load, PL planning cognitive load, WL writing cognitive load**

standardized estimates loadings on the hypothesized latent constructs were higher than the recommended value 0.50, showing a large effect size (Hair et al., 2010). The correlations among three factors were positive and significant at p<0.01 level. The discriminant validity was evidenced by moderately strong intercorrelations of the three factors ranging from 0.630 between reading cognitive load and planning cognitive load, and 0.696 with writing cognitive load, and 0.756 between planning cognitive load and writing cognitive load, revealing that these three factors were clearly correlated but also distinct constructs, as depicted in Table 4.

Table 4　Intercorrelations of cognitive loads and their relationships
with previous knowledge

| | Reading CL | Planning CL | Writing CL | Reading ability | Writing ability | Topic knowledge |
|---|---|---|---|---|---|---|
| Reading CL | 1 | 0.630** | 0.696** | −0.340** | −0.087 | −0.263** |
| Planning CL | | 1 | 0.756** | −0.216** | −0.045 | −0.245** |
| Writing CL | | | 1 | −0.282** | −0.116 | −0.239** |

∗∗ Correlation is significant at the .05 level (2-tailed)

- Predictive Validity Analysis

In terms of predictive validity, Table 2 shows the correlations between three cognitive loads and learners' previous knowledge: reading ability, writing abilities and topic knowledge. The results show that the three cognitive loads were significantly correlated with reading ability, and topic knowledge (p<0.05). However, there were no significant relationships of writing ability with cognitive load.

- Model Comparisons

Comparisons of plausible models are highly recommended for providing further evidence of construct validity in the questionnaire development process (Hair et al., 2010). So we proposed that three competing models be evaluated by using a series of CFA, including one factor model testing whether all these items load on one overall factor (Model 1); a five-factor uncorrelated model as evaluated in CFA (Model 2); a correlated factor model (Model 3) testing whether the five factors are related to one another. We resorted to the value of the $\chi^2$ difference with the corresponding change in the degrees of freedom to evaluate the significant differences between these models. On the whole, Model 3, the three-factor correlated model ($\chi^2$=2.55; df=674.08; p<0.001; TLI=0.95; CFI=0.97; RMSEA=0.057 [0.054, 0.062]; SRMR=0.047), had the best fit indices. On this basis, we retained Model 3 as the best model in our study. Figure 2 is a graphic display of the 16-item, three-factor correlated model (Model 3).

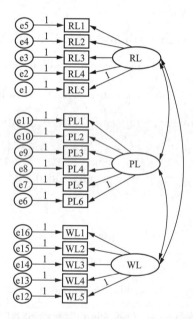

**Figure 2    Three-factor correlated model. RL reading cognitive load, PL planning cognitive load, WL writing cognitive load**

## 5. Discussion

Our study aimed to develop and validate a self-report instrument, the PBAW_CLS, to assess students' perceived cognitive load in project-based academic writing. The findings show that Chinese university students reported high cognitive load in the whole process of PBAW tasks. The factorial analyses through EFA and CFA with separate samples provide substantial evidence for the three-factor structure that includes reading, planning and writing related cognitive load. The results show the satisfactory psychometric qualities of the instrument in relation to the reliability, construct validity, and discriminant validity. The satisfactory predictive validity was also obtained through the significant correlations between these loads and previous knowledge. The three-factor correlated model with the best fit suggests that the three categories of cognitive loads were reliably distinguished but correlated on both conceptual and empirical grounds. So the scores of the 16 items can be collectively summed to represent a learner's overall level of cognitive load when doing PBAW tasks or calculated separately to reveal the load in different writing stages, with a higher score indicating a higher level of mental load. The negative correlations of reading and topic knowledge with the three loads reveal the essential relationship between the subjective knowledge owned by the learner and cognitive load in the sense of task complexity. The findings indicate that students who would like to increase their knowledge of reading or topic knowledge (e.g., improve the fast reading, critical reading and note-taking skill, comparing and contrasting reading, or learning for research related topic) tended to feel less cognitively loaded while writing academic papers. Part of our findings is in agreement with research findings along this line (e.g., Hyland, 2016; Grade and Zhang, 2013), suggesting that students, regardless of academic genres (e.g., argumentation, report or proposal), have an analogous psychological trait in their learning process. Improving subjective knowledge would be effective to lower PBAW tasks.

Three subcategories of CLs were found by the study. Factor 1, labeled as reading cognitive load (five items), refers to the difficulties of searching for valuable academic resources, understanding the research topic knowledge, comparing and contrasting different academic views, and find research gap. Poor L2 reading skills, limited vocabulary knowledge, and inadequate reading experience may pose challenges in the integrated writing process (Grabe & Zhang, 2013). Empirically, insufficient reading ability has been found to cause problems in locating and structuring the ideas of source texts and processing texts with expressions of low quality (Plakans, 2009). In China, EAP practitioners have reported learners with inadequate reading abilities have difficulty finding relevant information and understanding important academic concepts (Wang et al., 2015; Sun & Gong, 2017). Our findings also reveal that reading cognitive load was significantly correlated with students' reading ability and topic knowledge, which helps us understand that increasing students reading ability can lower their perceived reading load.

Factor 2, named as planning cognitive load (six items), includes finding the topic worth of study, clarifying the scope of knowledge involved in the topic, designing research methods, obtaining data, and analyzing data. Idea creation in an academic writing task is much more complex than in writing about daily life or personal experiences (Myles, 2002). For L2 students, the process is more cognitively challenging, considering the fact that they simultaneously engage in two difficult tasks: both constructing discipline knowledge and understanding texts in a foreign language with unfamiliar expressions (Bereiter & Scardamalia, 2014). Our findings also reseal that idea creating or planning cognitive load is related to reading ability and topic knowledge, which helps us understand that increasing students' previous knowledge in the two aspects can lower their perceived planning load.

Factor 3, named as writing cognitive load (five items), includes using appropriate academic language, selecting the content of literature review, comparing and synthesizing multiple articles, writing in their own language, and writing in proper structure. The development of text processing skills is an essential part of a writing course but is difficult even for many L1 students (Horning, 2009). In this process, the ability to use discipline-specific vocabulary, sentence patterns, textual structures, and styles within the field is required (Nagy & Townsend, 2012), but students are often found lacking in these abilities and overly reliant on copying source notes without proper citation (Neumann et al., 2019).

Students have also reported difficulties with expressing complex ideas in a second language and problems with developing confidence and a convincing academic voice (Hyland 2016). Our findings also reseal that idea translating or writing cognitive load is related to reading ability and topic knowledge, which helps us understand that increasing students' previous knowledge in the two aspects can lower their perceived planning load.

## 6. Summary

This study aimed to develop and validate the Project-based Academic Writing Cognitive Load Scale (PBAW_CLS) to measure cognitive load (CL) in second language writing (SLW). The PBAW_CLS is designed to assess CL across different academic writing genres, which can help teachers optimize intervention strategies and support self-regulated learning for students. The scale was developed based on cognitive load theory, writing cognitive models, and reports from learners. The study involved two phases. EFA and CFA supported a three-factor structure of the PBAW_CLS: Academic Reading Load, Idea Creating Load, and Text Processing Load. These factors were found to be reliable, valid, and distinct but correlated. The cognitive loads were significantly correlated with reading ability and topic knowledge but not with writing ability. The study contributes to the understanding of cognitive load in L2 writing and offers a tool for enhancing teaching and learning strategies in academic writing contexts.

## 7. Reference

Aghayani, B., & Hajmohammadi, E. (2019). Project-based learning: Promoting EFL learners writing skills. *LLT Journal: A Journal on Language and Language Teaching*, 22, 78–85.

Allen, N. J., & Hecht, T. D. (2004). The "romance of teams": Toward an understanding of its psychological underpinnings and implications. *Journal of Occupational and Organizational Psychology*, 77, 439–461.

Artini, L. P., Ratminings, N. M., & Padmadewi, N. N. (2018). Project based learning in EFL classes: Material development and impact of implementation. *Dutch Journal of Applied Linguistics*, (7), 26–44.

Bai, R., Hu, G., & Gu, Y. (2014). The relationship between writing strategies and English proficiency in Singapore primary schools. *Asia Pacific Education Researcher*, 23, 355–365.

Bereiter, C., & Scardamalia, M. (2014). Knowledge building and knowledge creation: One concept, two hills to climb. In S. Tan, H. So, & J. Yeo (Eds.), *Education innovation series* (pp. 35–52). Springer.

Berman, R., & Cheng, L. (2001). English academic language skills: Perceived difficulties by undergraduate and graduate students, and their academic achievement. *Canadian Journal of Applied Linguistics*, 4, 25–40.

Byrnes, H. (2014). Linking task and writing for language development: Evidence from a genre-based curricular approach. In H. Byrnes & R. M. Mancho'n (Eds.), *Task-based language learning: Insights from and for L2 writing* (pp. 237–263). Philadelphia, PA: Benjamins.

Cai, J. G. (2010). The feasibility study of EMI: A case analysis of public relation course of Fudan. *Foreign Languages in China (Zhongguo Waiyu)*, 7, 61–67.

Cai, J. G. (2012). EAP needs analysis and the study on teaching methodology. *Foreign Language Learning Theory and Practice (Waiyu Jiaoxue Lilun Yu Shijian)*, 2, 30–35.

Cai, Y., & Kunnan, A. J. (2019a). Mapping the fluctuating effect of strategy use ability on English reading performance for nursing students: A multi-layered moderation analysis approach. *Language Testing*, 37, 280–304.

Cai, Y., & Kunnan, A. J. (2019b). Detecting the language thresholds of the effect of background knowledge on a language for specific purposes reading performance: A case of the island ridge curve. *Journal of English for Academic Purposes*, 42, 100–795.

Choong, K. P. (2014). *Effects of task complexity on written production (Unpublished doctoral dissertation)*. Columbia University, New York.

Chinese Ministry of Education. (2020). College English curriculum requirements. *Higher Education Press*.

Clarke, M. A. (1980). The short circuit hypothesis of ESL reading – or when language competence interferes with reading performance. *The Modern Language Journal*, 64, 203–209.

Cohen, J. (1990). Statistical power analysis for the behavioral sciences. *Computers, Environment and Urban Systems*, (14), 71–78.

Crookes, G. (1989). Planning and interlanguage variation. *Studies in Second Language Acquisition*, (11), 177–193.

Cumming, A. (2013). Assessing integrated writing tasks for academic purposes: Promises and perils. *Language Assessment Quarterly*, 10, 1–8.

Cumming, A. (2014). Assessing integrated skills. In Kunnan, A. (Ed.), *Companion to language assessment* (pp. 216–229). Wiley-Blackwell.

Cumming, A., Lai, C., & Cho, H. (2016). Students' writing from sources for academic purposes: A synthesis of recent research. Journal of English for Academic Purposes, 23, 47–58.

Cummins, J. (1979). Linguistic interdependence and the educational development of bilingual children. Review of Educational Research, 49, 222–251.

Cummins, J. (2000). Language, power, and pedagogy: Bilingual children in the crossfire. Multilingual Matters.

Delaney, Y. A. (2008). Investigating the reading-to-write construct. Journal of English for Academic Purposes, 7, 140–150.

Deng, L., Chen, Q., & Zhang, Y. (2014). Developing Chinese EFL learners' generic competence: A genre-based and process-genre approach. New York, NY: Springer.

De La Paz, S. (2002). Explicitly teaching strategies, skills, and knowledge: Writing instruction in middle school classrooms. Journal of Educational Psychology, 94, 380–394.

DeVellis, R. F. (2012). Scale development: Theory and applications (3rd ed.). Thousand Oaks, CA: Sage.

Egbert, J. (2003). A study of flow theory in the foreign language classroom. The Modern Language Journal, 87, 499–518.

Ellis, R. (2003). Task-based language learning and teaching. Oxford University Press.

Enders, C. K. (2010). Applied missing data analysis. New York, NY: Guilford.

Evans, S., & Morrison, B. (2010). The first term at university: implications for EAP. ELT Journal, 65, 387–397.

Fan, X., & Sivo, S. A. (2007). Sensitivity of fit indices to model misspecification and model types. Multivariate Behavioral Research, 42(3), 509–529.

Ferris, D. (2009). Teaching college writing to diverse student populations. University of Michigan Press.

Field, A. P. (2009). Discovering statistics using SPSS: (and sex, drugs and rock "n" roll) (3rd ed.). London, UK: Sage.

Fitzgerald, J., & Shanahan, T. (2000). Reading and writing relations and their development. Educational Psychologist, 35, 39–50.

Flower, L., & Hayes, J. P. (1981). A cognitive process theory of writing. College Composition and Communication, 32, 365–387.

Galbraith, D., & Torrance, M. (2004). Revision in the context of different drafting strategies. Educational Studies in Language and Literature, 4, 37–52.

Gao, Y., Zhao, Y., Cheng, Y., & Zhou, Y. (2003). Motivation types of Chinese college undergraduates. Modern Foreign Languages (Quarterly), 26(1), 28–38.

Gilabert, R. (2005). Task complexity and L2 narrative oral production. Unpublished doctoral thesis. University of Barcelona.

Good, J. M., Osborne, K., & Birchfield, K. (2012). Placing data in the hands of discipline-specific decision makers: Campus-wide writing program assessment. Assessing Writing, 17, 140–149.

Gong, R. (2016). Exploring the effect of prewriting planning in EAP writing course context. Journal of University of Shanghai for Science and Technology (Shanghai Ligong Daxue Xuebao), 38, 28–35.

Grabe, W., & Stoller, F. L. (2013). Teaching and researching: Reading. Routledge.

Grabe, W., & Zhang, C. (2013). Reading and writing together: A critical component of English for academic purposes teaching and learning. TESOL Journal, 4, 9–24.

Grant, L., & Ginther, A. (2000). Using computer-tagged linguistic features to describe L2 writing differences. Journal of Second Language Writing, 9, 123–140.

Guo, P., Saab, N., Post, L. S., & Admiraal, W. (2020). A review of project-based learning in higher education: Student outcomes and measures. International Journal of Educational Research, 102, 101–586.

Hall, C. (1990). Managing the complexity of revising across languages. TESOL Quarterly, 24(1), 43–60.

Hair, J. F., Black, W. C., Babin, B. J., & Anderson, R. E. (2010). Multivariate data analysis: A global perspective (7th ed.). Upper Saddle River, NJ: Pearson.

Hayes, J. R. (1996). A new framework for understanding cognition and affect in writing. In C. M., Levy, & S., Ransdell (Eds.), The science of writing: Theories, methods, individual differences, and applications (pp. 1–27). New York/London: Routledge.

Hayes, J. R. (2012). Modeling and remodeling writing. Written Communication, 29(3), 369–388.

He, L., & Shi, L. (2012). Topic knowledge and ESL writing. Language Testing, 29(3), 443–464.

Hirvela, A. (2004). Connecting reading & writing in second language writing instruction. University of Michigan Press ELT.

Hu, L., & Bentler, P. M. (1999). Cutoff criteria for fit indexes in covariance structure analysis: Conventional criteria versus new alternatives. Structural Equation Modeling, 6, 1–55.

Hyland, F. (2016). Challenges faced by second language doctoral student writers in Hong Kong and their writing strategies. Australian Review of Applied Linguistics, 39, 158–180.

Hyland, K. (2007). Feedback on second language students' writing. Language Teaching Research, 11, 43–65.

Ishikawa, S. (2007). The effects of task complexity on the complexity, accuracy, and fluency of L2 written production. Journal of Second Language Writing, 16, 245–268.

Jackson, S., & Suethanapornkul, S. (2013). The effects of task complexity on L2 writing: A meta-analysis. Language Teaching Research, 17(4), 449–466.

Jarvis, S. (2002). Short texts, best-fitting curves and new measures of lexical diversity. Language Testing, 19(1), 59–82.

Jarvis, S., Grant, B., Bikowski, D., & Ferris, D. (2003). Exploring multiple profiles of highly rated learner compositions. Journal of Second Language Writing, 12, 255–276.

Johnson, M. D., Acevedo, A., & Mercado, L. (2012). The effects of planning sub-processes on L2 writing fluency, grammatical complexity, and lexical complexity. Journal of Second Language Writing, 21, 264–282.

Johnson, M. D. (2017). Cognitive task complexity and L2 written syntactic complexity, accuracy, lexical complexity and fluency: A research synthesis and meta-analysis. Journal of Second Language Writing, 37, 13–38.

Kang, E., & Han, Z. (2015). The efficacy of written corrective feedback in improving L2 written accuracy: A meta-analysis. Modern Language Journal, 99, 1–18.

Kellogg, R. T. (1996). A model of working memory in writing. In C. M. Levy, & S. Ransdell (Eds.), The science of writing: Theories, methods, individual differences, and applications (pp. 57–71). New York/London: Routledge.

Khabbazbashi, N. (2016). Topic and background knowledge effects on performance in speaking assessment. Language Testing, 34, 23–48.

Kim, Y. G. (2020a). Hierarchical and dynamic relations of language and cognitive skills to reading comprehension: Testing the direct and indirect effects model of reading (DIER). Journal of Educational Psychology, 112, 667–684.

Kim, Y. G. (2020b). Structural relations of language and cognitive skills, and topic knowledge to written composition: A test of the direct and indirect effects model of writing. British Journal of Educational Psychology, 90, 910–932.

Kline, R. B. (2011). Principles and practice of structural equation modeling (3rd ed.). New York, NY: Guilford.

Kormos, J. (2011). Task complexity and linguistic and discourse features of narrative writing performance. Journal of Second Language

Writing, 20, 240–252.

Kuiken, F., & Vedder, I. (2008). Cognitive task complexity and written output in Italian and French as a foreign language. Journal of Second Language Writing, 19, 48–60.

Kuiken, F., Mos, C., & Vedder, I. (2005). Cognitive task complexity and L2 writing performance. In R. Ellis (Ed.), Planning and task performance in a second language (pp. 235–249). Amsterdam: John Benjamins.

Lai, C., & Cho, H. (2016). Students' writing from sources for academic purposes: A synthesis of recent research. Journal of English for Academic Purposes, 23, 47–58.

Lee, I. (2014). Revisiting teacher feedback in EFL writing from sociocultural perspectives. TESOL Quarterly, 48(1), 201–213.

Lee, J. Y. (2020). Task closure and task complexity effects on L2 written performance. Journal of Second Language Writing, 50, 1–13.

Leki, I., Cumming, A., & Silva, T. (2008). A synthesis of research on second language writing in English. New York: Routledge.

Ma, G. (2005). The effects of motivation and effort on foreign language achievement. Journal of PLA University of Foreign Languages, 28(4), 37–41.

Manchón, R. M. (2014). The internal dimension of tasks: The interaction between task factors and learner factors in bringing about learning through writing. In H. Byrnes & R. M. Manchón (Eds.), Task-based language learning: Insights from and for L2 writing (pp. 27–52). Philadelphia, PA: Benjamins.

Matsuda, P. K. (2012). On the nature of second language writing: Replication in a postmodern field. Journal of Second Language Writing, 21(3), 300–302.

Mattus, M. (2007). Finding credible information: A challenge to students writing academic essays. Human IT: Journal for Information Technology Studies as a Human Science, 9, 1–28.

Mazzgutova, D., & Kormos, J. (2015). The effects of strategy use on writing performance in second language writing. Journal of Second Language Writing, 22, 19–32.

McCann, E. J., & Garcia, T. (1999). Maintaining motivation and regulating emotion: Measuring individual differences in academic volitional strategies. Learning and Individual Differences, 11(3), 259–279.

Myles, J. (2002). Second language writing and research: The writing process and error analysis in student texts. TESL-EJ, 6, 1–20.

Nagy, W. E., & Townsend, D. (2012). Words as tools: Learning academic vocabulary as language acquisition. Reading Research Quarterly, 47, 91–108.

Neumann, H., Leu, S., & McDonough, K. (2019). L2 writers' use of outside sources and the related challenges. Journal of English for Academic Purposes, 38, 106–120.

Norris, L., & Ortega, L. (2009). Syntactic complexity in second language writing development. Applied Linguistics, 30(4), 464–496.

Ong, J., & Zhang, L. J. (2013). Effects of the manipulation of cognitive processes on EFL writers' text quality. TESOL Quarterly, 47(2), 375–398.

Ortega, L. (2012). The role of the linguistic environment in second language acquisition. In S. Gass & A. Mackey (Eds.), The Routledge handbook of second language acquisition (pp. 271–286). New York: Routledge.

Park, J. (2016). Integrating reading and writing through extensive reading. ELT Journal, 70, 287–295.

Payant, C., McDonough, K., Uludag, P., & Lindberg, R. (2019). Predicting integrated writing task performance: Source comprehension, prewriting planning, and individual differences. Journal of English for Academic Purposes, 40, 87–97.

Perin, D., Keselman, A., & Monopoli, M. (2003). The academic writing of community college remedial students: Text and learner variables. Higher Education, 45, 19–42.

Plakans, L. (2009). The role of reading strategies in integrated L2 writing tasks. Journal of English for Academic Purposes, 8, 252–266.

Plakans, L. (2015). Integrated second language writing assessment: Why? What? How? Language and Linguistics Compass, 9, 159–167.

Qin, X., & Wen, Q. (2002). Internal structure of EFL motivation at the tertiary level in China. *Foreign Language Teaching and Research*, 34(1), 51–58.

Rahimi, M., & Zhang, L. J. (2018). Writing task complexity, students' motivational beliefs, anxiety and their writing production in English as a second language. *Reading and Writing*, 32, 761–786.

Raimes, A. (1985). What unskilled ESL students do as they write: A classroom study of composing. *TESOL Quarterly*, 19(2), 229–285.

Rau, D., & Sebrechts, M. M. (1996). Revision in the context of different drafting strategies. *Research in the Teaching of English*, 30(4), 407–436.

Raykov, T., & Marcoulides, G. A. (2008). *An introduction to applied multivariate analysis*. New York, NY: Routledge.

Roca de Larios, J., Martin, J., & Murphy, L. (2001). A temporal analysis of formulation processes in L1 and L2 writing. *Language Learning*, 51, 497–538.

Robinson, P. (2001). Task complexity, task difficulty, and task production: Exploring interactions in a componential framework. *Applied Linguistics*, 22(1), 27–57.

Rubin, J., Chamot, A. U., Harris, V., & Anderson, N. J. (2007). Intervening in the use of strategies. In A. D. Cohen & E. Macaro (Eds.), *Language learner strategies: Thirty years of research and practice* (pp. 141–160). Oxford, UK: Oxford University Press.

Ruiz-Funes, M. (2015). Exploring the potential of second/foreign language writing for language learning: The effects of task factors and learner variables. Journal of Second Language Writing, 28, 1–19.

Sasayama, S. (2016). Is a "complex" task really complex? Validating the assumption of cognitive task complexity. The Modern Language Journal, 100(1), 231–254.

Schwinger, M., Steinmayr, R., & Spinath, B. (2009). How do motivational regulation strategies affect achievement: Mediated by effort management and moderated by intelligence. Learning and Individual Differences, 19(4), 621–627.

Shanahan, T., & Shanahan, C. (2008). Teaching disciplinary literacy to adolescents: Rethinking content-area literacy. Harvard Educational Review, 78, 40–59.

Shintani, N. (2012). Input-based tasks and the acquisition of vocabulary and grammar: A process-product study. Language Teaching Research, 16, 253–279.

Silva, T. (1993). Toward an understanding of the distinct nature of L2 writing: The ESL research and its implications. TESOL Quarterly, 27, 657–677.

Silva, T., & Matsuda, P. K. (Eds.). (2010). Practicing theory in second language writing. West Lafayette, ID: Parlor Press.

Spivey, N. N. (1990). Transforming texts: Constructive processes in reading and writing. Written Communication, 7, 256–287.

Sun, X. J., & Gong, R. (2017). Investigating student perceptions toward a project-based EAP writing course in a blended learning environment. China ESP Study (Zhongguo ESP Yanjiu), 8, 87–95.

Tabari, M. A. (2021). Task preparedness and L2 written production: Investigating effects of planning modes on L2 learners' focus of attention and output. *Journal of Second Language Writing*, 52, 1–14.

Takimoto, M. (2007). The effects of input-based tasks on the development of learners' pragmatic proficiency. *Applied Linguistics*, 30, 1–25.

Tang, S. M., Lin, L. K., Mahmud, N., Ismail, K., & Zabidi, N. A. (2014). Technology integration in the form of digital storytelling: Mapping the concerns of four Malaysian ESL instructors. *Computer Assisted Language Learning*, 27, 311–329.

Teng, L. S., & Zhang, L. J. (2016). A questionnaire-based validation of multidimensional models of self-regulated learning strategies. *The Modern Language Journal*, 100, 674–701.

Trenkic, D., & Warmington, M. (2019). Language and literacy skills of home and international university students: How different are they, and does it matter? *Bilingualism: Language and Cognition*, 22, 349–365.

Uchihara, T., & Harada, T. (2018). Roles of vocabulary knowledge for success in English-medium instruction: Self-perceptions and academic outcomes of Japanese undergraduates. *TESOL Quarterly*, 52, 564–587.

Van Gog, T., & Paas, F. (2008). Instructional efficiency: Revisiting the original construct in educational research. *Educational Psychologist*, 43, 16–26.

Wang, X. H., Chen, M. H., & Li, X. X. (2015). Transition of college English teaching oriented towards EAP: Problems and countermeasures. *Foreign Language Learning Theory and Practice (Waiyu Jiaoxue Lilun Yu Shijian)*, 4, 55–58.

West, S. G., Finch, J. F., & Curran, P. J. (1995). Structural equation models with nonnormal variables: Problems and remedies. In Hoyle, R. H. (Ed.), *Structural equation modeling: Concepts, issues, and applications* (pp. 56–75). Sage.

Woodrow, L. (2011). College English writing affect: Self-efficacy and anxiety. *System*, 39(4), 510–522.

Wolters, C. A. (1998). Self-regulated learning and college students' regulation of motivation. *Journal of Educational Psychology*, 90(2), 224–235.

Wolters, C. A. (1999). The relation between high school students' motivational regulation and their use of learning strategies, effort, and classroom performance. *Learning and Individual Differences*, 11(3), 281–299.

Wolters, C. A. (2003). Regulation of motivation: Evaluating an underemphasized aspect of self-regulated learning. *Educational Psychologist*, 38(4), 189–205.

Wolters, C. A., & Benzon, M. B. (2013). Assessing and predicting college students' use of strategies for the self-regulation of motivation. *Journal of Experimental Education*, 81(2), 199–221.

Yang, L., & Gao, S. (2013). Beliefs and practices of Chinese university teachers in EFL writing instruction. *Language, Culture and Curriculum*, 26(2), 128–145.

Yeo, J. (2021). Challenging the connection between task perceptions and language use in L2 writing: Genre, cognitive task complexity, and linguistic complexity. *Journal of Second Language Writing*, 54, 1–14.

Yoon, H. J. (2021). Challenging the connection between task perceptions and language use in L2 writing: Genre, cognitive task complexity, and linguistic complexity. *Journal of Second Language Writing*, 54, 1–14.

Zalbidea, J. (2017). "One task fits all"? The roles of task complexity, modality, and working memory capacity in L2 performance. *The Modern Language Journal*, 101(2), 335–352.

Zhang, L. J. (2008). Constructivist pedagogy in strategic reading instruction: Exploring pathways to learner development in the English as a second language (ESL) classroom. *Instructional Sciences,* 36(2), 89–116.

Zhang, L. J. (2013). Second language writing as and for second language learning. Journal of Second Language Writing, 22(4), 446–447.

Zhang, L., Aryadoust, V., & Zhang, D. (2015). Taking stock of the effects of strategies-based instruction on writing in Chinese and English in Singapore primary schools. In R. E. Silver & W. Bokhorst-Heng (Eds.), *Quadrilingual education in Singapore: Pedagogical innovation in language education* (pp. 193–244). New York, NY: Springer.

ZhaoH. (2010). Investigating learners' use and understanding of peer and teacher feedback on writing: A comparative study in a Chinese English writing classroom. *Assessing Writing*, 15(1), 3–17.

Zheng, Y., & Cheng, L. (2008). Test review: College English test (CET) in China. *Language Testing*, 25(3), 408–417.

Zimmerman, B. J. (2013). From cognitive modeling to self-regulation: A social cognitive career path. *Educational Psychologist*, 48(3), 135–147.

Zimmerman, B. J., & Martinez-Pons, M. (1986). Development of a structured interview for assessing student use of self-regulated learning strategies. *American Educational Research Journal*, 23(4), 614–628.

# 第二部分
# 任务型学术英语写作认知负荷的
# 影响因素

# Part II
# Factors affecting cognitive load in
# PBAW

# 第四章　学术英语写作认知负荷的影响因素假设
## Chapter 4　Factors affecting cognitive load in PBAW tasks

**本章内容概要 Abstract of the chapter**

上一章我们研究了如何测量学习者主观感受的任务型学术英语写作的认知负荷。这种主观感受的负荷可能与任务本身的复杂度、学习者的知识储备、认知能力、情感动机，以及教学环境有关。影响学习者主观感知认知负荷的因素如果被明确，教学中就可以设计方案，对主观感知的认知负荷进行调节。在明确认知负荷测量方法的基础上，观察相关因素与学习者感知到的认知负荷的关联性，可以确定认知负荷的影响因素，进而对认知负荷进行调节。

在 PBAW 环境中，内在负荷由学习任务中涉及的要素的复杂性，以及交互性水平产生，与任务本身的复杂度相关，难以通过教学设计改变。影响写作任务内在认知负荷的因素包括体裁和内容的复杂性。由于认知负荷是主观感知的指标，学习者的知识储备、情感动机和思维特征等影响感知的负荷。外在负荷由任务信息呈现方式和学习活动环境产生，与教学设计相关。对于 PBAW 任务，影响外在负荷的学习环境包括教学支持、同伴合作，技术工具（AI）等。当学习者进行有助于新知识构建和进行长期记忆的认知活动时，产生相关负荷。从以上分析中可以总结出六个影响 PBAW 认知负荷的因素：1. 写作体裁；2. 学习者的先验知识和能力；3. 学习者的学习动机和情绪；4. 学习者使用的学习策略；5. 批判思维；6. 技术手段（AI）。但是这些因素是否真实影响PBAW学习过程中的认知负荷，以及如何影响认知负荷需要用实验研究观察。

## 1. Introduction

In the previous chapter, we investigated how to measure the cognitive load of project-based academic English writing as perceived by learners. This subjective perception of load may be related to the complexity of the task itself, the learners' knowledge base, cognitive abilities, emotional motivation, and the teaching environment. If the factors affecting the subjective perception of cognitive load are identified, it is possible to design interventions in teaching to regulate this subjectively perceived cognitive load. Based on the clarification of cognitive load measurement methods, observing the correlation between relevant factors and the cognitive load perceived by learners can identify the influencing factors of cognitive load, thereby allowing for its regulation. We will review related literature in the chapter and propose factors that may influencing learners' perceived cognitive load in PBAW context.

## 2. Literature Review

Paas and van Merriënboer (1994) distinguished causal and

assessment factors that determine the level of cognitive load. Causal factors include three main factors that affect cognitive load: characteristics of the learner (e.g., his cognitive skills), the task (e.g., task complexity with environment), and their mutual relations. Numerous factors with variance contribute to the level of cognitive load in English writing in addition to what has been mentioned above. For example, writing practice plays a role in affecting the cognitive load of a task, because with practice learners will accommodate the relevant knowledge in their long-term memory. A task which may seem very difficult when first attempted may end up requiring only a small amount of mental capacity after sufficient practice. Different language systems will affect the task load in writing as well. Chinese learners of English, especially the beginners, have difficulties in spelling the English words on hearing because they are used to link the written symbol to its meaning instead of its phoneme. The characteristics of writing systems across languages result in different awareness of writing systems. Chinese writers are clearly aware of morphemes in Chinese morphemic writing system rather than phonological units, but writing in English requires more phonological awareness. So the cognitive demands of coping with a new medium such as forming letters, attending to spelling and punctuation etc. may impede their writing performance for Chinese learners. Kirkland and Saunders (1991) have suggested a number of interacting internal and external constraints that determine cognitive load particularly related to summary writing. The following lists are the possible factors affecting the cognitive load of a L2 writing task in general: 1) The topic the student writes about; 2) The discourse mode, i. e., text type or genre that is required (e.g., narration, description, exposition or argumentation); 3) The time pressure required by the task; 4) Learner's L2 proficiency; 5) Learner's prior knowledge and expertise; 6) Learner's cognitive/metacognitive skills and learning style; 7) Writing apprehension; 8) Learning and instructional background... More may be added to the list. These factors seem to have their influences on the level of cognitive load (Paas, Touvinen, Tabbers, & Van Gervin, 2003).

Related to cognitive load theory, task complexity theory developed by Robinson (Robinson, 2001, 2005, 2007) in the field of L2 speaking tasks should be mentioned. Robinson made a delicate analysis on the factors affecting task complexity. Table 1 shows the three different types of task factors related to different levels of task complexity in his Cognition Hypothesis model.

Similar to cognitive load theory, Robinson considered task complexity, environment and learners' ability in the model. A task with few elements is less complex cognitively. For example, a task that requires describing a simple object has fewer elements than a task that requires analyzing a complex situation. If a task is focused on the here-and-now context, it is less complex. Tasks that involve thinking about past or future events or distant locations are more complex. When a task requires little prior knowledge, it is less complex. Tasks that demand extensive background knowledge are more complex. If a task does not involve learning new knowledge, it is less complex. Tasks that require learners to acquire and apply new knowledge are more complex.

We noticed affective variables e.g., motivation, anxiety and confidence were also being studied in relation to task complexity and speaking performance in this model. Motivation and self-efficacy or confidence are also variables frequently considered in cognitive load theory. According to emotion studies, negative emotions (e.g., anxiety and anger) exhaust working memory resources and incur a high cognitive load (Logan et al., 2011; Xie et al., 2023). On the other hand, positive emotions such as enjoyment can prevent students from experiencing such negative responses and reduce the high cognitive load caused by them (Logan et al., 2011; Wang & Guthrie, 2004).

According to Robinson's model, tasks with different levels of complexity can have an impact on various aspects of language production and learning. For example, more complex tasks may lead to more elaborate language output, greater cognitive processing, and potentially more language learning opportunities. However, very complex tasks may also overwhelm learners and lead to frustration.

**Table 1    Robinson's model of task complexity**

| Cognitive factors | Interactive factors | Difficulty factors |
|---|---|---|
| Task complexity<br>a) Resource directing e.g.,<br>　+/− few elements<br>　+/− Here-and-Now<br>　+/− no reasoning demands<br>　+/− spatial location<br>　+/− first person perspective<br>b) Resources dispersing e.g.,<br>　+/− planning<br>　+/− single task<br>　+/− prior knowledge<br>　+/− clear structure<br>　+/− few steps<br>　+/− sequence | Task conditions<br>a) participation variables<br>　e.g., one way/two way<br>　convergent/divergent<br>　open/closed<br>b) participant variables<br>　e.g., gender/familiarity<br>　power/solidarity | Task difficulty<br>a) affective variables e.g., motiv-<br>　ation/anxiety/confidence<br>b) ability variables e.g., working<br>　memory/aptitude/proficiency/<br>　intelligence |

## 3.  Cognitive load affecting factors in PBAW context

As illustrated in Chapter one, there are three kinds of cognitive loads: intrinsic, extrinsic and germane loads. These loads are aroused by task, learner and learning environment respectively. When studying affecting factors to the cognitive load PBAW activities, we consider the three kinds of load respectively.

*Intrinsic load* is generated by the level of element interactivity of the information presented by a learning task. Learners have to attend simultaneously to the elements in order to complete the task. It is task-related and can hardly be altered or manipulated by instructional design without changing the nature of the task or compromising understanding (Paas, Renkl, & Sweller, 2003; Pollock, Chandler, & Sweller, 2002).

It is beneficial to lower intrinsic cognitive load by artificially reducing element interactivity (Pollock, Chandler, & Sweller, 2002) or by developing learners' prior knowledge through pre-training before the final task is presented (Mayer & Moreno, 2003). As for writing tasks, the factors that affect the intrinsic cognitive load include genre and content schemata. Generally speaking, people feel narration and description are less cognitively challenging than argumentation; disciplinary related content will be more challenging than writing familiar topic.

From the simple analysis above, we can hypothesize that in the PBAW task, the cognitive load of writing may be related to the genre of writing, that is, opinion writing, research reports, and research proposal reports may affect the amount of cognitive load. Considering the writing experience of the Chinese college students in high school with short essay of less than 200 words as the main genres, academic writing based on research would be challenging for them; the prior knowledge and ability of learners, such as reading ability, writing ability, topic knowledge; their intelligence, memory, motivation and SRL strategies. Working as subjective resources, these factors would affect cognitive load of writing task.

Extraneous load of writing task

*Extraneous load* is imposed by the manner in which the task information is presented to learners and the learning activities required of learners. Therefore, it is instructional design-related. Unnecessary load can be added through a cumbersome design (Sweller, 1994). It interferes with schema construction and automation. There are a variety of methods which can be used to present instructional material. Examples of instructional techniques include written texts, pictures, diagrams, formal lectures and multimedia computer presentations. For English writing tasks, extraneous cognitive load involves the presentation modes of a writing task (e.g. picture vs. text). Time limits, the environment in which the student must function, and the conventions expected by the discourse community are also the external factors. For PBAW tasks, learning environment that may influence extrinsic load includes, among others, teaching scaffolding, such as one-to-one conference, lectures, feedback, writing sample, textbook, assessing rubric, writing team, literature resources and AI tools.

Germane load of writing task

When the load is related to the cognitive processing helpful to schema construction and storage into long-term memory, it is *germane load* (Sweller, van Merrienboer, & Paas, 1998; Pass & Kester, 2006). In instructional design the teacher should take the germane cognitive load into consideration. It ensures that the learner is focused on the learning processes. If the learner's attention is directed toward processes relevant to the construction of schemas, learning will be improved. Variability of problem situations increases germane cognitive load because it provides the Opportunity for learners to identify similar and relevant features to construct cognitive schemata (van Merriënboer & Sweller, 2005). It benefits subsequent performance on similar and transfer problems. Higher-level processes for achieving a deeper understanding or successful meaning conveyance are the very case of germane load as they involve sophisticated schemata construction and automation. Therefore, we hypothesize that directing learners' attention to high-level cognitive processes (such as critical thinking) contributes to germane load when learners are completing a writing task.

We noticed affective variables e.g., motivation, anxiety and confidence were also being studied in relation to task complexity and speaking performance. Motivation and self-efficacy or confidence are also variables frequently considered in cognitive load theory. According to emotion studies, negative emotions (e.g., anxiety and anger) exhaust working memory resources and incur a high cognitive load (Logan et al., 2011; Xie et al., 2023). On the other hand, positive emotions such as enjoyment can prevent students from experiencing such negative responses and reduce the high cognitive load caused by them (Logan et al., 2011; Wang & Guthrie, 2004). Here comes the hypothesis: motivation and emotion are factors influencing cognitive load.

## 4. PBAW cognitive load affecting factor hypotheses

To summarize, there are overall six hypotheses that we presumed for the PBAW influential factors:

- Hypothesis 1:

  The cognitive load of writing is related to the genre of writing, such as opinion writing, research reports, and research proposal. Genre can work as a variable in affecting the amount of cognitive load perceived by learners.

- Hypothesis 2:

  The prior knowledge of learners, such as reading ability, writing ability, and topic knowledge, may affect the cognitive load. The availability of knowledge influences the possibility of establishing new schema of knowledge in the learning process.

- Hypothesis 3:

  Motivation and positive emotion are factors influencing cognitive load, with negative emotions increasing cognitive load and positive emotions reducing it.

- Hypothesis 4:

  Learner's cognitive/metacognitive skills, and learning style can influence the cognitive load.

- Hypothesis 5:

  Directing learners' attention to high-level cognitive processes, such as critical thinking, contributes to germane load when learners are completing a writing task.

- Hypothesis 6:

  The learning environment, including teaching scaffolding, writing samples, textbooks, assessing rubrics, writing teams, literature resources, and AI tools, may influence extraneous cognitive load.

These hypotheses (as shown in figure 1 below) are derived from the analysis of cognitive load theory with the consideration of PBAW tasks in Chinese university. We will test these hypotheses in the following studies with data we collected in the past three years. The data we adopted came from Shanghai University of International Business and Economics. In the university, academic writing course has been provided since 2013. This is one of the earliest universities in China which changed from general English teaching to academic English teaching.

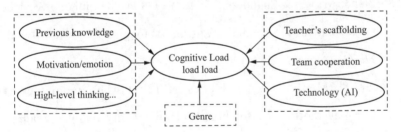

**Figure 1　hypothetical factors affecting PBAW cognitive load**

## 5. Summary

Through the careful examination of factors influencing intrinsic, extraneous, and germane loads, we have been able to formulate a series of hypotheses that shed light on the potential determinants of cognitive load in these tasks. Study these factors would shed insights into how educational interventions can be tailored to reduce unnecessary cognitive burdens and enhance learning outcomes. By considering the genre of writing, learner's prior knowledge, and the learning environment, educators can create more effective instructional designs that support schema construction and automate cognitive processes, leading to deeper understanding and more efficient learning. In the following chapters, experimental studies would be reported as to how these hypothetical factors influence Chinese university students when learning project-based academic writing.

## 6. References

Kirkland, M. R., & Saunders, M. A. P. (1991). Maximizing Student Performance in Summary Writing: Managing Cognitive Load. *TESOL Quarterly*, 25 (1).

Logan, S., Medford, E., & Hughes, N. (2011). The importance of intrinsic motivation for high and low ability readers' reading comprehension performance. *Learning and Individual Differences*, 21(1), 124–128.

Mayer, R. E., & Moreno, R. (2003). Nine ways to reduce cognitive load in multimedia learning. *Educational Psychologist*, 38, 43–52.

Paas, F., Renkl, A., & Sweller, J. (2003). Cognitive load theory and instructional design: Recent developments. *Educational Psychologist*, 38(1), 1–4.

Paas, F. G. W. C., & van Merriënboer, J. J. G. (1994a). Variability of worked examples and transfer of geometrical problem-solving skills: A cognitive-load approach. *Journal of Educational Psychology*, 86(1), 122–133.

Paas, F., Touvinen, J., Tabbers, H., & Van Gervin, A. J. L. (2003). Cognitive load measurement as a means to advance cognitive load theory. *Educational Psychologist*, 38(1), 63–71.

Pass, F., & Kester, L. (2006). Learner and Information Characteristics in the Design of Powerful Learning Environments. *Applied Cognitive Psychology*, 20(3), 281–85.

Pollock, E., Chandler, P., & Sweller, J. (2002). Assimilating complex information, *Learning and Instruction* 12(1), 61–86.

Robinson, P. (2001). Task complexity, cognitive resources, and syllabus design: A triadic framework for examining task influences on SLA. In P. Robinson (Ed.), *Cognition and Second Language Instruction* (pp.287–318). Cambridge: Cambridge University Press.

Robinson, P. (2005). Cognitive complexity and task sequencing: Studies in a componential framework for second language task design. *International Review of Applied Linguistics*, (43), 1–32.

Robinson, P. (2007). Criteria for classifying and sequencing pedagogic tasks. In Maria del Pilar García Mayo (Ed.) *Investigating Tasks in Formal Language Learning* (pp.7–26). Clevedon: Multilingual Matters.

Sweller, J. (1994). Cognitive load theory, learning difficulty and instructional design. *Learning and Instruction*, 4, 295–312.

Sweller, J., van Merrienboer, J. J. G., & Paas, F. (1998). Cognitive architecture and instructional design. *Educational Psychology Review*, 10(3), 251–296.

van Merriënboer, J. J. G., & Sweller, J. (2005). Cognitive load theory and complex learning: Recent developments and future directions. *Educational Psychology Review*, 17, 147–177.

Wang, J. H., & Guthrie, J. (2004). Modeling the effects of intrinsic motivation, extrinsic motivation, amount of reading, and past reading achievement on text comprehension between US and Chinese students. *Reading Research Quarterly*, 39(2), 162–186.

Xie, W., Ye, C., & Zhang, W. (2023). Negative emotion reduces visual working memory recall variability: A meta-analytical review. *Emotion*, 23(3), 859–871.

# 第五章　学习者阅读能力对认知负荷的影响
## Chapter 5　Influence of cognitive load from reading ability

**本章内容概要 Abstract of the chapter**

　　阅读能力在基于研究的写作任务中起着至关重要的作用，因为阅读是知识的来源。任务型学术报告写作是读写综合写作任务的一种，阅读理解能力对这类任务至关重要。因为读写相互依存，若不先理解原文材料，综合写作任务就无法完成。阅读还能调节写作过程中学习策略的有效性。在二语阅读中，阅读能力如果在一定水平之下，学生难以与二语文本进行互动。只有达到一定语言能力，学生才能在学术任务中表现良好，达不到阅读能力的学生在语言输入和输出任务中都会遇到困难。有研究提出阅读能力阈值可作为学生开始 PBAW 课程学习的门槛，但是具体的阅读能力要求尚无定论。

　　研究者对上海一所商科院校的学术英语写作课程进行了研究。研究发现，随着学习者英语阅读能力的提高，感知到的写作任务的认知负荷逐渐降低。但当阅读能力达到大学英语 4 级（CET4）测试中，阅读成绩 210 附近时，阅读水平的提高不再引起认知负荷的下降。认知负荷在这里趋于平稳（见图 3）。研究表明，当学习者的阅读能力到达 CET4 级 210 分，相当于欧洲语言参考框架的 B2 高端水平时，学习者感知到的认知负荷基本与阅读能力无关。此时，学习者可以完成英文阅读，掌握学科知识，进行分析写作。从而这个阅读水平可以认为是学习者进入任务型学术英语写作的基础水平。对于阅读水平不足以应对PBAW写作任务的学习者，研究者建议可以设计与专业相关的阅读训练，提高专业词汇、阅读速度、摘要写作能力。这样的训练可以避免用第二语言学习专业知识带来的交叉效应，减少认知负荷。本研究的价值在于为学习者选择课程提供前行语言能力评估。也为课程设计者提供教学内容参考。

## 1. Introduction

PBARW is an integrated reading/writing task (Grabe & Zhang, 2013). Reading comprehension ability is of vital importance in implementing such integrated tasks (Delaney, 2008; Payant et al., 2019; Park, 2016; Hirvela, 2004; Neumann et al., 2019). However, a lack of the reading ability required for integrated academic writing tasks is a common phenomenon (Plakans 2009, 2015; Perin et al., 2003; Ferris, 2009). In L2 reading, many researchers support a threshold reading level hypothesis that below a certain reading comprehension level, students will have difficulty in interacting with L2 texts (Cummins 1979, 2000; Clarke, 1980), transferring reading strategies (Cai & Kunnan, 2019a; Kim, 2020a), or activating background knowledge to facilitate comprehension (Cai & Kunnan, 2019b; Kim 2020b). Grabe and Zhang (2013) listed nine challenges met by L2 learners in reading/ writing integrated tasks, and three of them are directly related to insufficient reading comprehension ability, while the other six are, to varying degrees, indirectly related to it. However, the study of reading ability and challenges encountered in academic report writing tasks often focuses on master's and doctoral students (e.g., Hyland, 2016), and the reading-related challenges faced by undergraduates when carrying out project-based writing tasks have not been thoroughly studied before.

Failure to understand the relationship between reading comprehension ability and challenges may result in several obvious problems. Firstly, teachers may overlook the important role played by reading in an academic writing course, thereby ignoring the training of reading-related skills for those students who are struggling with difficult tasks (Grabe & Zhang, 2013; Hirvela, 2004; Horning, 2009). Secondly, challenges faced by students in the reading stage may give them a sense of frustration and hurt their motivation, disrupting further learning efforts (Kong & Wang, 2022). Moreover, insufficient reading ability can lower the effectiveness of utilizing learning strategies (Plakans, 2009; Cai & Kunnan, 2019a; Kim, 2020a) and learning efficiency, as language can only be acquired when the learner receives language input suitable to their ability level (Shintani, 2012; Takimoto, 2007). However, if the relationship between reading ability and challenges is well understood and, more ideally, if a reading comprehension threshold level is found beyond which reading comprehension is not a factor causing challenges, students can make judgments about their linguistic readiness for the project-based writing task. Teachers can also prepare a corresponding training curriculum for students whose reading comprehension level is below this threshold.

The present study aims to explore the relationship between English reading comprehension ability and language-related academic challenges experienced by students in a PBARW course. The study makes an academic and pedagogical contribution to course design, especially for academic writing teachers, by clarifying the importance of reading ability for successful PBARW performance, by finding a reading ability threshold level appropriate for students to begin PBARW tasks, and by helping teachers make decisions on the placement of students and provide effective instruction to linguistically insufficient learners.

## 2. Literature review

### 2.1 Difficulties faced by students in the academic writing process

Researchers have extensively explored the cognitive challenges or difficulties faced by L2 students in the composition process (Cumming et al., 2016; Hyland, 2016; Morrison & Evans, 2018; Evans & Morrison, 2010). Following the cognitive writing process theory (Flower & Hayes 1981; Hayes 2012; Teng & Zhang 2016), the PBARW process can be divided into three stages: information seeking and interpretation, idea creation before writing, and text processing.

Information seeking/interpreting is the initial stage of a PBARW task. During this process, students may encounter difficulties when they search for related literature to connect with their own (Mattus, 2007; Berman & Cheng, 2001; Hellekjaer, 2009). For EAP learners, seeking and interpreting conceptually complex sources of information has been observed to be challenging (Hirvela, 2004; Neumann et al., 2019). Learners' limited knowledge of disciplinary terminology and general academic vocabulary may prevent them from comprehending disciplinary textbooks and journals quickly and fully (Uchihara & Harada, 2018). Moreover, the challenges at this stage are more formidable for undergraduates because understanding complex theories and research methods used by prestigious scholars is cognitively taxing even at the postgraduate level (Hyland, 2016).

Idea creation is the second stage of a PBARW task. It involves multiple small tasks, such as critical evaluation of prior knowledge, raising research questions, and proposing solutions. Idea creation in an academic writing task is much more complex than in writing about daily life or personal experiences (Myles, 2002). For L2 students, the process is more cognitively challenging, considering the fact that they simultaneously engage in two difficult tasks: both constructing discipline knowledge and understanding texts in a foreign language that contains unfamiliar expressions (Bereiter & Scardamalia, 2014).

Text processing is the third writing stage that is both linguistically and structurally demanding (Rahmat, 2019). The development of text processing skills is an essential part of a writing course but is difficult even for many L1 students (Horning, 2009). In this process, the ability to use discipline-specific vocabulary, sentence patterns, textual structures, and styles within the field is required (Nagy & Townsend, 2012), but students are often found lacking in these abilities and overly reliant on copying source notes without proper citation (Neumann et al., 2019). Students have also reported difficulties with expressing complex ideas in a second language and problems with developing confidence and a convincing academic voice (Hyland 2016).

Based on the above-documented challenges students might face during the writing process, this study designed a questionnaire to measure the language-related challenges in a PBARW context. Measuring the challenges would reveal the cognitive load undertaken by students when engaging in PBARW tasks and provide a basis for exploring the relationship between the challenges they encounter and the language preparation readiness needed to deal with these challenges.

## 2.2 The importance of reading for reading/writing integrated writing tasks

Academic report writing is a part of reading/writing integrated writing tasks (Grabe & Zhang, 2013). Reading comprehension ability is of vital importance for the implementation of these integrated tasks (Delaney, 2008; Payant et al., 2019; Park, 2016; Hirvela, 2004; Neumann et al., 2019). An integrated task requires writers to comprehend source texts, synthesize source ideas, and express those ideas using appropriate stylistic conventions (Delaney, 2008; Knoch & Sitajalabhorn, 2013). As reading and writing draw on the same knowledge and cognitive systems and influence each other, an integrated writing task cannot be performed well if students do not first comprehend the source materials (Delaney, 2008; Payant et al., 2019; Park, 2016; Hirvela, 2004; Neumann et al., 2019).

Reading benefits writing through understanding topic knowledge and shaping knowledge representation at the semantic, syntactic, and pragmatic levels (Hayes, 2012; Grabe & Stoller, 2013). Proficient readers who are skilled at constructing a mental representation of the text and selecting important elements from it are likely to use these skills effectively during writing to shape the mental representations of the texts they compose and select relevant content (Spivey, 1990). Poor L2 reading skills, limited vocabulary knowledge, and inadequate reading experience may pose challenges in the integrated writing process (Grabe & Zhang, 2013). Empirically, insufficient reading ability has been found to cause problems in locating and structuring the ideas of source texts and processing texts with expressions of low quality (Plakans, 2009). In China, EAP practitioners have reported learners with inadequate reading abilities have difficulty finding relevant information and understanding important academic concepts (Wang et al., 2015; Sun & Gong, 2017).

Reading can also affect writing by moderating the effectiveness of learning strategies used, such as the effectiveness of self-regulation strategies (e.g., attention control), socio-emotional traits (e.g., motivation), and the effectiveness of activating mental presentation of topic knowledge in the writing process (Kim, 2020a, 2020b; Cai & Kunnan, 2019b). The constraining role reading ability plays on these strategies and knowledge is particularly germane to beginner writers. For more advanced writers, language proficiency is not likely to be as great a constraint, and these writing strategies and knowledge may make a greater contribution to writing (Kim, 2020b).

## 2.3 Reading ability threshold and challenges of PBARW tasks

In L2 reading, a threshold level refers to a level of reading competence below which students have difficulty interacting with L2 texts (Cummins 1979, 2000; Clarke 1980) or transferring reading strategies and background knowledge to improve comprehension (Cai & Kunnan 2019a; Cai & Kunnan 2019b). Students in an alternative or foreign language instructional environment will perform well on cognitive and academic tasks only when they have reached a certain threshold of language competence, while students with low levels of language proficiency will meet difficulties in both input and output tasks (Cummins 1979, 2000). Because ample evidence has shown that second-language writers simply cannot write effectively without sufficient comprehension of source materials, Cumming (2013, 2014) has proposed that the threshold level of reading abilities could differentiate students who are well prepared to begin academic studies from those who are not. Only students who have achieved a criterion level are able to integrate substantial content material into written forms.

To date, not many studies have systematically examined the relationship between reading ability threshold and the challenges of PBARW tasks, even though it is generally assumed that students of lower reading ability levels report more linguistic difficulties. Sun and Gong (2017) briefly mention in their study that Chinese undergraduates' reading ability was generally inconsistent with the reading materials required by PBARW tasks. Gong (2016) has studied the relationship between L2 proficiency and the usage of academic writing strategies, aiming to determine the proper language proficiency threshold value for writing strategies to work effectively. The author found that L2 proficiency moderated the effect of writing strategy use and suggested that EAP writing tasks suit students with an English proficiency of B1 or above, according to the Common European Framework of Reference for Languages (CEFR). This threshold conclusion, however, was arrived at from an argumentation essay writing task rather than a report writing task, which involves a more complex cognitive process.

The above literature shows that the PBARW teaching approach has gained widespread acceptance against the backdrop of the extensive implementation of EAP courses in China. However, the poor reading ability of the learners may pose formidable challenges during the integrated writing process, which PBARW belongs to. Teng and Zhang (2016), among other scholars, regarded writing as the most complex challenge in developing language proficiency. To our limited knowledge, little research has been done to scrutinize the association between reading ability and the challenges posed to undergraduate PBARW learners till now.

This study aims to examine the association between reading ability and PBARW challenges. We explore if there is a reading threshold level beyond which reading comprehension no longer poses challenges to PBARW learning and may even help learners effectively use writing strategies and topic knowledge to cope with PBARW challenges in writing tasks. The following three research questions will be addressed in this study:

- To what extent does English reading ability predict overall academic language-related challenges in PBARW tasks? We hypothesize that there is a strong association between the two.

- Does a reading threshold level exist, below which reading comprehension poses challenges in PBARW tasks, and beyond which reading comprehension stops directly affecting challenges met in the PBARW learning process? We hypothesize a reading ability threshold, below and beyond which the relationship between the two variables is different: the reading ability of the weaker group can predict challenges, while the reading ability of the good readers cannot.

- If the reading threshold level exists, how can different reading abilities, divided by the threshold, moderate the effects of topic knowledge and learning strategies on PBARW challenges? We hypothesize that only good readers can effectively use learning strategies and topic knowledge to meet PBARW obstacles.

## 3. Research method

### 3.1 Setting

The study was carried out at a business university in Shanghai, China, where students started PBARW learning during their second university year. PBARW tasks lasted for a semester, divided into eight sections. The course is provided exclusively for about 800 students with the best English proficiency. During the eight sections, students worked in groups, read authentic academic literature, chose research questions, collected data, and wrote academic reports of around 3000 words in English. During the learning process, four EAP teachers provided necessary scaffolding on searching for reliable academic information, writing different parts of reports, using proper citations, and so on. Two of the teachers have more than 10 years of teaching experience, and the other two are young teachers with an applied linguistic doctorate. Students' writing was accessed from five dimensions, covering writing focus, idea development, organization, style, and language convention

(Good, 2012).

## 3.2  Data collection

The current study utilized the following research instruments and measures:

- Project-Based Academic Writing Challenges Scale (PBAWCS)

A 19-item questionnaire about student perceptions of the challenges of PBARW tasks during the process of learning was prepared. Students responded via a six-point Likert scale, with answers ranging from 1 (not challenging at all) to 6 (very challenging). This instrument is referred to in the present study as the Project-Based Academic Writing Challenges Scale (PBAWCS). The PBAWCS was developed through a three-phase process: item generation, initial piloting, and psychometric evaluation.

Items in the PBAWCS were prepared according to social cognitive writing theory (Flower & Hayes, 1981; Hayes, 2012) and academic writing challenges elaborated in the literature (Grabe & Zhang, 2013; Hyland, 2016). The challenges possibly created in three sub-stages of writing activities were included in the questionnaire: information seeking/interpreting activities before writing, idea creation, and text processing activities. For content validity, 2 experts who possessed expertise in applied linguistics or academic writing were invited to scrutinize the initial pools, evaluating the theoretical rationale, the consistency of constructs and items, and the wording of questions. For face validity, we interviewed 8 students who had taken part in the project-based writing course via telephone. They were asked to evaluate the readability and clarity of the questionnaire. After addressing the questions raised by the experts and students, the revised questionnaire was formally used to measure the challenges of PBARW activity. Participants were asked to indicate the extent to which they thought the statement was consistent with their perceptions of challenges in the learning process.

We tested the validation of the constructs through exploratory factor analysis (EFA). All assumptions were met: Bartlett's test (p=0); KMO (MSA=0.96); and the scree plot suggested three overall factors. Three items loaded across two factors were eliminated. Confirmatory factor analysis (CFA) indicated the model had satisfactory fit: RMSEA was moderate ［0.06, 90% CI (0.05, 0.07)］, SRMR was excellent (0.05), CFI was satisfactory (0.96), and TLI (0.95) indicated little room for improvement (Hu & Bentler, 1999). The resulted 16 items related to the 3 factors indicating the challenges of Academic Reading (AR), Idea Creating (IC), and Text Processing (TP). The reliability of all three factors was very high, with 0.95, 0.94, and 0.95 respectively. It shows that the questionnaire was psychometrically reliable. Appendix A shows the details of the PBAWCS.

- Reading score on the College English Test (CET) band 4

We used the reading score of the College English Test (CET)

band 4 as a measure of English reading ability. The CET 4 is a standardized English proficiency test designed to assess whether university students meet the requirements of the college English course set by the National College English Syllabus for Non-English Majors. The participants took the CET 4 exam on June 21, 2020, two months before they took the PBARW course. In the reading section, students were required to read one article of about 1200 words and two articles of about 500 words to test their speed reading and reading for detail skills.

- Writing Strategy Scale (WSS)

    A 14-item questionnaire about self-regulated strategies was used in the survey. Items were prepared with reference to self-regulated writing strategies as elaborated in Teng & Zhang (2016). We made adjustments according to the PBARW process in our research context and checked its reliability. It was designed with a six-point Likert scale ranging from 1 (not at all true of me) to 6 (very true of me). The values of internal reliability for the instrument were 87, much higher than the benchmark value (.70). Appendix B shows the items on the WSS.

- Topic knowledge

    Topic knowledge was measured using 5 questions adapted from Khabbazbashi (2016). These questions measure the familiarity of the learners with the topic knowledge that they write on in the PBARW course. Appendix C shows the 5 items. It was designed with a six-point Likert scale ranging from 1 (not at all true of me) to 6 (very true of me). The values of internal reliability for the instrument were 89.

## 3.3 Participants and procedures

Though there was no institutional review board at this university that could examine our research aims and research design, we placed a very high premium on research ethics. We adhered to the principles of autonomy, beneficence, and justice. All participants were informed by their teachers of the purpose of the study, their privilege to choose whether to take part in the survey voluntarily, and how their confidentiality would be protected. Written informed consent was obtained from a total of 274 students, 143 female (52%), and 131 male (48%) before the survey. They agreed to participate in the study and complete an online survey in the eighteenth week of the semester. Their CET-4 reading scores were also collected. Five samples were taken away for missing data, and two outliners found later in piecewise regression analysis were also deleted. A total of 267 survey responses were ultimately analyzed. The mean CET 4 reading score of participants was 205 (SD=14.05), with the lowest score being 158 and the highest being 232. Using minimum conversion benchmarks from CET 4 to CEFR (Jin et al., 2022), the reading level of all these students was above the B1, with 82.0% of them above the B2 level (see Table 1 below).

Table 1    Frequency distribution of reading score

| CEFR level of reading | N |
|---|---|
| <B1 | 0 |
| ≥ B1 (CET reading above 149) | 48 (18.0%) |
| ≥ B2 (CET reading above 194) | 219 (82.0%) |

### 3.4  Data analyses

We used a three-stage statistical procedure to determine the relationship between reading ability and PBARW challenges met by the students in our sample.

To explore research question one, we used regression analysis to explore the association between reading ability and PBARW challenges.

To explore research question two, we used two-dimensional scatterplots between reading ability and PBARW challenges to find whether a threshold value of reading level exists. Moreover, we used ANOVA analysis to triangulate the existence of a reading ability threshold.

Lastly, we carried out piecewise multivariable regression analysis to study if reading ability, topic knowledge, and writing strategies had different effects on PBARW challenges in different reading ability groups separated by threshold level. This analysis formally addresses research question two and simultaneously explores whether reading ability moderates the effects of topic knowledge and learning strategies on PBARW challenges, which addresses research question three.

# 4. Results

## 4.1 The association of reading ability and PBARW challenges

The first research question explored to what extent reading ability can predict PBARW challenges. To answer this question, a regression model was used containing reading ability (the CET-4 reading score) as a potential predictor variable to explore the variance in student perceptions of the challenges associated with PBARW tasks. Table 2 displays descriptive statistics. Students' evaluation of PBARW challenges ranged from 1.0 to 6.00, with a mean of 3.33. The distributional properties, as indicated by skewness ($\leq 2$) and kurtosis ($<7$), were in the acceptable ranges (West et al., 1995).

Table 2　Descriptive analysis (n=267).

| Variable | Mean | SD | Min | Max | Skewness | Kurtosis |
|---|---|---|---|---|---|---|
| RS | 205 | 14.5 | 158 | 232 | −.802 | .550 |
| PC | 3.33 | 0.85 | 1.00 | 6.00 | .047 | .175 |
| TK | 4.43 | 0.86 | 1 | 6 | −.480 | .570 |
| WS | 4.22 | 0.78 | 1 | 6 | −.849 | 2.20 |

*Notes.*RS=reading score. PC=PBARW challenges. TK=topic knowledge. WS=writing strategies.

After comparing the data using regression models, we found, as Figure 1 shows, that the CET 4 reading score was a statistically significant predictor of challenges in PBARW by the quadratic curve regression model. The $R^2$ value was 0.069, confirmed by a significant $F$ statistic ($F$=9.846, $p$=.000), which means that 6.9% of the variance in PBARW challenges was explained by the reading ability. Although the $R^2$ value was small, the curve model was better fitted than the linear regression model ($R^2=0.045$). The curve model results in significantly smaller residual errors than a simple regression model. In the lower reading ability section, reading ability was negatively related to PBARW challenges. We found that the breaking point of the curve occurred at the reading scores around 210. From the pattern of the curve, it is very likely that there was a threshold beyond which the association between reading ability and PBARW challenges was different.

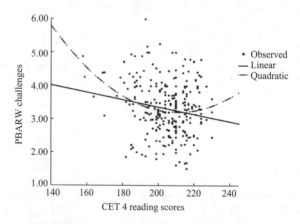

Figure 1　Reading score and PBARW challenges: scatterplot and regression lines.

## 4.2　Reading ability threshold

As shown by the two-dimensional scatterplots between reading ability and PBARW challenges in figure 1, visually we found a reading score of 210 might be a dividing point, but this needs to be further tested.

A one-way analysis of variance (ANOVA) was conducted with reading ability as the grouping factor and PBARW challenges as the dependent measure. The total scale of scores on the L2 reading measure, ranging from a minimum of 158 to a maximum of 232, was divided into five levels in equal intervals that each represented 20% of the scale, and we calculated challenge values for each of the five groups. Here we divided the scale into five parts in order that every group contained sufficient subjects.

Our next step was to compare the challenge differences between adjacent groups for the data now grouped into intervals by reading scores. As displayed in Table 3, the first three reading levels showed high challenges (the means were 3.95, 3.67 and 3.43 respectively). Reading level four and five revealed comparatively lower challenges (the means were 3.13 and 3.39 respectively). We found that there was an overall statistically significant effect of CET reading level on PBARW challenges ($F$=5.339, $p$=0.000). The post-hoc test revealed a statistically significant difference between level 3 and level 4. The challenges perceived by reading level 3 were significantly higher than those perceived by level 4. But the challenges for the subjects in the three lower reading proficiency-level groups were not different from each other. Similarly, the challenges for the two higher reading level groups also didn't differ from each other.

Table 3   Descriptive statistics of the CET reading score scales and PBAW challenge mean

| Variable | n | PBARW Challenge mean | SD | Min | Max |
|---|---|---|---|---|---|
| CETR level 1 (158–172) | 12 | 3.95 | .62 | 3.07 | 4.56 |
| CETR level 2 (173–187) | 24 | 3.67 | .91 | 2.01 | 5.24 |
| CETR level 3 (188–202) | 69 | 3.43 | .85 | 1.81 | 6.00 |
| CETR level 4 (203–217) | 123 | 3.13 | .78 | 1.00 | 5.00 |
| CETR level 5 (218–232) | 39 | 3.39 | .81 | 1.00 | 6.00 |

This result seems to indicate that there were two groupings of subjects based on their L2 reading levels: those with a lower level and those with a higher level, who demonstrated noticeably high and low PBARW challenges, respectively. The result agrees with the regression analysis of step one and provides support for the threshold hypothesis. Figure 2 below summarizes these patterns in a visual display of the mean differences of PBARW challenges according to different reading ability groups. A discernible challenge gap between group 3 and group 4 can

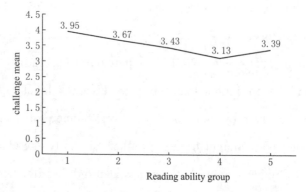

Figure 2   PBARW challenge means in different reading ability groups

be seen, confirming that a CET reading score of 210.46, the mean CET reading score of Group 4, may be enough to mitigate challenges met, beyond which challenges dissipate or level off. This result confirmed the visually observed reading ability threshold value in Figure 1.

## 4.3 The effects of reading abilities, divided by threshold, on PBARW challenges

Based on the curve regression plot and ANOVA analysis result, we formally test, with piecewise linear regression analysis, how the association of reading ability and PBARW challenges differs below and beyond the threshold. We divided the subjects into two groups according to their reading ability at the breakpoint of 210 and used reading scores to predict learning challenges. As suggested by related studies (Kim, 2020b; Plakans 2009), reading ability may moderate the effects of contributing elements such as topic knowledge and learning strategies on the reading/writing process, so we extended our study to include the predictive effects of topic knowledge and writing strategies on PBARW challenges in different reading ability groups. We controlled the possible influence of gender on challenges when doing the multiple regressions.

Before conducting the regression analysis, we completed the following preliminary analyses: An analysis of standard residuals was carried out, which showed that the data contained 2 outliers, which were taken out accordingly. The independent variables did not have multicollinearity (for the two models, VIF values are smaller than 1.32). The data met the assumption of independent errors (for the two models, Durbin-Watson values are 2.05 and 2.18, respectively). All these tests indicated that multiple regression was appropriate for the present data.

The result of the piecewise multivariable linear regression was summarized in Table 4. As shown by Table 4, as a whole, the three variables have significant relationships with PBARW challenges ($F$=6.511, $p$=.000; $F$=7.224, $p$=.000) and explain 12.6% and 27.0% of the variance in PBARW challenges for the two models, respectively. Considering that many other variables (e.g., learning time, learner personality, teaching methods, etc.) are possible to affect PBARW challenges, the variances explained by the three variables are considerable.

For the lower reading ability group, only reading ability predicted the challenges perceived ($B$=−0.321, $p$=.000). Topic knowledge and writing strategy did not predict PBARW challenges in this group. For the higher-reading ability group, both prior knowledge of the writing topic and writing strategies predicted the perceived sense of challenges negatively ($B$=−0.400, $p$=.000; $B$=−0.233, $p$=.004). However, reading ability in this group did not significantly predict the challenges ($B$=0.149, $p$=0.162).

**Table 4 Piecewise multiple regression models for PBARW challenges**

| Variable | Standardized Coefficients | | | | Partial coefficients correlation | | Model Summary | |
|---|---|---|---|---|---|---|---|---|
| | Beta | Sig. | Beta | Sig. | | | $R^2$ | |
| | Model 1 | | Model 2 | | Model 1 | Model 2 | Model 1 | Model 2 |
| Reading ability | −.321 | .000 | .149 | .162 | −.315 | .158 | .126 | .270 |
| Writing strategy | −.059 | .418 | −.400 | .000 | −.060 | −.405 | | |
| Topic knowledge | −.106 | .409 | −.233 | .004 | −.061 | −.230 | | |

*Notes.* Model 1 is the regression model for the low-reading ability group. Model 2 is the regression model for the high-reading ability group.

Figure 3 is the partial regression plot of PBARW challenges against reading scores. As shown by figure 3, the result provides evidence to suggest a qualitatively different relationship between PBARW challenges and reading ability at the level of 210. For low-level reading ability students, the improvement of their reading ability directly led to a decrease in challenges met, while for those students with a higher reading level, increased reading ability did not directly cause the change in PBARW challenges.

The squared partial correlation coefficients were often recommended to assess the relative contribution of individual variables in multiple regression analysis (e.g., Cohen, 1990). From the partial correlation coefficients (see Table 4), it can be seen that in the low reading ability group, reading ability was the best predictor of PBARW Challenges, explaining 9.92% of the challenge variance. In the high reading ability group, reading ability was a very weak predictor of PBARW Challenges,

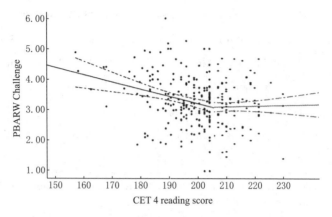

**Figure 3    Partial regression plot of PBARW challenges against
CET 4 reading scores with piecewise regression**

explaining only 2.5% of the challenge variance. This means that in the low reading ability group the improvement of reading ability directly mitigated PBARW challenges. But the mitigating effect was very weak in the high reading ability group. In contrast, in low reading ability group, the other two variables (writing strategy and topic knowledge variables) explained only 0.7% of the variance, while in the high reading ability group they explained 21.7% of the variance. This means that students who were better English readers were more likely than poor English readers to use their learning strategies and knowledge related to the topic to effectively meet the requirements of the task.

## 5. Discussion

Three questions were addressed in our research: firstly, we examined to what extent L2 reading ability could predict learning challenges in PBARW tasks; Secondly, we examined whether a distinct reading threshold level exists, below and above which reading ability has a different relationship with PBARW challenges; Thirdly, we studied if reading ability moderated the effects of topic knowledge and writing strategies on learning challenges.

For the first question, the results revealed that approximately 12.4% to 27.0% of the PBARW challenges met in a project-based writing course can be predicted, or, in other words, can be mitigated by L2 reading abilities. The higher the reading abilities, the more challenges can be mitigated. Our finding is in line with previous studies that highlighted the connection between reading ability and academic writing process and performance and suggested a tight interdependence of reading and writing activities (Grabe & Zhang, 2013; Park, 2016; Plakans, 2009; Plakans & Gebril, 2012; Payant et al., 2019). In PBARW tasks, reading helps writers make sense of the topic knowledge, understand data collecting/analyzing methods, and provide linguistic models in the text processing stage. This implies that although PBARW is an academic writing course, a successful approach to teaching it needs to help students reach the required reading ability threshold.

For the second question, our findings suggest that reading ability can predict learning challenges better using a quadratic curve regression model than a linear model. Piecewise regression analysis further shows there is a qualitative difference as to the effects of reading ability on challenges of PBARW at the breaking point of a CET reading score of around 210, beyond which reading ability does not directly predict challenges anymore. Thus, it is safe to establish a clear 'threshold' of reading ability suitable for PBARW tasks. The finding agrees with the threshold statement raised by Cumming (2013, 2014) that the threshold level of reading abilities can differentiate the students who are well prepared to begin academic studies from those who are not. Only students who have achieved the criterion level are able to integrate substantial content material into written forms. The study also corroborates previous PBARW research that found the requirements for reading ability in the PBARW tasks do not match students' reading abilities and therefore pose cognitive challenges during the task implementation process (Wang et al., 2015; Sun & Gong, 2017).

But our finding does not echo previous findings that a B2 reading level (CET-4 reading score of 194) may be high enough to mitigate the difficulties in the learning context where English is the main mediating language (Trenkic & Warmington, 2019) or the findings of Gong (2016), which show a B1 level (CET-4 reading score of 149) suits EAP writing in Chinese universities. Our study indicates that the PBARW task requires a higher level of English reading proficiency. The length of academic articles, the professional level of concepts involved, and the complexity of research methods used in academic articles all require higher reading abilities.

For the third question, we found that reading ability moderates the effects of topic knowledge and learning strategies on learning challenges. It was found that students who were good readers could effectively activate their topic knowledge or use learning strategies in dealing with the challenges they met in learning. This finding corroborates earlier studies suggesting that reading activities are of essential importance for source-based writing tasks because poor readers cannot use strategies appropriately (Plakans, 2009; Plakans & Gebril, 2012; Grabe & Zhang, 2013; Payant et al., 2019), and that undeveloped reading proficiency could place a limit on the extent to which topic knowledge can be coherently represented in L2 writing (Plakans & Gebril, 2012; Kim 2020b). It seems that only good L2 readers are free to process text; no excessive attention is drawn to linguistic concerns at the expense of idea integration or generation; there are no difficulties in using appropriate lexical and syntactic forms while expressing new ideas (Kim 2020a).

Given these findings, several implications regarding a PBARW teaching approach emerge. The results show reading ability is tightly related to learning challenges. This means that writing teachers should cover reading skills, providing reading exercises to help students improve their reading ability in order to lessen the challenges students may meet. As proposed by Grabe & Zhang (2013), reading and writing instruction should not be separated. Teachers and curricula need to focus explicit attention on reading comprehension activities with the texts that students must use in reading/writing tasks. In a PBARW context, students can be given explicit instruction on how to locate and interpret authentic academic literature and how to synthesize information from different texts effectively, which has been proven to be effective in improving academic writing ability.

The implication that there is a reading ability threshold at which the challenges met by students level off suggests that PBARW tasks might be easier for those students on the top level of B2 (CET-4 reading score of 210 in a Chinese context). The threshold level of English reading proficiency separates those who may or may not be able to comprehend source materials sufficiently well or write effectively. Integrated writing tasks, such as PBARW, are therefore appropriate only for students who have almost achieved or surpassed this threshold level of reading proficiency. In our understanding, this is the most powerful implication, showing that PBARW tasks suit students who have achieved criterion level reading abilities to integrate substantial content material into written forms. We generally follow the readiness theories that teaching PBARW before the attainment of reading ability may lead to unsuccessful outcomes or inefficient frustration (Fitzgerald & Shanahan, 2000).

With regard to students who have not yet reached the requisite threshold level for being able to do PBARW tasks effectively, we agree with Grabe and Zhang (2013) that integrated reading/writing training should be provided as early as possible. It is not sufficient to wait for students' general reading ability to be higher than CET-4 210 in order to begin PBARW tasks. Reading skills such as focusing students' attention on text organization and rhetorical patterns, developing L2 students' academic vocabulary, encouraging extensive reading related to course themes, and writing summaries to support students' reading/writing together (see also Shanahan & Shanahan, 2008) are all examples of useful training that can help students bridge any gap to reach the reading ability required by PBARW tasks.

This study has several limitations that we should note. We need to remain careful in the interpretation of our results. Although our visual analyses suggest that the threshold value lies at CET-4 210, our data does not allow discernment between a threshold of 210 and other potential values close to it through statistical tests. We thus have to remain cautious in interpreting our results. Our analyses clearly show evidence for a threshold mechanism in the relationship between reading ability and challenges met, but the precise value of the threshold analysis would require a larger sample size. Moreover, the mixed disciplines of the students may affect the results of this study. The challenges for "natural sciences" and "social sciences and humanities" differ. It has been found that students rely more heavily on language in the social sciences (Soruç et al., 2021). The business university students whom we surveyed in the study may have met higher language-related challenges compared with students from other disciplines.

## 6. Conclusions

This study leads to several theoretical and practical conclusions: In the same vein as Grabe and Zhang (2013), Plakans (2009, 2015), and Hirvela (2004), we emphasize the importance of reading ability in integrated reading/writing tasks and support the view empirically with a survey. Moreover, we find a reading ability threshold, below and beyond which reading ability has a qualitatively different association with the challenges of PBARW learning. This finding supports Cumming's proposal (2013, 2014) that a threshold level can differentiate the students who are well prepared to begin PBARW tasks from those who are not.

Practically, PBARW tasks are appropriate only for students who have almost achieved or surpassed this threshold level of reading proficiency. Learning PBARW before the attainment of reading ability may lead to unsuccessful outcomes or inefficient frustration (Fitzgerald & Shanahan, 2000). With regards to students who have not yet reached the requisite threshold, related training should be carried out to bridge any gap in the reading ability required.

In the future, the influence of reading ability on PBARW can be studied in different disciplines to test the association further. Secondly, while this study chose to focus on PBARW tasks as a homogeneous group, they actually include heterogeneous cognitive processes: some project-based report writing tasks require reading a large amount of literature, while other tasks may require more numerical calculation and need less reading. More research should therefore be done to study the reading threshold levels required by different PBARW tasks (Delaney, 2008).

## 7. References

Aghayani, B., & Hajmohammadi, E. (2019). Project-Based Learning: Promoting EFL Learners Writing Skills. *LLT Journal: A Journal on Language and Language Teaching*, *22*(1), 78–85. https://doi.org/10.24071/llt.v22i1.1727

Allen, N. J., & Hecht, T. D. (2004). The "romance of teams": Toward an understanding of its psychological underpinnings and implications. *Journal of Occupational and Organizational Psychology*, *77*(4), 439–461. https://doi.org/10.1348/0963179042596469

Artini, L. P., Ratminings, N. M., & Padmadewi, N. N. (2018). Project based learning in EFL classes: Material development and impact of implementation. *Dutch Journal of Applied Linguistics*, *7*(1), 26–44. https://doi.org/10.1075/dujal.17014.art

Bereiter, C., & Scardamalia, M. (2014). Knowledge building and knowledge creation: one concept, two hills to climb. In *Education innovation series* (pp. 35–52). https://doi.org/10.1007/978-981-287-047-6_3

Berman, R., & Cheng, L. (2001). English Academic language skills: perceived difficulties by undergraduate and graduate students, and their academic achievement. *Canadian Journal of Applied Linguistics*, 4(1), 25–40. https://eric.ed.gov/?id=EJ645304

Cai, J. G. (2010). The feasibility study of EMI: A case analysis of Public Relation course of Fudan. *Foreign Languages in China (Zhongguo Waiyu)*, 7(6), 61–67. DOI:10.13564/j.cnki.issn.1672-9382.2010.06.010.

Cai, J. G. (2012). EAP needs analysis and the study on teaching methodology. *Foreign Language Learning Theory and Practice (Waiyu Jiaoxue Lilun Yu Shijian)*, 2, 30–35. https://kns.cnki.net/kcms2/article/abstract?v=3uoqIhG8C44YLTlOAiTRKgchrJ08w1e7fm4X_1ttJAmmWNN5Ve0SBKZntFJuKVPnUA9sAvFBi1JtU-otlutV5910qv-HkN0w&uniplatform=NZKPT

Cai, Y., & Kunnan, A. J. (2019a). Mapping the fluctuating effect of strategy use ability on English reading performance for nursing students: A multi-layered moderation analysis approach. *Language Testing*, 37(2), 280–304. https://doi.org/10.1177/0265532219893384

Cai, Y., & Kunnan, A. J. (2019b). Detecting the language thresholds of the effect of background knowledge on a Language for Specific Purposes reading performance: A case of the island ridge curve. *Journal of English for Academic Purposes*, 42, 100795. https://doi.org/10.1016/j.jeap.2019.100795

Chinese Ministry of Education. (2020). *College English Curriculum Requirements*. Higher Education Press. https://ggkb.ntit.edu.

cn/2018/1112/c2948a23976/page.htm

Clarke, M. A. (1980). The short circuit hypothesis of ESL reading—or when language competence interferes with reading performance. *The Modern Language Journal*, *64*(2), 203–209. https://doi.org/10.1111/j.1540-4781.1980.tb05186.x

Cohen, J. (1990). Statistical power analysis for the behavioral sciences. *Computers, Environment and Urban Systems*, *14*(1), 71. https://doi.org/10.1016/0198-9715(90)90050-4

Cumming, A. (2013). Assessing integrated writing tasks for academic purposes: Promises and perils. *Language Assessment Quarterly*, *10*(1), 1–8. https://doi.org/10.1080/15434303.2011.622016

Cumming, A. (2014). *Assessing integrated skills*. In A. Kunnan (Ed.), *Companion to language assessment* (pp. 216–229). Wiley-Blackwell. https://doi.org/10.1002/9781118411360.wbcla131

Cumming, A., Lai, C., & Cho, H. (2016). Students' writing from sources for academic purposes: A synthesis of recent research. *Journal of English for Academic Purposes*, *23*, 47–58. https://doi.org/10.1016/j.jeap.2016.06.002

Cummins, J. (1979). Linguistic interdependence and the educational development of bilingual children. *Review of Educational Research*, *49*(2), 222–251. https://doi.org/10.3102/00346543049002222

Cummins, J. (2000). *Language, Power, and Pedagogy: Bilingual Children in the Crossfire*. Multilingual Matters. https://doi.

org/10.21832/9781853596773

Delaney, Y. A. (2008). Investigating the reading-to-write construct. *Journal of English for academic purposes*, *7*(3), 140–150. https://doi. org/10.1016/j.jeap.2008.04.001

Egbert, J. (2003). A Study of Flow Theory in the Foreign Language Classroom. *The Modern Language Journal*, *87*(4), 499–518. https:// doi.org/10.1111/1540-4781.00204

Ellis, R. (2003). *Task-based language learning and teaching*. Oxford university press. https://www.google.com.sg/books/edition/Task_ based_Language_Learning_and_Teachin/coO0bxnBeRgC?hl=zh- CN&gbpv=1

Evans, S., & Morrison, B. (2010). The first term at university: implications for EAP. *ELT Journal*, *65*(4), 387–397. https://doi.org/10.1093/elt/ccq072

Ferris, D. (2009). *Teaching college writing to diverse student populations*. University of Michigan Press. https://doi.org/10.3998/ mpub.263445

Fitzgerald, J., & Shanahan, T. (2000). Reading and writing relations and their development. *Educational Psychologist*, *35*(1), 39–50. https:// doi.org/10.1207/s15326985ep3501_5

Flower, L., & Hayes, J. P. (1981). A Cognitive Process Theory of Writing. *College Composition and Communication*, *32*(4), 365. https://doi.org/10.2307/356600

Gong, R., (2016). Exploring the Effect of Prewriting Planning in EAP Writing Course Context. *Journal of University of Shanghai for Science and Technology (Shanghai Ligong Daxue Xuebao), 38 (1)*, 28–35. https://kns.cnki.net/kcms2/article/abstract?v=3uoqIhG8C44YLTlOAiTRKibYlV5Vjs7ijP0rjQD-AVm 8oHBO0FTadlUw00YCgr7I1UtUZAZu_34OrwNBHCEKn75-DmPOnA3A&uniplatform=NZKPT

Good, J. M., Osborne, K., & Birchfield, K. (2012). Placing data in the hands of discipline-specific decision makers: Campus-wide writing program assessment. *Assessing Writing, 17*(3), 140–149. https://doi.org/10.1016/j.asw.2012.02.003

Grabe, W., & Stoller, F. L. (2013). *Teaching and researching: Reading.* Routledge. https://www.routledge.com/Teaching-and-Researching-Reading/Grabe-Stoller/p/book/9781138847941

Grabe, W., & Zhang, C. (2013). Reading and Writing Together: A Critical Component of English for Academic Purposes Teaching and Learning. *TESOL Journal, 4*(1), 9–24. https://doi.org/10.1002/tesj.65

Grant, S. (2017). Implementing project-based language teaching in an Asian context: a university EAP writing course case study from Macau. *Asian-Pacific Journal of Second and Foreign Language Education, 2*(1). https://doi.org/10.1186/s40862-017-0027-x

Guo, P., Saab, N., Post, L. S., & Admiraal, W. (2020). A review of project-based learning in higher education: Student outcomes and measures. *International Journal of Educational Research, 102*,

101586. https://doi.org/10.1016/j.ijer.2020.101586

Hayes, J. R. (2012). Modeling and remodeling writing. *Written communication*, *29*(3), 369–388. https://doi.org/10.1177/0741088312451260

Hellekjær, G. O. (2009). Academic English reading proficiency at the university level: A Norwegian case study. *Reading in a Foreign Language*, *21*(2), 198–222. http://files.eric.ed.gov/fulltext/EJ859587. pdf

Hirvela, A. (2004). *Connecting Reading & Writing in Second Language Writing Instruction*. University of Michigan Press ELT. https://doi. org/10.3998/mpub.8122864

Horning, A. (2009). A Potential to the Plagiarism Problem: Improving Reading. *Journal of Teaching Writing*, *25*(2), 143–175. https://journals.iupui.edu/index.php/teachingwriting/article/ download/18627/18635

Hu, L., & Bentler, P. M. (1999). Cutoff criteria for fit indexes in covariance structure analysis: Conventional criteria versus new alternatives. *Structural Equation Modeling*, *6*(1), 1–55. https://doi. org/10.1080/10705519909540118

Hyland, F. (2016). Challenges faced by second language doctoral student writers in Hong Kong and their writing strategies. *Australian Review of Applied Linguistics*, *39*(2), 158–180. https://doi.org/10.1075/ aral.39.2.04hyl

Jin, Y. Jie, W. & Wang, W. (2022). An Alignment Study of College

English Tests Band 4 & 6 and Standard Language Competence, *Foreign Language World* (Waiyu Jie) (02), 24–32. https://kns.cnki. net/kcms2/article/abstract?v=3uoqIhG8C44YLTlOAiTRKibYlV5Vj s7iJTKGjg9uTdeTsOI_ra5_XU8T4AGvM8I2DVmuF1zB5hHyHJqg wrSkJs9a0SkFvJaI&uniplatform=NZKPT

Khabbazbashi, N. (2016). Topic and background knowledge effects on performance in speaking assessment. *Language Testing, 34*(1), 23–48. https://doi.org/10.1177/0265532215595666

Kim, Y. G. (2020a). Hierarchical and dynamic relations of language and cognitive skills to reading comprehension: Testing the direct and indirect effects model of reading (DIER). *Journal of Educational Psychology, 112*(4), 667–684. https://doi.org/10.1037/edu0000407

Kim, Y. G. (2020b). Structural relations of language and cognitive skills, and topic knowledge to written composition: A test of the direct and indirect effects model of writing. *British Journal of Educational Psychology, 90*(4), 910–932. https://doi.org/10.1111/bjep.12330

Knoch, U., & Sitajalabhorn, W. (2013). A closer look at integrated writing tasks: Towards a more focussed definition for assessment purposes. *Assessing Writing, 18*(4), 300–308. https://doi.org/10.1016/j.asw.2013.09.003

Kong, Y., & Wang, C. (2022). The effects of self-efficacy on the use of self-regulated learning strategies and project-based writing performance. *International Journal of English for Academic*

*Purposes, 2022*(Spring), 21–39. https://doi.org/10.3828/ijeap.2022.3

Mattus, M. (2007). Finding credible information: a challenge to students writing academic essays. *Human IT: Journal for Information Technology Studies as a Human Science, 9*(2), 1–28. https://humanit.hb.se/article/download/105/105

Morrison, B., & Evans, S. (2018). Supporting non-native speaker student writers making the transition from school to an English-medium university. Language Learning in Higher Education, 8(1), 1–20. https://doi.org/10.1515/cercles-2018-0001

Myles, J. (2002). Second Language Writing and Research: The writing process and error analysis in student texts. *TESL-EJ, 6*(2), http://tesl-ej.org/wordpress/issues/volume6/ej22/ej22a1/?wscr

Nagy, W. E., & Townsend, D. (2012). Words as tools: Learning academic vocabulary as language acquisition. *Reading Research Quarterly, 47*(1), 91–108. https://doi.org/10.1002/rrq.011

Neumann, H., Leu, S., & McDonough, K. (2019). L2 writers' use of outside sources and the related challenges. *Journal of English for Academic Purposes, 38,* 106–120. https://doi.org/10.1016/j.jeap.2019.02.002

Park, J. (2016). Integrating reading and writing through extensive reading. *Elt Journal, 70*(3), 287–295. https://doi.org/10.1093/elt/ccv049

Payant, C., McDonough, K., Uludag, P., & Lindberg, R. (2019).

Predicting integrated writing task performance: Source comprehension, prewriting planning, and individual differences. *Journal of English for Academic Purposes*, *40*, 87–97. https://doi.org/10.1016/j.jeap.2019.06.001

Perin, D., Keselman, A., & Monopoli, M. (2003). The academic writing of community college remedial students: Text and learner variables. *Higher Education*, *45*(1), 19–42. https://doi.org/10.1023/A:1021237532056

Plakans, L. (2009). The role of reading strategies in integrated L2 writing tasks. *Journal of English for Academic Purposes*, *8*(4), 252–266. https://doi.org/10.1016/j.jeap.2009.05.001

Plakans, L. (2015). Integrated Second Language Writing Assessment: Why? What? How? *Language and Linguistics Compass*, *9*(4), 159–167. https://doi.org/10.1111/lnc3.12124

Plakans, L., & Gebril, A. (2012). A close investigation into source use in integrated second language writing tasks. *Assessing Writing*, *17*(1), 18–34. https://doi.org/10.1016/j.asw.2011.09.002

Poonpon, K. (2011). Enhancing English Skills Through Project-based Learning. *The English Teacher*, *40(1)*,1–10. https://meltajournals.com/index.php/TET/article/view/127

Rahmat, N. H. (2019). Problems with Rhetorical Problems among Academic Writers. *American Journal of Social Sciences and Humanities*, *4*(4), 506–515. https://doi.org/10.20448/801.44.506.515

Shanahan, T., & Shanahan, C. (2008). Teaching disciplinary literacy to adolescents: Rethinking content-area literacy. *Harvard educational review*, *78*(1), 40–59. https://doi.org/10.17763/haer.78.1.v62444321p602101

Shintani, N. (2012). Input-based tasks and the acquisition of vocabulary and grammar: A process-product study. *Language Teaching Research*, *16*(2), 253–279. https://doi.org/10.1177/1362168811431378

Soruç, A., Altay, M., Curle, S., & Yüksel, D. (2021). Students' academic language-related challenges in English Medium Instruction: The role of English proficiency and language gain. *System*, *103*, 102651. https://doi.org/10.1016/j.system.2021.102651

Spivey, N. N. (1990). Transforming Texts: Constructive Processes in Reading and Writing. *Written Communication*, 7, 256–287. https://doi.org/10.1177/0741088390007002004

Sun, X. J. & Gong, R. (2017). Investigating Student Perceptions Toward a Project-based EAP Writing Course in a Blended Learning Environment. *China ESP Study (zhongguo ESP Yanjiu)*, 8 (2), 87–95. https://kns.cnki.net/kcms2/article/abstract?v=3uoqIhG8C44wp2hFvIb_znleNvEqg4RtCv9vPRf2sA_DkgBLAdhhUGciQOfKdHw6MCYgVJt1j_rA7YnKR1lEd7o4G2nu_6Ej&uniplatform=NZKPT

Takimoto, M. (2007). The effects of Input-Based tasks on the development of learners' pragmatic proficiency. *Applied Linguistics*, *30*(1), 1–25. https://doi.org/10.1093/applin/amm049

Teng, L. S., & Zhang, L. J. (2016). A Questionnaire-Based validation of multidimensional models of Self-Regulated learning strategies. *The Modern Language Journal, 100*(3), 674–701. https://doi.org/10.1111/modl.12339

Thang, S. M., Lin, L. K., Mahmud, N., Ismail, K., & Zabidi, N. A. (2014). Technology integration in the form of digital storytelling: mapping the concerns of four Malaysian ESL instructors. *Computer Assisted Language Learning, 27*(4), 311–329. https://doi.org/10.1080/09588221.2014.903979

Trenkic, D., & Warmington, M. (2019). Language and literacy skills of home and international university students: How different are they, and does it matter? *Bilingualism: Language and Cognition, 22*(2), 349–365. https://doi.org/10.1017/s136672891700075x

Uchihara, T., & Harada, T. (2018). Roles of vocabulary knowledge for success in English-medium instruction: Self-perceptions and academic outcomes of Japanese undergraduates. *Tesol Quarterly, 52*(3), 564–587. https://doi.org/10.1002/tesq.453

Wang, X. H., Chen, M. H., & Li, X. X., (2015). Transition of College English Teaching Oriented towards EAP—problems and countermeasures. *Foreign Language Learning Theory and Practice (Waiyu Jiaoxue Lilun Yu Shijian),* 4, 55–58. https://kns.cnki.net/kcms2/article/abstract?v=3uoqIhG8C44YLTlOAiTRKibYlV5Vjs7ijP0rjQD-AVm8oHBO0FTadnEjCLNmZW0M3siRlEMJmPtY2zD99k1cyWUJ9 4U4OH4r&uniplatform=NZKPT

West, S. G., Finch, J. F., & Curran, P. J. (1995). Structural equation models with nonnormal variables: Problems and remedies. In R. H. Hoyle (Ed.), *Structural equation modeling: Concepts, issues, and applications* (pp. 56–75). Sage Publications, Inc. https://psycnet.apa.org/record/1995-97753-004

Yang, L.P., & Han, G., (2012). An Empirical Study on the Teaching of Academic Writing in College English Based on Project Based Learning Model. *Foreign Language World (Waiyu Jie), 5,* 8–16. https://kns.cnki.net/kcms2/article/abstract?v=3uoqIhG8C44YLTlOAiTRKgchrJ08w1e7fm4X_1ttJAnFAhSqFse0L0KG0fGgXN-MSP9oq3SSrm0c4p1xdwbkYRv8UuurmgUp&uniplatform=NZKPT

Ye, Y. (2020). EAP for undergraduate science and engineering students in an EFL context: What should we teach? *Ampersand, 7,* 100065. https://doi.org/10.1016/j.amper.2020.100065

# 第六章　先前知识对认知负荷的影响
## Chapter 6　Influence of cognitive load from previous knowledge

**本章内容概要 Abstract of the chapter**

　　认知负荷理论是理解学习过程中认知资源分配的关键理论。它将认知负荷分为外在、内在和相关三类，其中内在负荷受教育任务复杂性及学习者先验知识影响，学习者的先前知识与新知识之间的交互性是内在认知负荷的关键驱动因素。一般而言，先前知识有助于学习者降低元素交互性，从而降低认知负荷。然而，在某些复杂情境下，这种关系可能发生变化。例如，当问题涉及复杂系统时，低专业知识的学习者可能低估问题复杂性，报告较低内在负荷；而高专业知识的学习者可能因引入更多交互元素而增加认知负荷。

　　本章中的研究结果证实了这一发现。我们对 227 名大学学习者在 PBAW 写作的过程中感知的认知负荷进行观察，研究发现先前知识与学习者感知到的写作认知负荷并非线性关系。虽然先前知识最少的参与者所感知的认知负荷最高，但先前知识最多的参与者比较低水平的参与者所感知的任务复杂度显著的高。研究表明，认知负荷理论关于内在负荷和先前知识假设在大多数情况下存在，但应该进行细化，因为先前知识和报告的内在认知负荷之间的关系有时候被逆转。教学中应该尽量考虑任务设计时的不同解决方法，避免不必要的过于复杂的解决方案。

## 1. Introduction

Cognitive load theory asserts that it is important to analyze how complex a learning task or problem is for a specific learner (the intrinsic cognitive load), as this complexity determines whether a learner has enough working memory capacity remaining for productive cognitive activities or whether they are already overloaded by the task's complexity alone. The theory assumes that the higher a learner's prior knowledge, the lower the experienced complexity of a given learning task will be. In the terminology of cognitive load theory, higher learner expertise leads to *lower* cognitive load. However, in this paper we argue that higher learner expertise can, in some situations, lead to *higher* cognitive load. Particularly, in the case of problems involving complex systems, a learner with lower expertise may underestimate a problem's complexity and therefore report lower intrinsic load than a learner with higher expertise. This complication regarding the relation between expertise and intrinsic load is of theoretical as well as practical relevance, as it highlights that a lower expertise learner might need help to represent the problem in its true complexity, and a higher expertise learner may require help to manage the higher intrinsic load s/he might experience (Bannert, 2002). This study highlights topic knowledge where this atypical relationship between prior knowledge and cognitive load can be found. We suggest that the assumed relationship between cognitive load and prior knowledge, as represented in cognitive load theory, be refined to include such cases.

## 2. Literature Review

Cognitive load theory categorizes cognitive load into three distinct categories: extraneous, intrinsic, and germane (Sweller, 2010). Extraneous cognitive load arises predominantly from the inefficient design of educational content, causing learners to engage in avoidable mental exertions while processing the material. To enhance the learning experience, it is crucial to optimize instructional strategies and reduce extraneous load. Intrinsic and germane loads are closely related (Sweller et al., 2019), which is why certain authors, particularly those aiming to convey research insights to practitioners, prioritize intrinsic and extraneous loads over germane load (Lovell, 2020). The latest interpretations of cognitive load theory suggest that germane load does not add to the total load but instead aids in reallocating cognitive resources from extraneous tasks to manage intrinsic load (Sweller et al., 2019). Intrinsic load stems from the complexity of the educational task, which is influenced by the interactivity of task elements in relation to the learner's existing knowledge.

Element interactivity is the primary driver of intrinsic cognitive load and is comparable to the complexity of educational content (Paas et al., 2003; Sweller & Chandler, 1994) relative to the learner's prior knowledge. It encompasses both the quantity of elements that a learner must grasp and the interactions between these elements, all of which must be simultaneously retained in working memory during the learning process (Sweller, 2011). Low complexity and low element interactivity occur when each piece of information can be learned with minimal connections to other elements. This is typical for simple factual learning. For instance, when memorizing a list of new vocabulary, each word and its definition can be learned independently of the other words, leading to low element interactivity for each item. Conversely, high element interactivity might involve understanding the mechanics of a hydraulic car brake system. Merely learning the definitions of the individual components (e.g., cylinders, fluids) is insufficient. To grasp the underlying principles, a learner must comprehend how these elements interact (e.g., hydraulic multiplication principles, Van Gog & Sweller, 2015).

The reason why intrinsic load relates to prior knowledge of the learner is that prior knowledge usually helps a learner to reduce element interactivity. In classic situations investigated within cognitive load research, learners with higher prior knowledge already have chunked certain interacting elements from the given problem-solving scenario (or learning task) and stored within long-term memory. These learners can then draw upon these chunks of knowledge when engaging with the task, meaning that fewer elements and interactions must be held in working memory. Hence, an individual with higher prior knowledge will experience lower intrinsic load. Novices, on the other hand, need to deal with all presented elements and their interactions in working memory separately because these elements are not as yet chunked and stored within long-term memory.

These interrelations between prior knowledge and intrinsic load have been addressed in various studies (Ayres, 2006). For example, Clarke et al. (2005) developed specific prerequisite knowledge by pre-training for a subgroup of learners in relation to a task that required the learning of both spreadsheet skills and mathematical content. More specifically, the researchers investigated the effectiveness of pre-training basic spreadsheet skills that were required for learning specific mathematical concepts. They found that students with low prior knowledge of spreadsheets benefited from such a pre-training compared to high prior knowledge students who were already able to simultaneously deal with the spreadsheets and mathematical concepts (i.e., increased performance). As the pre-training changed the level of expertise of the learners when faced with the combined spreadsheet and mathematical task, it reduced the element interactivity the learners had to deal with in that final more complex task. This reduction allowed the initially low prior knowledge learners to successfully cope with the complexity of learning both spreadsheet skills and mathematical content (Sweller et al., 2019).

Despite the documented negative correlation between prior

knowledge and intrinsic load, there are scenarios where an additional factor may oppose the traditional mechanism described by cognitive load theory. An instance of this could be observed when individuals with varying levels of expertise read a text that discusses the debate on forest restructuring in light of climate change and are subsequently prompted to suggest a resolution. In this context, a learner with limited prior knowledge might solely focus on the elements mentioned in the text, perceiving them as the entirety of the factors necessary for solving the problem. Conversely, a learner with greater expertise is more likely to tap into their existing knowledge of additional factors that could be significant, even if they were not explicitly stated in the text. To effectively tackle such a problem, it is beneficial for learners to grasp the complexity of the issue by constructing a mental model, or situational model, as Kintsch and his colleagues have proposed (Kintsch, 1988; McNamara & Kintsch, 1996). In the process of building this mental model, learners incorporate not just the information explicitly stated in the problem but also the knowledge stored in their long-term memory. There is a possibility that prior knowledge, both relevant and irrelevant to the current context, is activated. This activation occurs when learners attempt to comprehend a problem presented in text, as explained by the established theory of text comprehension by Kintsch and his team (Kintsch, 1988; McNamara & Kintsch, 1996). When more knowledgeable learners leverage this relevant prior knowledge, their enhanced understanding can lead to a more thorough and effective approach to problem-solving, but they would introduce more elements that interact with one another, thereby increasing the complexity of their overall mental model. Conversely, novice students often fail to fully grasp the intricacy of systems (Booth-Sweeney & Sterman, 2007; Fanta et al., 2020).

In more skilled learners, the process associated with enhancing their mental model does not hinder the application of pre-existing knowledge structures as outlined in cognitive load theory studies. These experts could continue to leverage their stored knowledge structures to encode related informational elements from the text. This process of chunking might offset, to some extent or entirely, the complexity introduced by their more detailed mental model. However, if the enriched mental model contains more interactions than can be compensated for by the efficiency gains from the expert's prior knowledge, the overall intrinsic cognitive load could be amplified by their previous knowledge. Drawing from the aforementioned research on novice learners' tendency to underestimate the complexity of systems (Booth-Sweeney & Sterman, 2007; for ecological biology, see Fanta et al., 2020), it is hypothesized that the incorporation of prior knowledge might, in certain instances, surpass the chunking effect, resulting in a heightened intrinsic load for learners with greater expertise.

The issues previously examined demonstrate scenarios where the intricacy of a learner's understanding of a problem can escalate with greater prior knowledge. The key parallel between these examples is that the complexity of the problem representation could remain relatively simple if learners lack the capability or inclination to incorporate relevant information from their long-term memory into their problem-solving model.

We expect that the perceived cognitive load while doing PBAW tasks will be higher for learners with higher expertise in specific situations in which prior knowledge has the potential to add additional elements and interactions. More specifically, we expect that learners with higher expertise in topic knowledge will experience higher intrinsic load while doing tasks to which their prior knowledge can contribute additional relevant elements and interactions. Research question is:

- Does previous knowledge differ in predicting cognitive load among students with different levels of topic knowledge? If it does, to what extent do they differ?

## 3. Methods

### 3.1 Sample and setting

We assessed 227 PBAW participants, gender: 66.9% female, Mean of age=23.47 (2.42). 33.1% male, Mean of age=22.35 (2.10). All participants were postgraduates learning in a business university in Shanghai. These students took part in academic writing course using project-based teaching method. They are required to write research-based proposal while learning the course. Students were from business related majors.

## 3.2 Materials

- *Prior knowledge*

Prior knowledge included topic knowledge, English reading ability and academic research knowledge. Reading ability was included because PBAW depends on new topic knowledge gained from reading. Topic knowledge was assessed via four factual items, used to assess their knowledge on the writing topic (e.g., "I can lecture on the topic in detail" (Cronbach's $\alpha=.68$)). English reading ability was based on College English Test (band 4) reading score; Academic research knowledge was based on their self-reported score. We asked the participant how well they already judge their ability of doing academic research before the writing course. Participants rated their prior knowledge on a 0%–100% scale.

- *PBAW tasks*

PBARW tasks lasted for a semester, divided in 14 lectures. The course was provided for postgraduate students. During the 14 sections, students worked in groups of 2–3, read authentic academic literature, chose research questions, collected data, and wrote academic proposal of 2000 words in English. During the learning process, teachers provided necessary scaffolding on searching for reliable academic information, writing different parts of proposal, using proper citations, and so on.

- *Cognitive load*

We assessed cognitive load through the use of a subjective rating scale. We used the scale (PBAW_CLS) as described in Chapter 3, which is specially developed for PBAW teaching, and was validated to be reliable. With the scale 16 questions were used to measure the extent of perceived difficulties of the writing tasks. Cronbach's $\alpha$ was 81.

## 3.3 Procedure

At the beginning of the study, all participants provided informed consent and selected a compensation option in exchange for their participation. We assessed the demographic variables of age, sex, English reading ability, academic research ability, and their self-assessed knowledge of their discipline in the first week of the semester. In 14-weeks, students learned to write a research proposal with the guide of academic English teacher. Participants were asked to rate the cognitive load of the task at the end of the course after submitting their writing.

## 3.4 Analysis

Step one of the analyses was taken to address research question 1. We did regression analysis by predicting cognitive load with topic knowledge.

Step two of the analyses was taken to address research question 2. We divided students' previous knowledge into different parts according to different levels. Then we predicted cognitive load with previous knowledge in different groups respectively.

## 4. Results

## 4.1 Descriptive data

Descriptive statistical analyses revealed that the mean of the cognitive load was 3.44 (SD=1.17), α=.92. The mean score for topic knowledge was 3.48 (SD=1.12), for reading ability the mean was 207.1 (SD=10.30). The mean for academic research ability was 3.46 (SD=1.46). All items exhibited skewness and kurtosis values falling within the range of ±2, indicating reasonably normal distributions. Table 1 shows the descriptive statistics results.

Table 1　Descriptive statistics and correlations among target variables

|  | Mean | SD | Skewness | Kurtosis | 1 | 2 | 3 | 4 |
|---|---|---|---|---|---|---|---|---|
| 1. TK | 3.48 | 1.12 | −0.15 | −0.49 | 1 | | | |
| 2. ARA | 3.46 | 1.33 | −0.14 | −0.68 | 0.26* | 1 | | |
| 3. RA | 207.1 | 10.30 | −0.21 | −0.74 | 0.31** | 0.35** | 1 | |
| 4. CL | 3.44 | 1.17 | −0.03 | −0.56 | −0.41** | −0.37** | −0.33** | 1 |

Note: TK=topic knowledge; ARA=academic research ability; RA=reading ability; CL=cognitive load; *p<0.05; **p<0.01.

## 4.2  Results of bivariate correlations

We conducted a correlation analysis among the variables. The bivariate correlations of variables in this study are shown in Table 1. Topic knowledge displays a positive correlation with both the academic research ability (*r=0.26, p<.01*) and the reading ability (*r=0.31, p<.05*). Academic research ability was positively related to reading ability (*r=0.35, p<.01*). Topic knowledge, academic research ability and reading ability were all negatively correlated with cognitive load, with respective correlation coefficients of *r=−0.41, p<0.01; r=−0.37, p<0.01; and r=−0.33, p<0.01.*

## 4.3  Regression model comparison result

After comparing the data using regression models, we found, as

Fig. 1 shows, that the previous knowledge was a statistically significant predictor of cognitive load in PBARW by the cuboid curve regression model. The $R^2$ value was 0.096, confirmed by a significant $F$ statistic ($F$=7.882, $p$=.004), which means that 9.6% of the variance in PBAW cognitive load was explained by the previous knowledge. The cuboid model was better fitted than the linear regression model ($R^2$=0.085). It is also better fitted than the quadratic regression model ($R^2$=0.085). The cuboid model results in significantly smaller residual errors than the other two regression models. In both the lowest and highest previous knowledge section, previous knowledge was positively related to PBAW cognitive load, while in the middle part, previous knowledge was negatively related to cognitive load.

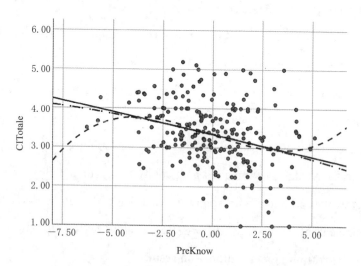

**Figure 1　previous knowledge and PBAW cognitive load: scatterplot and regression lines**

## 4.4 Comparison of cognitive load in different previous level groups

As shown by the two-dimensional scatterplots between previous knowledge and PBAW cognitive load in figure 1, visually, we found a level of −4.0 and 3.5 might be dividing points separating the effects of previous knowledge on cognitive load, but this needs to be further tested.

A one-way analysis of variance (ANOVA) was conducted with previous knowledge as the grouping factor and PBAW cognitive load as the dependent measure. The total scale of scores on the previous knowledge measure, ranging from a minimum of −6.0 to a maximum of 5.1, was divided into four levels at the breaking point of −4.0, 0 and 3.5, and we calculated cognitive load values for each of the four groups.

Our next step was to compare the cognitive differences between adjacent groups for the data now grouped into intervals by previous knowledge. As displayed in Table 2, the first three reading levels showed progressively lower loads (the means were 3.67, 3.54 and 3.12 respectively). Previous knowledge group four revealed comparatively higher cognitive load (the means were 3.22). We found that there was an overall statistically significant effect of previous knowledge on PBAW cognitive load ($F=5.339$, $p=0.000$). The post-hoc test revealed a statistically significant difference between level 3 and level 4. The cognitive load perceived by reading level 4 was significantly higher than those perceived by level 3.

Table 2 Cognitive loads of different previous knowledge

|  | cases | mean | SD | Max | Min |
|---|---|---|---|---|---|
| 1.00 | 5 | 3.6711 | .58650 | 2.79 | 4.27 |
| 2.00 | 111 | 3.5469 | .71006 | 1.70 | 5.19 |
| 3.00 | 82 | 3.1200 | .86425 | 1.00 | 5.00 |
| 4.00 | 23 | 3.2291 | 1.07328 | 1.00 | 5.00 |
| Total | 221 | 3.3416 | .82473 | 1.00 | 5.19 |

## 4.5 Effects of previous knowledge on PBAW cognitive load

Based on the curve regression plot and ANOVA analysis result, we test, with piecewise linear regression analysis, how the association of previous knowledge and PBAW cognitive load differs.

The result of the piecewise linear regression was summarized in Table 3. As shown by Table 3, as a whole, previous knowledge have significant relationships with PBAW cognitive load for level 2, 3 and 4 ($F_2$=7.224, $P_2$=.01; $F_3$=9.295, $P_3$=.000; $F_4$=6.224, $P_4$=.05) and explain 12.6% and 27.0% of the variance in PBAW cognitive load respectively. Considering that many other variables (e.g., learning time, learner personality, teaching methods, etc.) are possible to affect PBAW cognitive load, the variances explained by previous knowledge are considerable.

Table 3 Piecewise regression models for PBAW cognitive load

| Groups | Independent variable | B | t | p |
|---|---|---|---|---|
| 1 (*n*=5) | Previous Knowledge | .251 | .448 | .684 |
| 2 (*n*=111) | | −.184 | −2.358 | .031 |
| 3 (*n*=82) | | −.196 | −2.400 | .023 |
| 4 (*n*=23) | | .089 | .207 | .050 |

For the lowest previous knowledge group, previous knowledge did not predict PBAW cognitive load ($B$=0.251, $p$=.684). For the two groups 2 and 3 with middle level previous knowledge, previous knowledge negatively predicted the perceived sense of cognitive load ($B$=−0.184, $p$=.031; $B$=−0.196, $p$=.022). However, previous knowledge positively predicts the cognitive load in the highest-level group ($B$=0.089, $p$=0.05).

## 5. Discussion

We mainly used regression analysis to study the effects of learners' previous knowledge composed of topic knowledge, reading ability and academic research ability on PBAW cognitive load. It was found that different previous knowledge did not affect cognitive load in the same pattern:

For students with low reading ability, the activation of background knowledge did no good but might have added their perceived cognitive load. This is possible, as readers might have decoded the text wrongly while reading literature and doing planning, such that the miscoding again misled students to activate irrelevant background knowledge (Perfetti & Hart, 2001); or that even if they were able to activate certain relevant background knowledge while reading and writing, the activation was insufficient to some extent; or that they were able to activate relevant background knowledge but ended up using them wrongly when inferring meanings in the text.

For the students with middle level of previous knowledge, the effects of previous knowledge on cognitive load were a smooth descending slope. This result suggested that the potential beneficial effect of previous knowledge was gradually released and provided readers with foundational power to use it in a beneficial way (Perfetti & Hart, 2001).

But for the students with the highest previous knowledge, the cognitive load perceived was higher. The activated background knowledge may have been irrelevant to the task under writing, thereby leading to reduced effect of background knowledge that is executed. In a certain sense, this interpretation is consistent with Cai & Kunnan (2020) explanation of the mechanism of the topic knowledge on reading examination.

Hence, we have identified circumstances in which the typically assumed relation, higher prior knowledge leads to lower cognitive load, is reversed. This finding does not imply that cognitive load theory's assumptions about prior knowledge and cognitive load are generally disconfirmed. Instead, these finding should be a starting point to refine our understanding of the conditions under which prior knowledge increases and when it decreases cognitive load. Tentatively, we claim that prior knowledge increases cognitive load for tasks in which higher prior knowledge allows the learner to apprehend a task's unnessessary complexity. For the appropriate solution of such problems, additional information elements have to be added to the provided information in order to construct an adequate problem representation. These added prior knowledge elements, and their interactions, increase the complexity of the situational model of the problem, leading to higher cognitive load being experienced.

## 6. Implications

Cognitive load theory claims that intrinsic cognitive load depends upon task complexity and the learner's prior knowledge. Usually, it is assumed that more prior knowledge will reduce cognitive load, as multiple task elements chunked in long-term memory can be utilized within working memory with lower load implications. We propose that there might also be a different mechanism in specific situations by which prior knowledge leads to more complex problem representation and, thereby, intrinsic load is increased. This increase is likely when tasks have complexity not immediately apparent by the directly provided information. Consequently, low prior knowledge learners might underestimate the complexity whereas high prior knowledge might take the complexity of the problem more fully into account in their mental model of the problem.

Our findings do not only have theoretical but also practical implications. We showed that for students with lower knowledge of the writing topic, reading ability and academic research ability, improving these skills will lower their perceived sense of cognitive load. Considering our pattern of findings, there might be too much load in certain situations for students with high prior knowledge (even in the absence of sub-optimal instructional design; cf. expertise reversal effect, Kalyuga & Renkl, 2010). In such cases, it might be necessary to help learners with higher expertise to deal with their cognitive load. A complication here might be that the prior knowledge that is actually activated by the individual learners might be very different, as prior knowledge might be very diverse and learners might differ in how actively they bring their prior knowledge to bear on the problem. One possibility might be to raise the awareness of learners with high expertise in this issue and help them to self-manage their cognitive load. In other studies, learners managed to self-manage their cognitive load from poorly designed material that increased the extraneous load (Eitel et al., 2020). By informing learners about, for example, simplifying the situational model (such as within mathematical modelling), learners with high expertise might be able to manage their intrinsic cognitive load to benefit their learning.

## 7. Reference

Ayres, P. (2006). Using subjective measures to detect variations of intrinsic cognitive load within problems. Learning and Instruction, 16(5), 389–400.

Bannert, M. (2002). Managing cognitive load—Recent trends in cognitive load theory. Learning and Instruction, 12(1), 139–146.

Booth-Sweeney, L., & Sterman, J. D. (2007). Thinking about systems: Student and teacher conceptions of natural and social systems. System Dynamics Review, 23(2–3), 285–311.

Cai, Y., & Kunnan, A. J. (2020). Examining the inseparability of content knowledge from LSP reading ability: An approach combining bifactor-multidimensional item response theory and structural equation modeling. Language Assessment Quarterly, 15(2), 109–129.

Clarke, T., Ayres, P., & Sweller, J. (2005). The impact of sequencing and prior knowledge on learning mathematics through spreadsheet applications. Educational Technology Research and Development, 53(3), 15–24.

Dörnyei, Z., & Ryan, S. (2015). Learning strategies and self-regulation. In Z. Dörnyei & S. Ryan (Eds.), The psychology of the language learner revisited. New York and London: Routledge.

Eitel, A., Endres, T., & Renkl, A. (2020). Self-management as a bridge between cognitive load and self-regulated learning: The illustrative case of seductive details. Educational Psychology Review, 32(4), 1073–1087.

Fanta, D., Braeutigam, J., & Riess, W. (2020). Fostering systems thinking in student teachers of biology and geography—An intervention study. Journal of Biological Education, 54(3), 226–244.

Griffiths, C., & Inceçay, G. (2016). New directions in language learning strategy research: Engaging with the complexity of strategy use. In New directions in language learning psychology (pp. 25–38). New York: Springer.

Kalyuga, S., & Renkl, A. (2010). Expertise reversal effect and its instructional implications: Introduction to the special issue. Instructional Science, 38(3), 209–215.

Kintsch, W. (1988). The role of knowledge in discourse comprehension: A construction-integration model. Psychological Review, 95(2), 163–182.

Lovell, O. (2020). Sweller's cognitive load theory in action. John Catt Educational.

McNamara, D. S., & Kintsch, W. (1996). Learning from texts: Effects of prior knowledge and text coherence. Discourse Processes, 22(3), 247–288.

Oxford, R. (2017). Teaching and researching language learning strategies: Self-regulation in context (2nd ed.). New York: Routledge.

Paas, F., Renkl, A., & Sweller, J. (2003). Cognitive load theory and instructional design: Recent developments. Educational Psychologist, 38(1), 1–4.

Perfetti, C. A., & Hart, L. (2001). The lexical quality hypothesis. In L. T. Verhoeven, C. Elbro, & P. Reitsma (Eds.), Precursors of functional literacy (Vol. 11, pp. 67–86). Amsterdam and Philadelphia, PA: John Benjamins.

Renkl, A. (2022). Using worked examples for ill-structured learning content. In C. E. Overson, C. M. Hakala, L. L. Kordonowy, & V. A. Benassi (Eds.), In their own words: What scholars want you to know about why and how to apply the science of learning in your academic setting. Society for the Teaching of Psychology (APA, Division 2).

Sweller, J. (2010). Element interactivity and intrinsic, extraneous and germane cognitive load. Educational Psychology Review, 22, 123–138.

Sweller, J. (2011). Cognitive load theory. In Psychology of learning and motivation (Vol. 55, pp. 37–76). Academic Press.

Sweller, J., & Chandler, P. (1994). Why some material is difficult to learn. Cognition and Instruction, 12(3), 185–233.

Sweller, J., van Merriënboer, J. J., & Paas, F. (2019). Cognitive architecture and instructional design: 20 years later. Educational Psychology Review, 31(2), 261–292.

Van Gog, T., & Sweller, J. (2015). Not new, but nearly forgotten: The testing effect decreases or even disappears as the complexity of learning materials increases. Educational Psychology Review, 27(2), 247–264.

# 第七章　积极情绪对认知负荷的影响

## Chapter 7　Influence of cognitive load from writing enjoyment

### 本章内容概要 Abstract of the chapter

　　动机和情感是可能降低PBAW认知负荷的心理因素。写作乐趣与认知负荷的关系复杂：根据情感研究，消极情绪会消耗工作记忆资源并导致高认知负荷，而积极情绪如写作乐趣则可预防消极情绪反应，减少认知负荷。从神经心理学的多巴胺假说来看，写作乐趣可提高大脑多巴胺水平，进而提升学习者的努力投入，减少认知负荷对写作的负面影响。但也可能因引发额外认知负担而加剧认知负荷对写作的负面影响。

　　本研究招募了417名学生，调查了他们的写作乐趣、进行学术写作时感知到的认知负荷以及写作能力。通过研究感知到的认知负荷在写作乐趣和写作成就之间的中介效应，我们发现：1）写作乐趣直接正面影响写作能力；2）写作乐趣有助于减轻认知负荷对写作表现的负面影响。这一发现显示了在学术写作课程中提高写作乐趣的重要性。在教学中，PBAW教师应该采取策略提高学习者的写作愉悦感，比如，教师可以把写作的选题权利交给学习者，把小组成员的组织权利交给学习者，鼓励学习者的进步，增加写作效能感，对学习者提供更多的积极反馈。

# 1. Introduction

As discussed in earlier chapters, students often face obstacles when tackling PBAW tasks. This perceived challenge can subsequently have an adverse impact on their writing performance. However, cognitive load is influenced by the characteristics of the learners, such as their emotions (Fraser et al., 2012; Schrader & Kalyuga, 2023) and their natural drive (Minkley et al., 2021). Despite this knowledge, there is limited understanding of how students' perception of cognitive load might interact with their motivation to influence writing performance. Considering the widely recognized beneficial impact of motivation on learning outcomes (Guthrie & Wigfield, 2023; Nalipay et al., 2020), we propose that the positive emotion for academic writing could lessen the perceived cognitive load and mitigate its detrimental impact on writing performance. This study investigated the interaction between students' cognitive load perception and their writing enjoyment in shaping PBAW performance. To accomplish this objective, we utilized data from a survey involving 417 students who were enrolled in a PBAW course at a university in Shanghai to study the association between cognitive load, writing motivation and PBAW performance.

# 2. Literature Review

## 2.1 Writing enjoyment and writing performance

In recent years, the positive turn in second language acquisition

(SLA) (MacIntyre et al., 2016) has led to a surge in interest in the role of positive emotions in the language learning process. One emotion that has received much attention is foreign language enjoyment (FLE; Botes et al., 2022). FLE is defined as the joy and pleasure learners experience when learning or using a language (Teimouri, 2017) and it is conceptualized as a dynamic variable (Dewaele & Dewaele, 2017) that encompasses multiple dimensions beyond joy and pleasure, such as intellectual focus, heightened attention, and optimal challenge (Boudreau et al., 2018). In general education, enjoyment is understood as feeling satisfied with one's participation in an activity (Ainley & Hidi, 2014) and scholars have linked it to confidence and strong coping abilities in the face of challenges (Izard, 1977). In recent SLA studies, FLE has been found to increase learners' willingness to communicate (Khajavy et al., 2018), enhance learner motivation (e.g., Pekrun et al., 2007), and positively affect performance (Dewaele & Alfawzan, 2018). Similar to anxiety, FLE has been reconceptualized as a skill-specific construct. Specifically, L2 writing enjoyment has been defined as "learners' experience of joy and pleasure while writing in a second language" (Papi et al., 2022, p. 383).

Enjoyment occurs when writing contents match writers' preferences (Fulmer & Frijters, 2011) and when students genuinely engage in an activity (Ibrahim, 2020). An important note is that enjoyment is not only conceptualized as a key component of intrinsic motivation, as reviewed above but also a type of achievement emotion by control-value theorists (Pekrun, 2006). In many cases, enjoyment is used interchangeably as either a form of motivation or positive emotion (e.g., Miyamoto et al., 2018).

Only a few studies have used this construct to investigate its role in L2 enjoyment and written performance. Tahmouresi and Papi (2021) used course grades and an adapted 4-item scale measuring joy (Teimouri, 2017) to examine the association between L2 writing enjoyment and achievement. The authors found that L2 writing enjoyment unexpectedly did not predict achievement nor was there a significant relationship between the variables. In contrast, Zhu et al. (2022) used an integrated argumentative writing task (i.e., tasks that require learners to deploy skills beyond writing (e.g., reading) to complete the task to explore the relationship between L2 writing enjoyment and task performance. In this study, task performance was assessed using the rubrics contextual awareness, citation and synthesis, opinion and argument, and organization and expression, while L2 writing enjoyment was measured with a general FLE instrument (Saito et al., 2018). Findings showed that L2 writing enjoyment functioned as a mediator between learner motivation and performance and only had a moderate direct effect on task performance. No conclusive insights into the role of L2 writing enjoyment in L2 written task performance can be drawn from these limited studies.

## 2.2  Writing enjoyment and cognitive load

The relevant literature has shown a complex relation between enjoyment of writing and perceived cognitive load. According to emotion studies, negative emotions (e.g., anxiety and anger) exhaust working memory resources and incur a high cognitive load (Logan et al., 2011; Xie et al., 2023). On the other hand, positive emotions such as enjoyment can prevent students from experiencing such negative responses and reduce the high cognitive load caused by them (Logan et al., 2011; Wang & Guthrie, 2004). This is because academic enjoyment usually accompanies a sense of pleasure (Guthrie & Wigfield, 2000). According to the dopamine hypothesis in neuropsychology (Ashby & Isen, 1999), positive affect such as writing enjoyment can enhance brain dopamine levels, increasing the working memory resources for other cognitive activities.

Writing enjoyment may reduce the quantity of perceived cognitive load by deteriorating its effect on writing achievement. This argument is based on two relevant hypotheses: the dopamine hypothesis we mentioned earlier, and the facilitating hypothesis (Cai et al., 2024). The dopamine hypothesis suggests that positive emotions could stimulate the secretion of dopamine, which can improve writers' cognitive flexibility (i.e., the ability to combine ideas creatively) and, hence, the efficiency of cognitive processing. This amplified cognitive processing, therefore, can cancel off or attenuate the negative effect of perceived cognitive load on reading performance. Similar to the dopamine hypothesis, the facilitating hypothesis holds that positive emotions (e.g., enjoyment) increase the availability of resources by modulating learners' effort investment (Isen, 1987; Oaksford et al., 1996).

Contrary to the aforementioned assumptions, it's possible that a sense of enjoyment while writing could intensify the detrimental impact of perceived cognitive demands. This could occur because emotions, whether they are adverse (such as anxiety, concern, or uncertainty) or positive (like happiness, curiosity, or pleasure), act as additional cognitive burdens (Plass & Kalyuga, 2019). The arousal of emotions would likely instigate an extra cognitive burden (which we can refer to as emotionally-induced cognitive load, or EICL), causing a redirection of the finite capacity of working memory towards the emotion, thus resulting in less cognitive capacity available for learning processes (Plass & Kalyuga, 2019).

Empirical research has demonstrated a connection between emotions and cognition. Fraser et al. (2012) analyzed the link between emotional states and cognitive demands within the context of simulation-based training. Their exploratory factor analysis identified two main dimensions of emotion: activation (encompassing feelings such as satisfaction, happiness, exhilaration, arousal, and alertness) and peacefulness (including calmness, relaxation, and peacefulness). The regression analysis they conducted revealed that activation had a positive correlation with cognitive load, whereas peacefulness was inversely related to it. The potential for positive emotion to increase cognitive load has also been noted in numerous additional studies (for example, Costley & Lange, 2018; Skulmowski & Xu, 2022). When positive emotions are superimposed on cognitive load perceptions, they might exacerbate the negative impact of perceived cognitive load. In the psychological literature, this potentially adverse effect of positive emotions has been recorded and has received confirmatory evidence (Gruber et al., 2011; Oaksford et al., 1996). However, the extent to which this adverse aspect of emotion also pertains to the pleasure derived from writing, and particularly how it interacts with perceived cognitive load to influence writing performance, remains an open question.

In conclusion, this literature review underscores the importance of writing motivation, cognitive load and performance of academic English writing. Understanding the effects of positive emotion on cognitive load and writing achievement would help researchers understand the relationship between cognitive load and emotions, and inspire teachers to plan the PBAW course in a more efficient manner. The study addressed two research questions:

1) How does writing enjoyment and perceived cognitive load influence writing achievement in project-based writing (PBW) activities?

2) How does writing enjoyment influence PBW achievement indirectly through perceived cognitive load?

# 3. Method

## 3.1 Participants

Participants of the study were 417 students at a Chinese economics university enrolled in academic writing courses. The academic writing course used project-based teaching method, which required students to choose their writing topics freely and finish research proposal writing in a semester with the scaffolding from teachers. The participants' general language proficiency ranged from High B1 to High C1 according to the Common European Framework of Reference for Languages (CEFR). The mean age of the respondents was 20.5, ranging between 19 and 22. The sample consisted of 162 males and 255 females majoring in different fields of study. This skewness reflects the gender ratio of the university which is favored by female students who are perceived to perform better in foreign language learning. All the participants took part in the survey voluntarily.

## 3.2 Data collection procedures

The researchers collect data from the participants in the July 2024. The course ran from early February to early July. Students received academic writing instruction on writing process and research proposal genre knowledge. Students were asked to do small-scale research in groups of three to four, and submitted individual academic reports of around 2,000 words at the end of the term. At the end of the course, the questionnaire was sent to participants through an online platform (Wen

Juan Xing, Changsha Ranxing Company) by one of the researchers, who was also teaching the course. The students were informed clearly about the purpose of the study, and informed that their participation in the study was voluntary. Then the teacher insfructed the participants how to complete the questionnaire. The confidentiality and anonymity of their responses were ensured. The students completed the questionnaire during their regular writing class time.

### 3.3 Instruments

• Writing enjoyment

Writing enjoyment refers to the intrinsic interest in writing. The researchers asked students to endorse their agreement on three items addressing their interest in writing activities on a six-point scale (1=Strongly Disagree, 6=Strongly Agree). The descriptive statistics and reliability estimates of students' writing enjoyment are shown in Table 1. The three items were "I like academic writing" ($M$=3.98, $SD$=1.20), "I like attending academic writing class" ($M$=3.94, $SD$=1.15), and "I like to devote my time in academic writing" ($M$=3.76, $SD$=1.20). The Cronbach's Alpha for the three items was α=0.86.

• Perceived cognitive load for academic writing task

The cognitive load of the research proposal writing task was measured by a subjective self-reporting instrument of 13 items with reference to cognitive measurement scale of Li and Wang (2024), and project-based writing challenge scale by Wang et al (2023). We adjusted the questionnaire according to the writing process of research proposal to match the writing tasks of the study. Students were asked to evaluate the perceived degree of difficulties they felt of the writing task in the writing process, with a 6-point scale (1=not difficult at all, 6=very difficult). The 13 items could be divided into two categories: the idea-planning load with 6 items showing the cognitive load that the learners perceived when searching for academic information, reading and learning academic knowledge, and planning their own writing; the writing load with 7 items showing the cognitive load that the learners perceived when translation ideas into text and revising. The overall internal consistency was good as assessed by Cronbach's alpha value 0.921. The mean of the perceived cognitive load in our sample was $M=4.00$ ($SD=0.76$).

- Academic writing achievement

We invited participants to honestly estimate their own writing achievement from 1 to 6 points with 1 indicating very low and 6 indicating very high. As the questionnaire asked no personal information of name or student ID, the self-reported writing achievement can be regarded as highly reliable showing the actual writing achievement (Pike, 1996). The mean of the self-reported writing achievement in our sample was $M=4.02$ ($SD=1.07$).

- Statistic Analysis

We took two steps to apply a structural equation modeling (SEM) analysis in the study. It is believed that SEM analysis can identify sources of the misfit of data models and prevent problems of nonconvergence (Mueller &Hancock, 2008). Firstly, we evaluated the measurement models of the questionnaire. The reliability and validity of the questionnaire were checked with CFAs using software-AMOS program Version 22.0 (Arbuckle, 2013). This was designed to check whether the data we collected fit the hypothesized measurement models. Informed by the CFA results, we proposed a mediation model and evaluated it by SEM. Several goodness of fit indices was reported in order to check model fits, including the ratio of chi-square ($\chi^2$) divided by the degree of freedom (df), the comparative fit index (CFI), the Tucker-Lewis index (TLI), the root mean square error of approximation (RMSEA), and the standardized root mean square residual (SRMR). We applied Hu and Bentler's (1999) cut-off values found that CFI and TLI were lower than .95; RMSEA lower than .06; and SRMR no larger than .08, showing a good model fit. In addition, chi-square/df ratio values lower than 2.5 were considered in our study to represent an acceptable model (Byrne, 1991).

## 4. Results

### 4.1 CFA Model Fit Results

Table 1 shows the CFA fit results for perceived cognitive load (Model1) with the fit results for two subscales (Model 1a and Model 1b), and writing enjoyment (Model 2). The CFA model fit results showed that the measurement scales were reliable and could be used safely for further analysis.

**Table 1 CFA Model Fit Results**

| Model | $\chi^2$ | df | $\chi^2/df$ | p | RMSEA | SRMR | CFI | TLI |
|---|---|---|---|---|---|---|---|---|
| Model 1a | 21.432 | 12 | 1.936 | .412 | .018 (.000, .102) | .037 | .991 | .983 |
| Model 1b | 3.75 | 5 | .751 | .585 | .000 (.000, .000) | .011 | .983 | .978 |
| Model 1 | .000 | 0 | .000 | .000 | .000 (.000, .000) | .000 | 1.000 | 1.000 |
| Model 2 | .000 | 0 | .000 | .000 | .000 (.000, .000) | .000 | 1.000 | 1.000 |

Note: Model 1a=idea planning cognitive load; Model 1b=writing cognitive load; Model 1=perceived cognitive load; Model 2=writing.

## 4.2 Descriptive Statistics

Table 2 provides the descriptive statistics, based on the mean of the two scales, and correlations related to the writing enjoyment, perceived cognitive load and writing achievement. As shown, writing enjoyment were negatively associated with perceived idea-planning, writing loads, and positively associated with writing achievement. The two perceived cognitive load variables were positively associated with writing achievement.

**Table 2 Descriptive Statistics**

| | V1 | V2 | V3 |
|---|---|---|---|
| **V1.** | 1 | −.1.44** | −.163** |
| **V2.** | | 1 | .242** |
| **V3.** | | | 1 |
| **Mean** | 4.45 | 3.86 | 4.02 |
| **SD** | 1.04 | 1.05 | 1.07 |

Note: V1=perceived cognitive load ;V2=Reading enjoyment; V3=Writing achievement.

## 4.3 Mediation Model Evaluation

The next step was to specify a SEM to evaluate how writing enjoyment, being mediated by perceived cognitive load, affected academic writing achievement. A critical condition for testing the mediation effect is that there should be significant relationships between predictors and dependent variables (Hayes, 2013). Therefore, we checked the correlations of these variables including writing enjoyment, perceived cognitive load, and academic writing achievement. Table 2 shows the correlations between the dependent and independent variables. These provide sufficient justification for an investigation into mediation effects among these constructs. Therefore, a partial mediation model was proposed, including both direct and mediation paths from the predictors to the outcome variables (writing enjoyment→writing achievement; writing enjoyment→perceived cognitive load→writing achievement). The structure of the hypothesized partial mediation model is shown in Fig. 1.

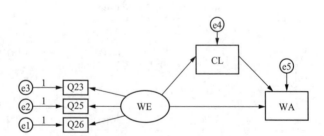

**Figure 1　A partial mediation model with both mediation and direct paths from writing enjoyment to writing achievement**

Note: WE=writing enjoyment; WA=writing achievement; CL=cognitive load.

The SEM results revealed an acceptable model fit, with $\chi^2(4)=5.858$; $\chi^2/df=1.46$; $p=0.216>0.05$; *CFI*=.99; *TLI*=.98; RMSEA 90% confidence *interval*=.04 [.00, .09]; *SRMR*=.06. On this basis, we retained the partial mediation structure of writing enjoyment on writing achievement. Figure 2 shows the standardized regression coefficients between writing enjoyment and writing achievement, mediated by perceived cognitive load. The path diagram of the model shows the standardized estimates of the causal paths for both the direct and indirect effects. It is apparently indicated that writing enjoyment, as a whole, generated both direct and indirect effects on academic writing achievement, mediated by perceived cognitive load. In specific terms, the significant direct paths were found from writing enjoyment to writing achievement ($\beta$=.27, $p<.01$); the significant indirect paths were found from writing enjoyment, through perceived cognitive load ($\beta$=−.17, $p$=0) to writing performance ($\beta$=−.12, $p<.01$). In total, 14.70% of the variance in writing performance was accounted for by the predictor variables.

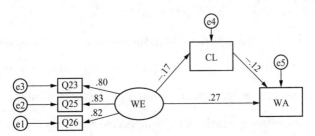

**Figure 2　A partial mediation model with both mediation and direct paths from writing enjoyment to writing achievement**

Note: WE=writing enjoyment; WA=writing achievement; CL=cognitive load; All path coefficients are significant with p<.01.

To test the significance of the mediator effects, we used a bootstrapping procedure with bias-corrected confidence estimates. In the study, 95% confidence interval of the indirect effects was obtained using 2000 bootstrap resamples (Preacher &Hayes, 2008). We evaluated the following mediation paths: writing enjoyment $\rightarrow$ cognitive load $\rightarrow$ writing achievement. We found there was a significant mediator effect ($\beta$=.019, $p$<.006); lower bounds=.016; upper bounds=.057

To summarize, in this study writing enjoyment had significantly strong positive effects on writing achievement. In addition, self-efficacy had a partial mediation effect on writing performance through cognitive strategies: through negative association with perceived cognitive load, writing enjoyment baffled the negative effect of cognitive load on writing achievement.

## 5. Discussion

This study aimed to examine the effect of writing enjoyment on cognitive load and on PBAW performance.

### 5.1 Perceived cognitive load, writing enjoyment and writing achievement

Our findings suggest that writing enjoyment positively predicted writing achievement, echoing prior research indicating that psychological factors such as enjoyment and motivation significantly influence students' learning outcomes (Pajares, 2003; Pekrun et al., 2012). This finding is consistent with existing studies examining the relationship between writing enjoyment and writing achievement (Tabari et al., 2024; Zumbrunn et al., 2019). In PBAW tasks, students enjoying academic writing are more ready to read literature articles that match their academic interests (Fulmer & Frijters, 2011) and share their thoughts with others. Through these reading and writing activities, they have more motivation to devote time to improving their researching and writing skills. Enhancement in all these aspects contributes to writing achievement development (Grabe, 2009).

Conversely, we found that perceived cognitive load negatively predicted writing achievement, in line with cognitive load theory (CLT) positing that excessive demands on working memory can hinder performance (Paas et al., 2003). This finding is also compatible with CLT contentions that higher cognitive load levels can undermine students' learning performance (Van Merriënboer et al., 2003). Perceived cognitive load can affect writing in two ways: in the condition of PBAW tasks, learners would prioritize their cognitive resources for processing all disciplinarily novel information related to reading and researching (DeStefano & LeFevre, 2007). As the activation of previous knowledge and establishing new knowledge is highly demanding on mental resources. The higher intrinsic cognitive load felt means that the learner needs to activate more previous knowledge (sometimes irrelevant and wrong connection was activated), and the higher difficult for the learners to gain good writing performance because of the limitation of working memory (Cho et al., 2015; Sweller, 1994).

Besides, learning the PBAW tasks is relate to the extraneous load. PBAW tasks require searching, reading large number of academic resources. Learners may have found academic resources too difficult for them to understand, or met a research model too complicated for them to replicate, or cooperated with team members with poor cooperating spirit, or gaining useless support from teachers. To deal with these problems students must allocate extra cognitive resources, which would compete against the mental resources that would otherwise be allocated for the perceived intrinsic load (DeStefano & LeFevre, 2007; Lehmann & Seufert, 2020). The dual findings on writing enjoyment and cognitive load reveal that, while academic writing inherently poses significant cognitive challenges, individual perceptions of enjoyment can mitigate these demands, fostering more productive and less stressful writing experiences.

## 5.2  The Indirect Effect of Writing Enjoyment on Writing Achievement

Further analysis demonstrated the indirect effect of writing enjoyment on writing achievement, mediated by perceived cognitive load. Specifically, we found that writing enjoyment negatively influenced cognitive load, which in turn had a positive effect on writing achievement. An interpretation of the deteriorating function of enjoyment in the relation between cognitive load and writing achievement relates to the mental noise aroused by enjoyment. It is consistent with the conclusion by Fraser et al. (2012) that high-intensity emotions are likely to lead to distraction. This unnecessary consumption of mental energy might be responsible for the deteriorating effect of writing enjoyment on the relationship between perceived cognitive load and writing achievement. On the other hand, we assume that with higher level of enjoyment, students may devote more efforts into learning, forming new schema of knowledge, and decreasing the perceived intrinsic cognitive load. According to Ayres (2006), facilitating germane load equals to decreasing intrinsic load, because as expertise develops, element interactivity (intrinsic load) decreases when the interactions become learnt and incorporated into schemas.

## 6. Implications

This mediation pathway suggests that enjoyment not only promotes a positive writing experience but also reduces the perceived burden of the writing task, thereby improving academic outcomes. These results emphasize the buffering role of psychological factors like enjoyment in the face of cognitively demanding tasks. Teachers and educators can leverage this insight by fostering enjoyable learning environments that alleviate cognitive strain and foster writing proficiency.

Our study offers valuable implications for both academic writing instruction and curriculum design. Firstly, it highlights the significance of nurturing students' writing enjoyment as a means to counterbalance the negative impact of cognitive load on writing achievement. To achieve this, educators can employ engaging writing activities, incorporate personalized instruction, and provide constructive feedback that promotes a sense of accomplishment and enthusiasm for writing.

Secondly, reducing the perceived cognitive load of writing tasks through strategic instructional interventions can be beneficial. For instance, introducing modularized writing tasks, using scaffolded instructions, and fostering peer support networks can all contribute to lowering cognitive demands and making the writing process more manageable.

Finally, educators should recognize the synergy between motivation, self-efficacy, and cognitive load. Encouraging positive teacher-student interactions, reinforcing students' beliefs in their writing abilities, and cultivating self-regulatory skills can reinforce this relationship, further amplifying the benefits of writing enjoyment and mitigating the impact of cognitive load.

Despite the insights provided by this study, there are some limitations to be acknowledged. Firstly, writing achievement was self-reported by the participants, which may be subject to biases and inconsistencies. Future research should consider employing more objective measures of writing proficiency, such as blind-graded essays or performance-based assessments. Secondly, the study was conducted within a specific population of students from a Chinese economics university, limiting the generalizability of the findings. Broader cross-cultural studies could help identify universal trends and culture-specific variations in the relationships between writing enjoyment, cognitive load, and writing achievement. Lastly, while our model accounts for direct and indirect effects, there may be other variables influencing these relationships that were not explored in this study. Future research should aim to uncover potential confounding factors and develop more comprehensive models of writing performance.

In conclusion, our findings offer a nuanced understanding of the intricate interplay between writing enjoyment, cognitive load, and writing achievement. By recognizing and leveraging these relationships, educators can enhance students' academic writing experience and outcomes.

## 7. References

Arbuckle, J. L. (2013). IBM SPSS Amos 22 user's guide. Crawfordville: Amos Development Corporation.

Ashby, F. G., & Isen, A. M. (1999). A neuropsychological theory of positive affect and its influence on cognition. Psychological Review, 106(3), 529–550. https://doi.org/10.1037/0033-295x.106.3.529.

Ayres, P. (2006). Using subjective measures to detect variations of intrinsic cognitive load within problems. *Learning and Instruction*, *16*(5), 389–400. https://doi.org/10.1016/j.learninstruc.2006.09.001.

Botes, L., Dewaele, J.-M., & MacIntyre, P. D. (2022). Foreign language enjoyment: Concept, measurement, and implications for language learning and teaching. System, 104, 102–114. https://doi.org/10.1016/j.system.2021.102–114.

Boudreau, F., Gernigon, C., & Roy, M. (2018). The role of flow in second language writing: A study of French immersion students. Canadian Modern Language Review, 74(4), 489–511. https://doi.org/10.3138/cmp.74.4.489.

Byrne, B. M. (1991). The Maslach burnout inventory: Validating factorial structure and invariance across intermediate, secondary, and university educators. Multivariate Behavioral Research, 26(4), 583–605.

Costley, J., & Lange, C. (2018). The moderating effects of group work on the relationship between motivation and cognitive load. The International Review of Research in Open and Distributed Learning, 19(1), 69–90. https://doi.org/10.19173/irrodl.v19i1.3325.

Dewaele, J.-M., & Alfawzan, M. (2018). Anxiety and enjoyment in L2 Arabic, French, German, and Russian: A trilingual investigation. Studies in Second Language Learning and Teaching, 8(4), 635–670. https://doi.org/10.14746/ssllt.2018.8.4.4.

Dewaele, J.-M., & Dewaele, J. (2017). Foreign language enjoyment and anxiety: An introduction. In J.-M. Dewaele & J. Dewaele (Eds.), Foreign language enjoyment and anxiety (pp. 1–10). Multilingual Matters.

DeStefano, D., & LeFevre, J.-A. (2007). Cognitive load in hypertext reading: A review. Computers in Human Behavior, 23(3), 1616–1641.

https://doi.org/10.1016/j.chb.2005.08.012.

Fraser, K., Ma, I., Teteris, E., Baxter, H., Wright, B., & McLaughlin, K. (2012). Emotion, cognitive load and learning outcomes during simulation training. Medical Education, 46(11), 1055–1062. https://doi.org/10.1111/j.1365-2923.2012.04355.x.

Fulmer, S. M., & Frijters, J. C. (2011). Motivation during an excessively challenging reading task: The buffering role of relative topic interest. The Journal of Experimental Education, 79(2), 185–208. https://doi.org/10.1080/00220973.2010.481503.

Gruber, J., Mauss, I. B., & Tamir, M. (2011). A dark side of happiness? How, when, and why happiness is not always good. Perspectives on Psychological Science, 6(3), 222–233. https://doi.org/10.1177/1745691611406927.

Guthrie, J. T., & Wigfield, A. (2000). Engagement and motivation in reading. In M. L. Kamil, P. B. Mosenthal, P. D. Pearson, & R. Barr (Eds.), Handbook of reading research (pp. 403–422). Erlbaum.

Guthrie, J. T., & Wigfield, A. (2023). Roles of motivation and engagement in teaching the English language arts. In J. T. Guthrie & A. Wigfield (Eds.), Handbook of research on teaching the English language arts (pp. 267–293). Routledge.

Hayes, A. F. (2013). Introduction to mediation, moderation, and conditional process analysis: A regression-based approach. New York: Guilford.

Hu, L. T., & Bentler, P. M. (1999). Cutoff criteria for fit indexes in covariance structure analysis: Conventional criteria versus new alternatives. Structural Equation Modeling, 6, 1–55. doi:10.1080/10705519909540118.

Isen, A. M. (1987). Positive affect, cognitive processes, and social behavior. In L. Berkowitiz (Ed.), Advances in experimental social psychology (pp. 203–253). Elsevier.

Ibrahim, D. K. (2020). The role of enjoyment in second language learning: A systematic review. System, 93, 102–113. https://doi.org/10.1016/j.system.2020.102–113.

Izard, C. E. (1977). Human emotions. Plenum Press.

Khajavy, G., Dewaele, J.-M., & Power, M. (2018). The role of foreign language enjoyment and anxiety in L2 communication: Evidence from Iranian and British learners of English. System, 76, 53–68. https://doi.org/10.1016/j.system.2018.07.004.

Lehmann, J., & Seufert, T. (2020). The interaction between text modality and the learner's modality preference influences comprehension and cognitive load. Frontiers in Psychology, 10, 2820. https://doi.org/10.3389/fpsyg.2019.02820.

Li, J., & Wang, J. (2024). A measure of EFL argumentative writing cognitive load: Scale development and validation. Journal of Second Language Writing, 63, 101095. https://doi.org/10.1016/j.jslw.2024.101095.

Logan, S., Medford, E., & Hughes, N. (2011). The importance of intrinsic motivation for high and low ability readers' reading comprehension performance. Learning and Individual Differences, 21(1), 124–128. https://doi.org/10.1016/j.lindif.2010.09.011.

MacIntyre, P. D., Boudreau, F., & Gregersen, T. (2016). Positive psychology and SLA: The role of positive emotions, motivation, and self-regulation. In P. D. MacIntyre, T. Gregersen, & S. Mercer (Eds.), Positive psychology in SLA (pp. 3–18). Multilingual Matters.

Minkley, N., Xu, K. M., & Krell, M. (2021). Analyzing relationships between causal and assessment factors of cognitive load: Associations between objective and subjective measures of cognitive load, stress, interest, and self-concept. Frontiers in Education, 6, 632907. https://doi.org/10.3389/feduc.2021.632907.

Miyamoto, Y., Sato, M., & Samim, M. (2024). The role of language learning emotions in predicting L2 achievement: A meta-analysis. Language Teaching Research, 22(6), 729–746. https://doi.org/10.1177/1362168817729911.

Mueller, R. O., & Hancock, G. R. (2008). Best practices in structural equation modeling. In J. W. Osborne (Ed.), Best practices in quantitative methods (pp. 488–508). Thousand Oaks: Sage.

Nalipay, M. J. N., Cai, Y., & King, R. B. (2020). Why do girls do better in reading than boys? How parental emotional contagion explains gender differences in reading achievement. Psychology in the Schools, 57(2), 310–319. https://doi.org/10.1002/pits.22330.

Oaksford, M., Morris, F., Grainger, B., & Williams, J. M. G. (1996).

Mood, reasoning, and central executive processes. Journal of Experimental Psychology: Learning, Memory, and Cognition, 22(2), 476–492. https://doi.org/10.1037/0278-7393.22.2.476.

Paas, F. (1992). Training strategies for attaining transfer of problem-solving skills in statistics: A cognitive-load approach. Journal of Educational Psychology, (4), 429–434. https://doi.org/10.1037/0022-0663.84.4.429.

Paas, F., Tuovinen, J. E., Tabbers, H., & Van Gerven, P. W. M. (2003). Cognitive load measurement as a means to advance cognitive load theory. Educational Psychologist, 38(1), 63–71. https://doi.org/10.1207/S15326985EP3801_8.

Pajares, F. (2003). Self-efficacy, beliefs, and achievement in writing: A review of the literature. Reading & Writing Quarterly: Overcoming Learning Difficulties, 19(2), 139–158. https://doi.org/10.1037/a0013462.

Papi, M., Tahmouresi, S., & Merza, S. (2022). L2 writing enjoyment: Concept, measurement, and effects on L2 writing achievement. Language Teaching Research. Advance online publication. https://doi.org/10.1177/13621688221090301.

Pekrun, R. (2006). The control-value theory of achievement emotions: Assumptions, corollaries, and implications for educational research and practice. Educational Psychology Review, 18(4), 315–341. https://doi.org/10.1007/s10648-006-9029-9.

Pekrun, R., Frenzel, A. C., Goetz, T., & Perry, R. P. (2007). The control-value theory of achievement emotions: An integrative approach to emotions in education. In P. A. Schutz & R. Pekrun (Eds.), Emotion in education (pp. 13–36). Academic Press.

Plass, J. L., & Kalyuga, S. (1999). Four ways of considering emotion in cognitive load theory. Educational Psychology Review, 31(2), 339–359. https://doi.org/10.1007/s10648-019-09473-5.

Preacher, K. J., & Hayes, A. F. (2008). Asymptotic and resampling strategies for assessing and comparing indirect effects in multiple mediator models. Behavior Research Methods, 40(3), 879–891. https://doi.org/10.3758/BRM.40.3.879.

Pike, A. W. (1996). Self-reported measures of academic achievement: A review. Educational Psychology Review, 8(3), 211–231.

Saito, Y., Dewaele, J.-M., & Pfenninger, B. (2018). The effects of integrated speaking and writing tasks on L2 anxiety, enjoyment, and performance: A pilot study. Language Teaching Research, 22(1), 45–63. https://doi.org/10.1177/1362168816680650.

Skulmowski, A., & Xu, K. M. (2022). Understanding cognitive load in digital and online learning: A new perspective on extraneous cognitive load. Educational Psychology Review, 34(1), 171–196. https://doi.org/10.1007/s10648-021-09624-7.

Sweller, J. (1988). Cognitive load during problem solving: Effects on learning. Cognitive Science, 12(2), 257–285. https://doi.org/10.1016/0364-0213(88)90023-7.

Sweller, J. (1994). Cognitive load theory, learning difficulty, and instructional design. Learning and Instruction, 4(4), 295–312. https://doi.org/10.1016/0959-4752(94)90003-5.

Tabari, M., Khajavy, G. H., & Goetze, J. (2024). Mapping the interactions between task sequencing, anxiety, and enjoyment in L2 writing development. Journal of Second Language Writing, 65(2024), 101116. https://doi.org/10.1016/j.jslw.2024.101116.

Tahmouresi, S., & Papi, M. (2021). L2 writing enjoyment and achievement: A mixed-methods study. Language Teaching Research. Advance online publication. https://doi.org/10.1177/13621688211007866.

Teimouri, M. (2017). The role of enjoyment in foreign language learning. In J.-M. Dewaele & J. Dewaele (Eds.), Foreign language enjoyment and anxiety (pp. 97–116). Multilingual Matters.

Van Merriënboer, J. J., Kirschner, P. A., & Kester, L. (2003). Taking the load off a learner's mind: Instructional design for complex learning. Educational Psychologist, 38(1), 5–13. https://doi.org/10.1207/S15326985E P3801_2.

Wang, C., You, X., & Lu, J. (2023). Reading ability and challenges in a project-based academic report writing course: A test of the threshold hypothesis. Language Teaching Research, 1212118. https://doi.org/10.1177/13621688231212118.

Wang, J. H., & Guthrie, J. (2004). Modeling the effects of intrinsic motivation, extrinsic motivation, amount of reading, and past reading achievement on text comprehension between US and Chinese students. *Reading Research Quarterly*, 39(2), 162–186. https://doi. org/10.1598/RRQ.39.2.2.

Xie, W., Ye, C., & Zhang, W. (2023). Negative emotion reduces visual working memory recall variability: A meta-analytical review. *Emotion*, 23(3), 859–871. https://doi.org/10.1037/emo0001139.

Zhu, C., Li, S., & Zhang, L. J. (2022). The role of L2 writing enjoyment in the relationship between learner motivation and performance: A structural equation modeling analysis. *Language Teaching Research*. Advance online publication. https://doi. org/10.1177/13621688221090302.

### Appendix 1    Research Proposal Writing Cognitive Load Scale (RPWCLS)

| *Prompt: Please choose one number that most properly suits the degree of difficulties you perceived when writing research proposal: 1 means not difficult at all; 6 means very difficult* | | | | | | |
|---|---|---|---|---|---|---|
| 1. Looking for academic literature | 1 | 2 | 3 | 4 | 5 | 6 |
| 2. Taking notes while reading | 1 | 2 | 3 | 4 | 5 | 6 |
| 3. Summarizing while reading | 1 | 2 | 3 | 4 | 5 | 6 |
| 4. Synthesizing while reading | 1 | 2 | 3 | 4 | 5 | 6 |
| 5. Deciding a research topic to write on | 1 | 2 | 3 | 4 | 5 | 6 |
| 6. Understanding the knowledge related to the topic | 1 | 2 | 3 | 4 | 5 | 6 |
| 7. Designing research method | 1 | 2 | 3 | 4 | 5 | 6 |
| 8. Listing the outline of research proposal | 1 | 2 | 3 | 4 | 5 | 6 |
| 9. Translating ideas into texts | 1 | 2 | 3 | 4 | 5 | 6 |
| 10. Writing with focus | 1 | 2 | 3 | 4 | 5 | 6 |
| 11. Writing with clear structure | 1 | 2 | 3 | 4 | 5 | 6 |
| 12. Writing with good convention | 1 | 2 | 3 | 4 | 5 | 6 |
| 13. Writing with good academic style | 1 | 2 | 3 | 4 | 5 | 6 |

# 第八章　教学支持对认知负荷的影响
# Chapter 8　Influence of cognitive load from teaching scaffolding

**本章内容概要 Abstract of the chapter**

本章探讨教师在项目式学术英语写作（PBAW）课程中的支持作用对学生认知负荷和学习努力程度的影响。基于建构主义的 PBL 课程倡导最小化指导，对缺乏必要知识储备的新手学习者来说，任务的难度可能导致无效学习。本章讨论了教师支持、学习动机与认知负荷的关系。在 PBAW 课程中，尽管学习者有较大探索空间，但如果缺乏动机和投入，优化认知负荷的效果有限。动机对于学生应对复杂学习任务至关重要。任务的重要性、有用性、自我效能等会影响学习努力程度，而教师提供的支持也会影响学习者对学习任务的认知。教师的外部指导可以提供知识构建所需的执行指导，促进学习动机，降低不必要的认知负荷。

研究以 227 名参加学术写作课程的学生为对象进行调查。课程在上海对外经济贸易大学开展，采用项目式教学法，学生在一学期内完成研究提案写作等任务。研究使用问卷调查收集数据，测量工具包括教师支持量表、学习努力程度量表和认知负荷量表，并运用结构方程模型进行分析。研究结果显示，教师支持通过提高学习者的努力程度，间接减少学习者感知的认知负荷。但研究未发现教师支持对降低认知负荷有直接作用。

　　本章的案例表明，PBAW 课程中教师支持可以影响学习者的努力程度，继而影响认知负荷。研究回应了对 PBL 课程的批评，强调根据认知负荷理论设计 PBAW 课程的可能性。实践中教师应提供必要的支持，如给予更多反馈、组织更多的小组辅导，提供个性化帮助，讲授写作知识等。对于本科生新手来说，在高度复杂的 PBAW 任务中，教师指导尤其重要。表 2 为 PBAW 课程中教师给予支持的示例。在不同的教学目标与学习对象中，教学支持内容需要调整。但总体而言，教学支持通过学习者的投入会减少学习者感知的认知负荷。

## 1. Introduction

　　PBL teaching is criticized (Paul et al., 2006) as lacking considering the structures that constitute human cognitive architecture and evidence from empirical studies over the past half-century and that minimally guided instruction is less effective and less efficient than instructional approaches which place a strong emphasis on guidance of the student learning process. In effect, PBAW course puts strong emphasis on scaffolding from the tutor. The chapter explains why tutor's scaffolding is needed not only in providing PBAW related knowledge, but also important in decreasing learners' cognitive load. The author propose that scaffolding can directly lower learner's cognitive load and indirectly facilitate writing efforts, improve learner's knowledge and lower intrinsic load. We employed 227 undergraduates and observed the relationship between PBAW teaching and learners' cognitive load.

## 2. Literature review

### 2.1 Criticism of PBL teaching method

Constructivist approaches, on which PBAW is based on, advocate for minimal guidance to allow learners to construct knowledge, this approach is criticized as leading to ineffective learning, especially for novices who lack the necessary prior knowledge. For example, in the article "Why Minimal Guidance During Instruction Does Not Work: An Analysis of the Failure of Constructivist, Discovery, Problem-Based, Experiential, and Inquiry-Based Teaching", Kirschner et al., (2006) discusses the effectiveness of instructional guidance during teaching. The authors argue that minimal guidance in instruction is less effective than guided instruction based on cognitive architecture, expert-novice differences, and cognitive load. They argued that human cognitive structure, including working memory and long-term memory, plays a crucial role in learning. Effective learning requires consideration of these structures. The limited previous knowledge owned by novice learners is not enough to support complex construction of new knowledge. Experts have well-developed cognitive structures that facilitate problem-solving and learning, whereas novices lack these structures, necessitating more guidance. Minimally guided instruction can overwhelm working memory, leading to less effective learning, especially for novices. But direct guidance, such as worked examples and process worksheets, supports cognitive processing during learning and is more effective than minimal guidance.

The criticism in the above reminds the PBAW designers the importance of lowering cognitive load by providing adequate support to learners. Scaffolding is necessary in the whole learning process and these scaffolding may lower learners' cognitive loads from at least two aspects: enhancing research and academic writing knowledge, and writing motivation.

## 2.2 Teacher's scaffolding and motivation

PBAW course has the advantage of giving students large space of exploration without unnecessary teaching and related extraneous cognitive load. However, optimizing the cognitive load has little effect unless learners are motivated and actually invest mental effort in processing the instructions. Authentic learning tasks based on real-life tasks are often difficult to understand and learners who choose real-life problem to solve have to deal with complicated and interactive factors. In confronting these problems, motivation is undoubtedly identified especially as a critical dimension that determines learning success (Frankola, 2001). PBL course designers and researchers need to determine the motivational effects of instructional conditions, and identify teaching strategies that assist students to deal with high intrinsic cognitive load going with complex learning tasks.

Motivating students to achieve success in dealing with complex learning task should be the topic of practical concern to PBAW instructional designers, and of theoretical concern to researchers. Important variables that have been identified as motivators for learning effort are perceived importance, usefulness, and the value of engaging in a task (Pintrich & Schrauben, 1992). Student perceptions of their ability to accomplish the task, that is, their self-efficacy (Bandura, 1982), has been found to affect effort and achievement (Salomon, 1983, 1984). Task characteristics such as task difficulty can be instrumental in providing cues as to the efficiency of effort. If the effort expenditure is perceived as a waste of energy or as unnecessary for success, learners will not be motivated to exert sufficient mental effort. Also, learner preconceptions about the effort required by a learning task influence the effort expenditure (Cennamo, 1993). These preconceptions are influenced not only by task characteristics, but also by the scaffolding provided by teachers. In particular, the schemas formulated from past experiences will determine how a learner perceives a learning task in terms of the amount of mental effort needed to deal with it successfully.

## 2.3 Teacher's scaffolding and cognitive load

Cognitive load theory posits that long-term memory (LTM) structures are crucial for preventing cognitive overload and guiding cognitive processing during complex learning tasks (Sweller, 2003; Van Merrienboer & Sweller, 2005). However, in authentic educational contexts, we often encounter cognitive challenges that necessitate the understanding and deliberate application of sophisticated knowledge frameworks. In these settings, executive functions or control are inextricably linked to the operational schemas of knowledge. When the long-term memory (LTM) possesses relevant schemas, working memory (WM) can efficiently manage intricate cognitive activities and organize complex environments. However, in the absence of comprehensive schemas to offer executive guidance in new situations, individuals default to general search strategies (Newell & Simon, 1972).

Although search-and-test strategies can eventually help achieve learning goals, they are inefficient due to the high cognitive load they impose on working memory, potentially leading to cognitive overload (Sweller, 1988). A more effective alternative is external instruction, which can provide the executive guidance needed for knowledge construction and elaboration. This guidance acts as a substitute for the missing schema-based guidance during the initial learning stages, instructing learners on how to manage situations or solve tasks, either through explicit instructions or by presenting worked examples (Efklides, 2008).

The role of direct instruction is thus to furnish the external executive guidance that compensates for the lack of internal schema-based guidance, thereby reducing unnecessary cognitive load. Cognitive load theory seeks to identify instructional methods that offer optimal executive guidance in various learning contexts, such as for learners with different levels of prior knowledge. If instruction primarily serves as a substitute for unavailable LTM schema-based guidance, instructional design should replicate the key characteristics and types of schemas related to a specific domain. This approach can help students learn stable information patterns and categorization schemes, enabling them to effectively apply relevant knowledge to various situations without incurring additional cognitive load.

## 2.4 Motivation, effort and cognitive load

Not many studies have been done on learners' motivation of learning and cognitive load. Evans (2024) found teacher's instruction can be effective in reducing students' perceptions of cognitive load, and the benefits extend to autonomous motivation, engagement, and (lower) disengagement. Engagement of learning, or learning effort, can bring about changes in overall cognitive load, because levels of learner prior knowledge are not constant, shown to be lower as demonstrated by Ayres (2006). Intrinsic load can be lowered after instruction and learning engagement as Ayres (2006) argued. A task is difficult because a number of elements have to be assimilated simultaneously. When expertise develops, element interactivity (intrinsic load) decreases as the interactions become learnt and incorporated into schemas (Kalyuga et al., 2003; Renkl & Atkinson, 2003). As problem solvers are able to recognize changes in element interactivity within problems, subjective measures directly linked to intrinsic cognitive load can find the change. Research on instruction converges with these findings. Load reduction instruction was positively correlated with academic motivation, learning effort, and school achievement in a study of high school mathematics students (Martin & Evans, 2018). In a study of high school science students, engagement mediated the effects of load reduction instruction on achievement, with large effects at both student and classroom levels (Martin, Ginns, Burns, Kennett, Munro-Smith, et al., 2021b).

## 3. The study

Based on the literature review, we did a survey on how teaching influences students' cognitive load and learning effort. The study aims to know if teacher's scaffolding in PBAW benefits learners' by directly lowering their cognitive load and indirectly through enhancing their learning effort. The theoretical model is shown in Figure 1 below.

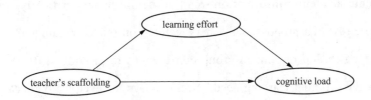

**Figure 1　Theoretical model of the study**

## 4. Research method

### 4.1 PBAW course instruction

The study was carried out at Shanghai University of International Business and Economics, China, where students started PBAW learning during their second university year. PBAW tasks lasted for a semester, separated into eight sections. The course is provided exclusively for about 800 students with the best English proficiency. During the eight sections, students worked in groups, read authentic academic literature, chose research questions, collected data, and wrote academic reports of around 2400 words in English. Students' writing was accessed from five dimensions, covering writing focus, idea development, organization, style, and language convention (Good, 2012).

During the eight sections, two writing teachers lectured on reading/writing strategies and genre knowledge to students distributed across six classes. Students were divided into small groups. They chose writing topics freely with group members, but each student read and wrote individually. The first four sections were used for students to locate academic information, read academic papers critically, and write research proposals. Teachers lectured on related reading/writing strategies and organized group conferences to provide scaffolding for the different learning needs. Sections five to seven were allocated for writing reports. Teachers, with the help of teaching assistants, lectured on genre knowledge pertaining to academic reports and gave brief feedback on unfinished drafts. Section eight was for peer review and revision. In addition to regular teaching, teachers provide group conference to give scaffolding according to different needs. Details of the course arrangement is summarized with table 1.

Table 1    Instruction in the PBAW course

| Meeting time | Teaching theme | Teaching and learning process |
| --- | --- | --- |
| 1st meeting | Locating reliable academic information | Teacher gives lecture and students search online |
| 2nd meeting | Taking notes, summarizing, and synthesizing | Teacher shows writing procedure and samples |
| 3rd meeting | Writing a research proposal | Teacher shows samples and lectures on genre and language support |
| 4th meeting | Collecting and analyzing data | Teacher lectures on research method, students choose research method |
| Group conference with teacher | | |
| 5th meeting | Writing the introduction part | Teacher lectures on genre and language support |
| 6th meeting | Writing the body part | |
| 7th meeting | Writing the conclusion part | |
| 8th meeting | Revising | Revise based on the feedback from the teacher and classmates |

## 4.2 Participants

Participants of the study were 227 students enrolled in academic writing course. The academic writing course used project-based teaching method, which required students to choose their writing topics freely and finish research proposal writing in a semester with the scaffolding provided by teachers. The participants' general language proficiency ranged from High B1 to High C1 according to the Common European Framework of Reference for Languages (CEFR). The mean age of the respondents was 20.5, ranging between 19 and 22. The sample consisted of 102 males and 125 females majoring in different fields of study. This skewness reflects the gender ratio of the university which is favored by female students who are perceived to perform better in foreign language learning. All the participants took part in the survey voluntarily.

## 4.3 Data Collection Procedures

The researchers collect data from the participants in the July 2024. The course ran from early February to early July. Students received academic writing instruction on writing process and report genre knowledge. At the end of the course, the questionnaire was sent to participants through an online platform (Wen Juan Xing, Changsha Ranxing Company) by one of the researchers, who was also teaching the course. The students were informed clearly about the purpose of the study, and told that their participation in the study was voluntary. Then the teacher told the participants how to complete the questionnaire. The confidentiality and anonymity of their responses were ensured. The students completed the questionnaire during their regular writing class time.

## 4.4 Instruments

• Teacher scaffolding scale

Instruction scaffolding scale is used to measure the scaffolding provided by teachers in PBAW course. The researchers asked students to endorse their agreement on three items addressing the scaffolding provided by the teacher in teaching activities on a six-point scale (1=Strongly Disagree, 6=Strongly Agree). The three items were "Teacher provided useful researching and writing related lecture in the semester" (M=4.50, SD=1.09), "Teacher provided useful group conference in the semester" (M=4.65, SD=1.09), and

"Teaching provided useful feedback in the semester" (M=4.70, SD=1.05). The Cronbach's Alpha for the three items was α=0.93.

- Effort of learning

We used one item to measure the effort of learning, "When learning the course, I put forth my best effort". Students were asked to evaluate the perceived degree of efforts they felt used in the writing process, with a 6-point scale (1=very little effort, 6=very best effort). The mean of the perceived learning effort in our sample was 4.70 (SD=0.89).

- Cognitive Load

The cognitive load of the research proposal writing task was measured by a subjective self-reporting instrument of 16 items in PBAW_CLS. Students were asked to evaluate the perceived degree of difficulties they felt of the writing task in the writing process, with a 6-point scale (1=not difficult at all, 6=very difficult). The overall internal consistency was good as assessed by Cronbach's alpha value 0.921. The mean of the perceived cognitive load in our sample was 4.00 (SD=0.76).

- Analysis

Firstly, we evaluated the measurement models of the questionnaire. The reliability and validity of the questionnaire were checked with CFAs using software-AMOS program Version 22.0 (Arbuckle, 2013). This was designed to check whether the data we collected fit the hypothesized measurement models. Informed by the CFA results, we proposed a mediation model and evaluated it by SEM. Several goodness of fit indices was reported in order to check model fits, including the ratio of chi-square ($\chi^2$) divided by the degree of freedom (df), the comparative fit index (CFI), the Tucker-Lewis index (TLI), the root mean square error of approximation (RMSEA), and the standardized root mean square residual (SRMR). We applied Hu and Bentler's (1999) cut-off values found that CFI and TLI were lower than .95; RMSEA lower than .06; and SRMR no larger than .08, showing a good model fit. In addition, chi-square/df ratio values lower than 2.5 were considered in our study to represent an acceptable model (Byrne, 1991).

## 5. Results

### 5.1 CFA Model Fit Results

Table 1 shows the CFA fit results for cognitive load (Model 1) with the fit results for two subscales (Model 1a, 1b and 1c), and teacher's scaffolding scale (Model 2). The CFA model fit results showed that the measurement scales were reliable and could be used safely for further analysis.

**Table 1    CFA Model Fit Results**

| Model | $\chi^2$ | df | $\chi^2$/df | p | RMSEA | SRMR | CFI | TLI |
|---|---|---|---|---|---|---|---|---|
| Model 1a | 10.437 | 7 | 1.436 | .112 | .028 (.000, .102) | .030 | .994 | .981 |
| Model 1b | 3.75 | 5 | .751 | .585 | .000 (.000, .000) | .011 | .983 | .978 |
| Model 1c | 10.512 | 7 | 1.502 | .161 | .047(.000, .103) | .002 | .995 | .989 |
| Model 1 | .000 | 0 | .000 | .000 | .000 (.000, .000) | .000 | 1.000 | 1.000 |
| Model 2 | .000 | 0 | .000 | .000 | .000 (.000, .000) | .000 | 1.000 | 1.000 |

Note:  Model 1a=reading cognitive load; Model 1b=planning cognitive load; Model 1c=writing cognitive load; Model 1=cognitive load; Model 2=teacher's scaffolding.

## 5.2 Descriptive Statistics

Table 2 provides the descriptive statistics, based on the mean of the two scales, and correlations related to the teacher's scaffolding, cognitive load and effort of learning. As shown, cognitive load was significantly associated with learning effort, but not significantly with teacher's scaffolding. Teacher's scaffolding was significantly associated with learning effort.

**Table 2    Descriptive Statistics**

|  | **V1** | **V2** | **V3** |
|---|---|---|---|
| Cognitive load | 1 | −1.65** | −.022 |
| Learning effort |  | 1 | .176** |
| Teacher's scaffolding |  |  | 1 |
| Mean | 3.33 | 4.70 | 4.61 |
| SD | .89 | .82 | 1.01 |

## 5.3 Mediation Model Evaluation

The next step was to specify a SEM to evaluate how teacher's scaffolding, being mediated by learning effort, affected cognitive load. A critical condition for testing the mediation effect is that there should be significant relationships between predictors and dependent variables (Hayes, 2013). Therefore, we checked the correlations of these variables including the three variables. Table 2 shows the correlations between the dependent and independent variables. As there was no significant association between teacher's scaffolding and cognitive load, a complete mediation model was proposed, only including the mediation paths from the predictor to the outcome variable (teacher's scaffolding→Effort of learning→cognitive load).

The SEM results revealed an acceptable model fit, with $\chi^2$ (12)=12.386; $\chi^2$/df=1.02; p=0.415>0.05; CFI=.99; TLI=.99; RMSEA 90% confidence interval=.04 [.00, .09]; SRMR=.06. On this basis, we retained the complete mediation structure of teaching scaffolding on cognitive load. Figure 2 shows the standardized regression coefficients between teaching scaffolding and cognitive load, mediated by learning effort. The path diagram of the model shows the standardized estimates of the causal paths only for the indirect effect. In specific terms, the significant indirect paths were found from teaching scaffolding, through the effort of learning (β=.16, p=0) to cognitive load (β=−.18, p<.01). In total, 3.70% of the variance in cognitive load was accounted for by the predictor variable.

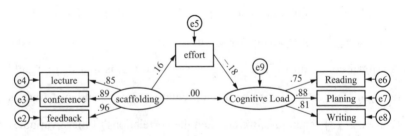

**Figure 2   A complete mediation model**

To summarize, in this study teacher's scaffolding had significant positive effects on students' learning efforts. In addition, students' learning efforts had a negative effect on cognitive load. The study shows that in PBAW course, instructions provided in our case do not directly lead to the lowering of cognitive load, but it indirectly enforces learning efforts and lowering the cognitive load.

## 6. Discussion

Our study shows teacher's scaffolding positively influence motivation by improving learning effort. It shows in PBAW course teachers can influence learners by motivating them into making more efforts into learning. The finding agrees with Evans et al. (2024). We also found that learning effort negatively associated with cognitive load. The finding agrees with Ayres (2006) in that by learning and establishing new schemas, the previous knowledge was increased, and intrinsic cognitive load was decreased. Combining the two findings we clearly show the indirect effect of teacher's scaffolding in influencing cognitive load positively. However, it should be pointed out that in the case being studied, the baffling effect of scaffolding on cognitive load was low (only 3.7% of the total effect), and more scaffolding should be encouraged in the teaching process.

We did not find the direct effect of scaffolding in decreasing cognitive load, which is different from Evans et al. (2024). The scaffolding in PBAW had not been specially aimed to lower perceived cognitive load, while Evans et al. (2024) had focused on it. The finding also demonstrated that without being associated learning efforts, scaffolding provided by the teacher would not bring about change of cognitive load, and might not benefit writing performance.

## 7. Implications

The study showed PBAW scaffolding can influence the perceived cognitive load, although only under the condition of being associated with learning effort. This finding replies the criticism of PBL course, by emphasizing the possibility of designing PBAW course according to cognitive load theory. The finding broadens the previous knowledge on the relationship between motivation and cognitive load. The benefit of PBAW lies in that when students are in the center of learning, teacher is free to choose only necessary knowledge to provide to the whole class or to the needed small groups. In the case being studied, group conference is good time to find problems faced by students and provide in time support.

In practice teachers should provide enough scaffolding such as giving more feedback, organizing more tutorial and lecturing more researching and writing related lectures. Instruction is needed in supporting highly complicated PBAW tasks, especially for undergraduates who are novice in the field. The indirect effects of scaffolding on cognitive load also shows that teachers could design support directly aiming at lowering cognitive load such as using more students' report as samples, or lowering task complexity, which will be mentioned in Chapter 13.

This study is limited in that only the mediating effect of learners' motivation is considered when observing teachers' scaffolding effects on cognitive load. As shown by literature review, scaffolding of writing and researching knowledge may directly increase learners' previous knowledge and decrease the number of interactive factors related to intrinsic load in solving problems. This means that if increased knowledge can be studied as the mediator, more significant effects on cognitive loads may have been observed. In the future, researchers were encouraged to measure intrinsic load multiple times in the whole learning process to study the change of intrinsic load with teachers' scaffolding.

## 8. References

Ayres, P. (2006). Impact of reducing intrinsic cognitive load on learning in a mathematical domain. Applied Cognitive Psychology, 20, 287–298.

Bandura, A. (1982). Self-efficacy mechanisms in human agency. American Psychologist, 37, 122–147.

Byrne, B. M. (1991). The Maslach burnout inventory: Validating factorial structure and invariance across intermediate, secondary, and university educators. Multivariate Behavioral Research, 26(4), 583–605.

Cennamo, K. S. (1993). Learning from video: Factors influencing learners' preconceptions and invested mental effort. Educational Technology Research and Development, 41(3), 33–45.

Efklides, A. (2008). Metacognition: defining its facets and levels of functioning in relation to self- and co-regulation. European Psychologist, 13, 277–287.

Evans, P., & Martin, A. J. (2024). Load reduction instruction: Multilevel effects for motivation, engagement, and achievement in mathematics. Educational Psychology, 1–19.

Frankola, K. (2001). Why online learners drop out. Workforce, 80, 53–60.

Hayes, A. F. (2013). Introduction to mediation, moderation, and conditional process analysis: A regression-based approach. New York: Guilford.

Hu, L. T., & Bentler, P. M. (1999). Cutoff criteria for fit indexes in covariance structure analysis: Conventional criteria versus new alternatives. Structural Equation Modeling, 6, 1–55. doi:10.1080/1070551990954013.18.

Kalyuga, S., Ayres, P., Chandler, P., & Sweller, J. (2003). The expertise reversal effect. Educational Psychologist, 38, 23–31.

Kirschner, Paul A., Sweller, John, & Clark, Richard E. (2006). Why Minimal Guidance During Instruction Does Not Work: An Analysis of the Failure of Constructivist, Discovery, Problem-Based, Experiential, and Inquiry-Based Teaching. Educational Psychologist, 41(2), 75–86.

Martin, A. J., & Evans, P. (2018). Load reduction instruction: Exploring a framework that assesses explicit instruction through to independent learning. Teaching and Teacher Education, 73, 203–214.

Martin, A. J., Ginns, P., Burns, E. C., Kennett, R., Munro-Smith, V., Collie, R. J., & Pearson, J. (2021b). Assessing instructional cognitive load in the context of students' psychological challenge and threat orientations: A multi-level latent profile analysis of students and classrooms. Frontiers in Psychology, 12.

Newell, A., & Simon, G. (1972). Human problem solving. Englewood Cliffs, NJ: Prentice-Hall.

Pintrich, P. R., & Schrauben, B. (1992). Students' motivational beliefs and their cognitive engagement in classroom academic tasks. In D. H. Schunk & J. L. Meece (Eds.), Student perceptions in the classroom (pp. 149–183). Hillsdale, NJ: Erlbaum.

Renkl, A., & Atkinson, R. K. (2003). Structuring the transition from example study to problem solving in cognitive skills acquisition: A cognitive load perspective. Educational Psychologist, 38, 15–22.

Salomon, G. (1983). The differential investment of mental effort in learning from different sources. Educational Psychologist, 18, 42–50.

Salomon, G. (1984). Television is "easy" and print is "tough": The differential investment of mental effort as a function of perceptions and attributions. Journal of Educational Psychology, 76, 647–658.

Sweller, J. (1988). Cognitive load during problem solving: Effects on learning. Cognitive Science, 12, 257 Sweller, J. (1988). Cognitive load during problem solving: Effects on learning. Cognitive Science, 12, 257–285.

Sweller, J. (2003). Evolution of human cognitive architecture. In B. Ross (Ed.), The psychology of learning and motivation (Vol. 43, pp. 215–266). San Diego, CA: Academic.

Van Merrienboer, J. J. G., & Sweller, J. (2005). Cognitive load theory and complex learning: Recent developments and future directions. Educational Psychology Review, 17(2), 147–177.

# 第九章　自主学习策略对认知负荷的影响

**Chapter 9　Influence of cognitive load from self-regulation strategy**

## 本章内容概要 Abstract of the chapter

　　过去几十年中，自我调控策略和认知负荷一直是最有影响力的两个概念。作为学习者的主体行为特征，自我调控学习策略的应用可能对认知负荷产生影响。本文旨在将这两个概念联系起来，以更好地阐释学习者自我调控学习策略与认知负荷的关联性。PBAW 学习环境要求学习者自我调控他们的学习过程，学习者需要设定目标和计划，使用写作策略并监控他们的学习进度。然而，自我调控策略是否可以降低认知负荷，并促进写作成绩，有赖于学习者的认知资源是否充足。在学术写作任务中，认知资源包括学习者的学术阅读能力、专业知识、研究能力等。在认知资源不足的情况下自我调控可能导致认知负荷的增加。本文分析了内在、外在和相关认知负荷与自我调控策略的关系，并用两个实验研究展现了自我调控学习策略、学习者的资源和认知负荷的关系。

　　在研究一中，274 名学生参与调查。研究者将学生按阅读能力分为高、低两组。通过分段多元回归分析，研究发现，高阅读能力组中自我调控学习策略与认知负荷显著相关，且学习策略能负向预测认知负荷（策略使用越多，认知负荷越低）；低阅读能力组中只有阅读能力能预测认知负荷，自我调控学习策略对其无影响。在研究二中，

165 名学生参与了调查。高阅读能力组中阅读能力和读写策略都能预测写作表现，低阅读能力组只有阅读能力能预测写作表现。低阅读能力学生难以有效使用学习策略影响写作表现，而高阅读能力学生在运用策略方面更有能力。研究表明，PBAW 课程在设定写作任务和教学写作策略时，需要考虑学习者的认知资源是否充分，只有在认知资源充分的情况下，学习策略才可能发挥效用。

## 1. Introduction

Self-regulated learning strategies are defined as "self-generated thoughts, feelings, and actions that are planned and cyclically adapted to the attainment of personal goals" (Zimmerman, 2005). Cognitive load theory focuses on the cognitive demands placed on learners and distinguishes between intrinsic, extraneous, and germane load (Kalyuga, 2011). While these two theories have developed independently, there may be a potential connection between them.

Previous attempts to merge self-regulated learning and cognitive load theory have been limited. As noted in this Chapter, learning and instruction aimed to bridge these theories (De Bruin & van Merriënboer, 2017), highlight their commonalities such as the use of learners' subjective estimates and a focus on self-directed learning situations. However, differences remain, with cognitive load theory concentrating on complex cognitive skill acquisition often in abstract domains like science and mathematics (Kalyuga, 2011), while self-regulated learning tends to focus on conceptual knowledge acquisition (Zimmerman, 2005). This chapter presents research that includes two experiments. The two studies investigate if self-regulated learning strategies taken by undergraduates could influence their perceived cognitive load and writing performance. Study 1 examines how self-regulated learning strategies influence cognitive load with a survey of 227 undergraduates. Study 2 studies how self-regulated learning strategies influence writing performance with a survey of 165 undergraduates. The results show that students' reading ability, as a resource of learning PBAW, limits their ability to use self-regulated learning strategies to influence cognitive load and writing performance. Only good readers can effectively use these strategies to decrease cognitive load and positively impact writing performance.

This research has important implications for teaching. For students with lower reading ability, courses aiming to improve their reading ability, topic knowledge, and less complicated linguistic training would be beneficial. For learners with more expertise (reading ability and other resources), instructional self-regulated learning strategies can help decrease cognitive demands as these learners have enough competence to gain knowledge with cognitive resources and learning strategies, indicating a shift towards greater self-sufficiency (Seufert, 2018). By understanding the interplay between self-regulated learning and cognitive load theory, educators can design instructional strategies that support self-regulatory processes and manage cognitive load effectively.

## 2. Literature Review

### 2.1 Self-regulated learning (SRL) and cognitive load theory (CLT)

Education is a dynamic journey that requires individuals to be adept at self-regulation. To excel, learners must establish objectives and strategize their educational trajectory, employing various techniques and continuously assessing their progress towards these goals. If they find themselves off course, they must adapt and modify their approach. This self-directed management of learning is an additional layer to the act of learning itself and can potentially strain learners' cognitive resources. To gain insight into the cognitive demands of self-regulated learning, it is essential to connect two significant strands in educational research: self-regulated learning and cognitive load. Previous attempts to merge these concepts have been limited, and this paper aims to explore their interaction. To establish a link between cognitive load and learning self-regulation, we must first define these concepts individually.

Zimmerman (2005) defines self-regulation as "self-generated thoughts, feelings, and actions that are planned and cyclically adapted to the attainment of personal goals" (p. 14). Models of Self-Regulated Learning (SRL) emphasize the cyclic nature of self-regulation, with feedback and adjustment loops throughout the learning process (e.g., Schmitz & Wiese, 2006; Winne & Hadwin, 1998; Zimmerman, 2005).

Kalyuga (2011) notes the interdependence of germane and intrinsic load, suggesting that focusing germane resources on task elements enhances learning success. This distinction is crucial for self-regulation, as it differentiates between task demands and learner-driven decisions. CLT provides instructional design guidelines to optimize learning by considering cognitive system capabilities. It has been instrumental in multimedia learning research, offering principles to reduce extraneous load and enhance germane resource investment. The theory aims to equip educators with strategies to regulate learning processes effectively. In summary, self-regulation models highlight the dynamic interplay of cognitive, metacognitive, and motivational factors during learning, while CLT offers a cognitive framework to predict and enhance learning outcomes through instructional design.

## 2.2 Similarities and differences of the two theories

The Self-Regulated Learning (SRL) and Cognitive Load Theory (CLT) both originated in the 1980s and have since developed into significant areas of educational research. Despite their common ground in learning and memory psychology and their focus on self-directed learning, they have largely evolved independently. Research aimed to bridge these theories, highlighting their commonalities such as the use of learners' subjective estimates and a focus on self-directed learning situations. However, differences remain, with CLT concentrating on complex cognitive skill acquisition, often in abstract domains like science and mathematics, while SRL tends to focus on conceptual knowledge acquisition.

The goals of SRL and CLT also diverge. CLT aims to generate new instructional techniques, whereas SRL has been more focused on describing and fostering learning processes, although it also contributes to instructional design through empirical studies. SRL emphasizes the learner as the agent of regulation, whereas CLT seeks to regulate learning through instructional design, often aiming to reduce extraneous cognitive load and enhance germane load.

SRL models encompass cognitive, metacognitive, motivational, and emotional aspects of learning, influencing a learner's regulatory behavior. In contrast, CLT primarily focuses on cognitive aspects, with less consideration of motivational or affective states. There have been attempts to introduce metacognitive load as a separate category, but these have not significantly influenced the current CLT debate.

SRL views learning as a dynamic process, with past experiences shaping current strategies and an emphasis on the adaptability of learning approaches. CLT, however, tends to present a more static view, with cognitive demands determined by task complexity and instructional design relative to prior knowledge. Some researchers have challenged this static view, advocating for a more dynamic understanding of cognitive load that accounts for learner goals and activities.

In summary, while SRL and CLT share some foundational concepts, they differ in their focus, goals, and conceptual breadth, with SRL taking a broader, more dynamic approach to learning regulation and CLT concentrating on cognitive aspects and instructional design to manage cognitive load.

## 2.3 Bridge the two theories

Integrating Self-Regulated Learning (SRL) and Cognitive Load Theory (CLT) could significantly benefit learning processes. While SRL values learner autonomy and metacognition, CLT focuses on task-related cognitive demands. De Bruin & van Merriënboer (2017) attempted to connect these theories, showcasing empirical studies that examined how SRL strategies affect cognitive load and how imposed cognitive loads influence self-regulatory behaviors.

The planning phase of self-regulated learning entails analyzing the learning situation and setting goals to select strategies (Zimmerman, 2002). Its intrinsic cognitive load is related to task complexity, with more complex tasks leading to higher planning loads. This phase also involves metacognitive knowledge, as learners assess their abilities and strategies, increasing cognitive demand (Flavell, 1979). Specific goal setting can further raise cognitive load, particularly when learners analyze and link their current and target states (Wirth, Künsting, & Leutner, 2009). Despite this, learners can apply strategies flexibly, though specific goals might sometimes limit these options. To alleviate the intrinsic load, Van Merriënboer and Sluijsmans (2009) suggest simplifying tasks and gradually increasing complexity. Sharing task selection control with a system that offers a preselected, appropriate set of tasks can also help. Extraneous load during planning may be caused by the structure of the learning environment or by distractions. In non-linear environments like hypertexts, planning and goal-setting can be difficult (de Stefano & LeFevre, 2007), but graphic organizers and information prompts can provide support. Finally, the effort in planning constitutes germane load. Prompts and implementation intentions can encourage self-regulation and initiate learning activities (Zheng, 2016; Gollwitzer, 1999). Implementation intentions have been shown to facilitate text-picture integration, reduce extraneous load, and promote germane resource investment (Stalbovs, Scheiter, & Gerjets, 2015), highlighting the significance of managing intrinsic and germane loads in the planning phase for effective self-regulated learning.

After planning and then learners employ cognitive strategies to tackle tasks, involving both cognitive and metacognitive strategies. Intrinsic load during this phase depends on task complexity; metacognitive monitoring activities can be particularly demanding, as shown by Stark et al. (2002). To ease this load, van Merrienboer and Sluijsman (2009) recommend a step-by-step approach, such as starting with simpler tasks. Extraneous load can occur when the dual execution of cognitive and metacognitive strategies hinders learning, especially with complex tasks (Van Gog, Kester, & Paas, 2011). Glogger-Frey et al.

(2017) found higher extraneous load in self-regulated tasks, suggesting that self-regulation can deepen task analysis but may also increase load. Reducing extraneous load could involve guidance strategies like process worksheets or prompts. Germane load in this phase can be fostered by activities that enhance learning and metacognition, such as drawing (Schleinschok et al., 2017). Feedback can improve self-assessment accuracy (van Loon et al., 2017), and prompts can activate cognitive strategies and monitoring, potentially boosting learning (Zheng, 2016). However, more research is needed on how these approaches affect cognitive load.

The third aspect is that, whether self-regulation modulates intrinsic, extraneous and germane load and thus results in lower or higher learning performance, depends on learners' resources. Learners with high levels of prior knowledge will perceive tasks as less intrinsically loading and they will be able to compensate for additional extraneously loading aspects (expertise reversal effect; Kalyuga, 2007). Also high memory capacity is a protective factor when facing high task demands. Despite such cognitive features metacognitive knowledge and skills will also influence load. Monitoring for example might be less loading if learners are used to observe and possess monitoring strategies. Also, cognitive learning strategies that are automated will reduce potential loading effects. And not least motivational and emotional characteristics will influence the amount of perceived load or the amount of invested effort

(Zander, 2010). All these aptitudes interact with instructional affordances and should be taken into account when modeling the interplay between SRL and CLT.

## 2.4  Interaction model of SRL and CLT

The interaction between Self-Regulated Learning (SRL) and Cognitive Load Theory (CLT) can be depicted through a model that centers around the task at hand, which includes both the learning task itself and the self-regulatory elements involved in managing it (see Figure 1). These elements can be intrinsic or extraneous. The model suggests that the difficulty of the task creates a load (a combination of intrinsic and extraneous factors) that interacts with the learner's available resources. As task difficulty and imposed load increase, resources may deplete. The intersection of task load and learner resources marks the point where self-regulation becomes necessary. In scenarios where tasks are simple, learners may not need to engage in self-regulation because their resources are more than adequate, and perceived load is low. Conversely, when tasks are excessively challenging, self-regulation may not be feasible as resources are insufficient, and the load is excessively high (e.g., Moos, 2013). Optimal self-regulation occurs with tasks of moderate difficulty, where resources and load are balanced, allowing learners to effectively utilize their resources and improve task management. This model also considers the impact of learner characteristics, such as prior knowledge. For instance, novice learners may find initial tasks challenging but can be assisted by prompts that help initiate self-regulatory processes, as shown by Nückles et al. (2010). Over time, as learners gain expertise, the demands of the task decrease, and they may no longer require prompts, indicating a shift in the model towards greater self-sufficiency. This framework can guide research into how SRL and CLT interrelate, provided that robust and process-oriented measures for both self-regulation and cognitive load are employed. It can elucidate how different instructional strategies may either support or impede self-regulatory processes and cognitive load.

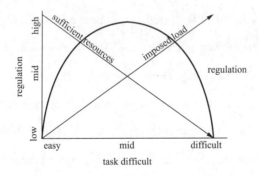

Figure 1　Interplay of regulation and cognitive load (source: Seufert, 2018)

## 3. The studies

Considering the complex interaction of SRL and CLT, we used two experiments to research if SRL strategies taken by undergraduates could influence their perceived cognitive load and writing performance. In study 1, we did research on how SRL strategies influence cognitive load with a survey of 227 undergraduates; In study 2 we studied how SRL strategies influence writing performance with a survey of 165 undergraduates. The two studies were combined to show if PBAW learners had enough SRL strategies to influence their learning process and performance. As PBAW is reading based writing activity, and reading ability is one of prerequired resources for carrying out PBAW tasks, we use reading ability as resource to study the complex relationship between SRL strategy and CL.

## 3.1　Study 1

### 3.1.1　Setting

In the study PBARW lasted for a semester, separated into eight sections. The course is provided exclusively for about 800 students with the best English proficiency. During the eight sections, students worked in groups, read authentic academic literature, chose research questions, collected data, and wrote academic reports of around 2400 words in English. During the learning process, four EAP teachers provided necessary scaffolding on searching for reliable academic information, writing different parts of reports, using proper citations, and so on. Two of the teachers have more than 10 years of teaching experience, and the other two are young teachers with an applied linguistic doctorate.

### 3.1.2　Data collection

The current study utilized the following research instruments and measures:

- Project-Based Academic Writing Challenges Scale (PBAW_CLS)

  The 16-item PBAW_CLS was employed to measure perceived cognitive load after they finished doing the task (see appendix 1 for detail). Students responded via a six-point Likert scale, with answers ranging from 1 (not challenging at all) to 6 (very challenging). Confirmatory factor analysis (CFA) indicated the model had satisfactory fit: RMSEA was moderate (0.06, 90% CI (0.05, 0.07)), SRMR was excellent (0.05), CFI was satisfactory (0.96), and TLI (0.95) indicated little room for improvement (Hu & Bentler, 1999). The resulted 16 items related to the 3 factors indicating the challenges of Academic Reading (AR), Idea Creating (IC), and Text Processing (TP). The reliability of all three factors was very high, with 0.95, 0.94, and 0.95 respectively. It shows that the questionnaire was psychometrically reliable.

- Reading score on the College English Test (CET) band 4

  We used the reading score of the College English Test (CET) band 4 as a measure of English reading ability. The CET 4 is a standardized English proficiency test designed to assess whether university students meet the requirements of the college English course set by the National College English Syllabus for Non-English Majors. The participants took the CET 4 exam on June 21, 2020, two months before they took the PBARW course. In the reading section, students were required to read one article of about 1200 words and two articles of about 500 words to test their speed reading and reading for detail skills.

- Reading/Writing Strategy Scale (RWSS)

A 14-item questionnaire about self-regulated strategies was used in the survey (See appendix 2 for detail). Items were prepared with reference to self-regulated writing strategies as elaborated in Teng & Zhang (2016). We made adjustments according to the PBARW process in our research context and checked its reliability. It was designed with a six-point Likert scale ranging from 1 (not at all true of me) to 6 (very true of me). The values of internal reliability for the instrument were .87, much higher than the benchmark value (.70).

### 3.1.3 Participants and procedures

All participants were informed by their teachers of the purpose of the study, their privilege to choose whether to take part in the survey voluntarily, and how their confidentiality would be protected. Written informed consent was obtained from a total of 274 students, 143 female (52%), and 131 male (48%) before the survey. They agreed to participate in the study and complete an online survey in the eighteenth week of the semester. Their CET-4 reading scores were also collected. Five samples were taken away for missing data, and two outliners found later in piecewise regression analysis were also deleted. A total of 267 survey responses were ultimately analyzed. The mean CET 4 reading score of participants was 207 (SD=14.05), with the lowest score being 158 and the highest being 232. Using minimum conversion benchmarks from CET 4 to CEFR (Jin et al., 2022), the reading level of all these students was above the B1, with 82.0% of them above the B2 level (see Table 1 below).

Table 1　Frequency distribution of reading score

| CEFR level of reading | N |
|---|---|
| <B1 | 0 |
| ≥ B1 (CET reading above149) | 48 (18.0%) |
| ≥ B2 (CET reading above194) | 219 (82.0%) |

### 3.1.4  Data analyses

We use a three-stage statistical procedure to determine the relationship between reading ability, SRL strategy and CL met by the students in our sample.

Firstly, we separated students into two groups according to their reading ability into higher reading ability and lower reading ability groups at the mean score of CET reading Band 4 (207).

Secondly, we carried out piecewise multivariable regression analysis to study if self-regulated learning strategies had different effects on cognitive load in different reading ability groups separated by threshold level.

### 3.1.5  Results

- Descriptive and correlational statistics

Table 2 displays descriptive statistics. Students' evaluation of PBAW cognitive load ranged from 1.0 to 6.00, with a mean of 3.33. The distributional properties, as indicated by skewness ( ≤ 2) and kurtosis (<7), were in the acceptable ranges (West et al., 1995). SRL strategies ranged from 1 to 6 with

4.22 as the mean score. We found SRL strategy score and PBAW cognitive load was not significantly related as shown in table 2. But as we divided students into two groups with higher and lower reading abilities, as shown in Table 3, PBAW cognitive load and SRL strategies were significantly corelated for the higher reading ability group with 125 students (r=−0.209; p=0.033); while in the lower reading ability group with 142 students, the two variables were still not significantly corelated (r=.084; p=0.360).

**Table 2    Descriptive and correlational analysis (n=274)**

| Variable | Mean | SD | Min | Max | Skewness | Kurtosis | PC | SRLS |
|---|---|---|---|---|---|---|---|---|
| RS | 207 | 14.5 | 158 | 232 | −.802 | .550 | / | / |
| PC | 3.33 | 0.85 | 1.00 | 6.00 | .047 | .175 | 1 | −0.51 |
| SRLS | 4.22 | 0.78 | 1 | 6 | −.849 | 2.20 | −0.51 | 1 |

Notes. RS=reading score. PC=PBAW cognitive load.  SRLS=self-regulated learning strategies.

**Table 3    correlation analysis**

| Reading ability groups | | | SRL strategy | Cognitive Load |
|---|---|---|---|---|
| Lower reading ability | SRL strategy | Pearson correlation | 1 | .084 |
| | | Sig. | | .360 |
| | | n | 122 | 122 |
| | Cognitive Load | Pearson correlation | .084 | 1 |
| | | Sig. | .360 | |
| | | n | 122 | 122 |
| Higher reading ability | SRL strategy | Pearson correlation | 1 | −.209* |
| | | Sig. | | .033 |
| | | n | 105 | 105 |
| | Cognitive Load | Pearson correlation | −.209* | 1 |
| | | Sig. | .033 | |
| | | n | 105 | 105 |
| * 0.05 | | | | |

- The effects of SRL strategies, divided by reading ability, on PBAW cognitive load

We tested, with piecewise linear regression analysis, how the SRL strategies influenced PBAW cognitive load. We divided the subjects into two groups according to their reading ability at the breakpoint of 207 and used learning strategies to predict cognitive load. As suggested by related studies (Kim, 2020b; Plakans 2009), reading ability may moderate the effects of contributing elements such as topic knowledge and learning strategies on the reading/writing process, so we extended our study to include the predictive effects of reading ability on PBAW cognitive load in different reading ability groups. We controlled the possible influence of gender on cognitive load when doing the multiple regressions.

Before conducting the regression analysis, we completed the following preliminary analyses: An analysis of standard residuals was carried out, which showed that the data contained 2 outliers, which were taken out accordingly. The independent variables did not have multicollinearity (for the two models, VIF values are smaller than 1.32). The data met the assumption of independent errors (for the two models, Durbin-Watson values are 2.05 and 2.18, respectively). All these tests indicated that multiple regression was appropriate for the present data.

The result of the piecewise multivariable linear regression was summarized in Table 4. As shown by Table 4, as a whole, the two variables have significant relationships with PBAW challenges ($F$=6.511, $p$=.000; $F$=7.224, $p$=.000) and explain 10.2% and 8.5% of the variance in PBAW challenges for the two models, respectively. For the lower reading ability group, only reading ability predicted the cognitive load perceived ($\beta$=−0.321, $p$=.000). SRL strategy did not predict PBAW cognitive load in this group. For the higher-reading ability group, SRL strategies predicted the perceived sense of challenges negatively ($\beta$=−0.400, $p$=.000; $\beta$=−0.233, $p$=.004). This means that students who were better English readers were more likely than poor English readers to use their learning strategies related to the topic to effectively meet the requirements of the task.

Table 4　Piecewise multiple regression models for PBAW cognitive load

| Variable | Standardized Coefficients | | | | Partial correlation coefficients | | Model Summary | |
|---|---|---|---|---|---|---|---|---|
| | Beta | Sig. | Beta | Sig. | | | $R^2$ | |
| | Model 1 | | Model 2 | | Model 1 | Model 2 | Model 1 | Model 2 |
| Reading ability | −.321 | .000 | .149 | .162 | −.315 | .158 | .102 | .085 |
| Writing strategy | −.059 | .418 | −.400 | .000 | −.060 | −.405 | | |

Notes. Model 1 is the regression model for the low-reading ability group. Model 2 is the regression model for the high-reading ability group.

## 3.2  Study 2  SRL strategy and PBAW performance

### 3.2.1  Participants

The study employed a mixed-methods approach, combining quantitative and qualitative research methods. Volunteers were recruited from six PBAW classes, totaling 165 participants for a questionnaire survey. These participants were second-year university students, distributed across four majors: International Trade (25.1%, n=41), Public Management (18.2%, n=30), Finance (24.0%, n=40), and Accounting (32.7%, n=54). The average age of participants was 21.08 years (SD=0.97), with females making up 57% of the sample (n=94). An additional 16 students participated in a qualitative survey, submitting their learning journals biweekly throughout the study. Despite the absence of an institutional review board to review our research aims and design, we prioritized research ethics. All participants were informed about the study's purpose, their right to choose participation, and the measures taken to ensure their confidentiality. Written consent was obtained from all participants.

### 3.2.2 Instruments and procedures

The following instruments were used in the study:

- We used the same SRL strategy questionnaire as in study 1.

- PBAW papers

Students' academic writings were collected one week after the end of the course. These writings were used to indicate their PBARW performance. Each student was required to write a research report of 2,400 words, including at least 10 references to academic articles in English. The overall quality of the reports was scored using Good et al.'s (2012) discipline-specific writing rubric (See Appendix 3 for reference). These analytical writing criteria measure five aspects of writing performance: focus, content, organization, style, and English language conventions. Two raters attended a workshop to standardize their understanding of the writing rubric. Inter-rater reliability and intra-rater reliability were at acceptable levels, with 0.80 and 0.90 respectively. In total, 165 reports were scored, with an average score of 21.58 (SD=1.58) out of 25. As the PBARW reports are much longer than the essays required by IELTS or TOEFL, the scoring and rescoring of 165 reports took approximately two weeks.

- Reading score on the College English Test (CET) Band 4
- learning journal

To track students' learning experiences, learning journals were used in the study. Although writing journals require a time investment, it is considered conducive to improving writers' reflective thinking ability (Lee, 2015). Sixteen informants volunteered to write learning journals biweekly. The informants were encouraged, but not required to note the strategies they had adopted during the writing process, as well as difficulties they had encountered while learning. Each journal was limited to 200 words. Altogether, we collected eight entries per informant, totaling 128 entries. The journals were not graded or corrected, and students received brief feedback only if they posed questions. See Appendix 4 for reference of the journal themes.

### 3.2.3 Data analyses

We used a segmented multivariate regression analysis to determine if reading ability separates the effectiveness of strategies on writing performance. Then we analyzed the learning journals to further understand the challenges faced by the participants. Lastly, we used t test to compare the SRL strategies used by learners with higher and lower reading abilities.

### 3.2.4 Results

We divided students into two groups based on a CET-4 reading score breakpoint of 207. The results of the segmental regression show that in the higher reading ability group, both reading ability and reading/writing strategies predicted the PBARW performance (with $\beta=0.246$, $p=0.021$ and $\beta=0.260$, $p=0.015$ respectively). In the lower reading level group, only reading ability predicted the PBARW performance ($\beta=0.228$, $p=0.044$). These results indicate that while reading ability can predict writing performance in both groups, only good readers can use reading/writing strategies to influence PBARW performance.

Figure 2 shows the partial regression plot of PBARW scores against strategies at different reading levels, divided by the CET-4 reading score of 207. The regression lines suggest a qualitatively different relationship between PBARW scores and reading/writing strategies in higher (on the right) and lower (on the left) reading ability groups. For the lower group, the use of additional strategies did not lead to higher PBARW scores, and the regression line nearly levels off. In contrast, for the higher group, increased use of strategies clearly led to higher writing scores. This indicates that the lower-reading-ability students cannot effectively use integrated strategies to influence their writing performance.

Learning journals from six students belonging to the lower reading abilities revealed that they found applying the strategies from the PBARW course considerably challenging. The repeated theme in their journals was the difficulty caused by low reading comprehension ability such as a lack of fast reading ability to judge the value of the literature. Twenty-three percent of the learning journal entries from students with lower reading abilities mentioned the challenge of fast reading, while this percentage was only 7.5 percent among students with higher reading abilities. As expressed by Zhu (in the lower reading-ability group), "I think the most difficult part is literature locating, fast reading, and determining the value of the literature. There are too many terms. I have to use translating software, but it is time-consuming." Yang (in the lower reading-ability group) wrote, "Usually, useful articles are hard to understand, while the easy-to-understand articles are not worth reading."

However, the journals from students with higher reading abilities demonstrated greater competence in employing the strategies. Fewer than 10 percent of these students mentioned challenges in using reading/ writing strategies. Some students exhibited a high level of competence in engaging in writerly reading and mining information from texts. For instance, Ma (in the higher reading-ability group) wrote, "I compared many articles before deciding on the definition of the term for my paper." She also explored rhetorical functions of academic reports by

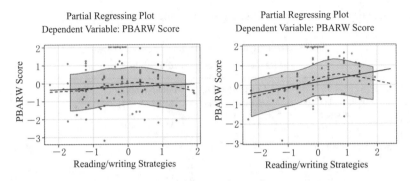

Partial Regressing Plot
Dependent Variable: PBARW Score

Partial Regressing Plot
Dependent Variable: PBARW Score

**Figure 2**　**Partial regression plot of PBARW scores against SRL
strategies with segmental regression**

analyzing multiple articles and learned statistics by reading textbooks in English.

The results of T-tests, as shown in Table 5, revealed that reading/writing strategies were significantly more frequently adopted by students of higher reading ability ($p$ values for all the strategies were lower than 0.05). A detailed comparison (*see Appendix 5 for reference*) showed almost all the strategies that were significantly more used by good readers were, directly or indirectly, based on good comprehension of source materials, such as the strategy "I reflected on the advantages and disadvantages of the literature" in the prewriting stage, the strategy "I found a gap in the previous literature." in the proposing stage, and the strategy "I referred to the expressions used in samples" in the translating stage. Considering the fact that all the reading/writing strategies were taught in the PBARW course, this finding suggests that students with higher reading ability are more competent in utilizing the strategies, especially those that necessitate good reading comprehension.

Table 5  Reading/writing strategies comparison between
the learners of different reading abilities

| Reading/Writing strategies | Lower-reading ability (N=82) | | Higher-reading ability (N=83) | | t | p |
|---|---|---|---|---|---|---|
| | M | SD | M | SD | | |
| Locating/reading strategies | 4.73 | 1.12 | 5.20 | 1.18 | −2.677** | 0.008 |
| Proposing strategies | 4.75 | 1.08 | 5.16 | 1.10 | −2.382* | 0.018 |
| Translating strategies | 4.75 | 0.95 | 5.10 | 1.04 | −2.267* | 0.025 |
| Revising strategies | 4.960 | 0.99 | 5.25 | 1.03 | −2.189* | 0.030 |

Note: *p<0.05. **p<0.01.

## 4. Discussion

We used two studies to observe the effects of SRL strategies on PBARW process and product. Findings showed that students' resources (reading ability) limit their competence to use SRL strategies in influencing cognitive load or writing performance. Findings showed that divided by reading ability, only the good readers used SRL strategies effectively to decrease cognitive load and positively influenced writing performance. The finding agrees with the model proposed by Seufert, T. (2020) that the difficulty of learning task creates a load (a combination of intrinsic and extraneous factors) that interacts with the learner's available resources. For students with lower reading ability (about half of the learners in the two studies), task difficulty imposed too high load for resources (SRL strategies) to confront effectively. These learners may find initial tasks challenging but cannot help themselves with scaffolding provided. For these students, preparing courses aiming to improve their reading ability, topic knowledge and more strategies would be benefiting. For learners with more expertise (reading ability and other resources), the demands of the task can be decreased with more knowledges gained in the learning process, indicating a shift in the model towards greater self-sufficiency. This framework can guide research into how SRL and CLT interrelate, provided that robust and process-oriented measures for both self-regulation and cognitive load are employed. It can further elucidate how different instructional strategies may either support or impede self-regulatory processes and cognitive load.

## 5. References

Aghayani, B., & Hajmohammadi, E. (2019). Project-based Learning: Promoting EFL Learners Writing Skills. LLT Journal: A Journal on Language and Language Teaching, 22(1), 78–85. https://doi.org/10.24071/llt.v22i1.1727

Bai, B., & Wang, J. (2020). Conceptualizing self-regulated reading-to-write in ESL/EFL writing and investigating its relationships to motivation and writing competence. Language Teaching Research, 27(5), 1193–1216. https://doi.org/10.1177/1362168820971740

Cheong, C. M., Zhu, X., & Liao, X. (2017). Differences between the relationship of L1 learners' performance in integrated writing with both independent listening and independent reading cognitive skills. Reading and Writing, 31(4), 779–811. https://doi.org/10.1007/s11145-017-9811-8

De Bruin, A. B., & van Merriënboer, J. J. (2017). Bridging cognitive load and self-regulated learning research. Learning and Instruction, 52, 1–98.

Flavell, J. H. (1979). Metacognition and cognitive monitoring: A new area of cognitive-developmental inquiry. American Psychologist, 34, 906.

Glogger-Frey, I., Gaus, K., & Renkl, A. (2017). Learning from direct instruction: Best prepared by several self-regulated or guided invention activities? Learning and Instruction, 51, 26–35.

Gollwitzer, P. M. (1999). Implementation intentions: Strong effects of simple plans. American Psychologist, 54, 493.

Grabe, W., & Zhang, C. (2013). Reading and Writing Together: a critical component of English for academic purposes teaching and learning. TESOL Journal, 4(1), 9–24. https://doi.org/10.1002/tesj.65

Hinkel, E. (2003). Simplicity without elegance: Features of sentences in L1 and L2 academic texts. TESOL Quarterly, 37, 275–301. https://doi.org/10.2307/3588505

Hyland, K. (2005). Representing readers in writing: Student and expert practices. Linguistics and Education, 16(4), 363–377. https://doi.org/10.1016/j.linged.2006.05.002

Jin, Y. Jie, W. & Wang, W. (2022). An Alignment Study of College English Tests Band 4 & 6 and Standard Language Competence, Foreign Language World (Waiyu Jie) (02), 24–32.

Kalyuga, S. (2007). Expertise reversal effect and its implications for learner-tailored instruction. Educational Psychology Review, 19, 509–539.

Kalyuga, S. (2011). Cognitive load theory: How many types of load does it really need? Educational Psychology Review, 23, 1–19.

Kellogg, R. T., Whiteford, A. P., Turner, C. E., Cahill, M. J., & Mertens, A. (2013). Working memory in written Composition: a progress report. Journal of Writing Research, 5(2), 159–190. https://doi.org/10.17239/jowr-2013.05.02.1

Kong, Y., & Wang, C. (2022). The effects of self-efficacy on the use of self-regulated learning strategies and project-based writing performance. International Journal of English for Academic Purposes, 2022(Spring), 21–39. https://doi.org/10.3828/ijeap.2022.3

Lee, S. (2015). Joining the "literacy club": when reading meets blogging. ELT Journal, 69(4), 373–382. https://doi.org/10.1093/elt/ccv030

Li, J. (2014). The role of reading and writing in summarization as an integrated task. Language Testing in Asia, 4(1). https://doi.org/10.1186/2229-0443-4-3

Li, J., & Schmitt, N. (2009). The acquisition of lexical phrases in academic writing: A longitudinal case study. Journal of Second Language

Writing, 18(2), 85–102. https://doi.org/10.1016/j.jslw.2009.02.001

Lundstrom, K., & Baker, W. (2009). To give is better than to receive: The benefits of peer review to the reviewer's own writing. Journal of Second Language Writing, 18(1), 30–43. https://doi.org/10.1016/j.jslw.2008.06.002

McCulloch, S. (2013). Investigating the reading-to-write processes and source use of L2 postgraduate students in real-life academic tasks: An exploratory study. Journal of English for Academic Purposes, 12(2), 136–147. https://doi.org/10.1016/j.jeap.2012.11.009

Moos, D. (2013). Examining hypermedia Learning: The role of cognitive load and self-regulated learning. Journal of Educational Multimedia and Hypermedia, 22, 39–61.

Nückles, M., Hübner, S., Dümer, S., & Renkl, A. (2010). Expertise reversal effects in writing-to-learn. Instructional Science, 38, 237–258.

Paul, J., & Criado, A. R. (2020). The art of writing literature review: What do we know and what do we need to know? International Business Review, 29(4), 101717. https://doi.org/10.1016/j.ibusrev.2020.101717

Payant, C., McDonough, K., Uludag, P., & Lindberg, R. (2019). Predicting integrated writing task performance: Source comprehension, prewriting planning, and individual differences. Journal of English for Academic Purposes, 40, 87–97. https://doi.org/10.1016/j.jeap.2019.06.001

Perfetti, C. A., & Stafura, J. Z. (2014). Word knowledge in a theory of reading comprehension. Scientific Studies of Reading, 18(1), 22–37.

https://doi.org/10.1080/10888438.2013.827687

Plakans, L. (2009). The role of reading strategies in integrated L2 writing tasks. Journal of English for Academic Purposes, 8(4), 252–266. https://doi.org/10.1016/j.jeap.2009.05.001

Plakans, L., & Gebril, A. (2013). Using multiple texts in an integrated writing assessment: Source text use as a predictor of score. Journal of Second Language Writing, 22(3), 217–230. https://doi.org/10.1016/j.jslw.2013.02.003

Sawaki, Y., Quinlan, T., & Lee, Y. W. (2013). Understanding learner strengths and weaknesses: Assessing performance on an integrated writing task. Language Assessment Quarterly, 10(1), 73–95. https://doi.org/10.1080/15434303.2011.633305

Schleinschok, K., Eitel, A., & Scheiter, K. (2017). Do drawing tasks improve monitoring and control during learning from text? Learning and Instruction, 51, 10–25.

Seufert, T. (2018). Building bridges between Self-Regulation and cognitive load—an invitation for a broad and differentiated attempt. Educational Psychology Review, 32(4), 1151–1162. https://doi.org/10.1007/s10648-020-09574-6

Schmitz, B., & Wiese, B. S. (2006). New perspectives for the evaluation of training sessions in self-regulated learning: Time-series analyses of diary data. Contemporary Educational Psychology, 31, 64–96. https://doi.org/10.1016/j.cedpsych.2005.09.002

Stark, R., Mandl, H., Gruber, H., & Renkl, A. (2002). Conditions and effects of example elaboration. Learning and Instruction, 12, 39–60. https://doi.org/10.1016/S0959-4752(02)00003-5

Van Gog, T., Kester, L., & Paas, F. (2011). Effects of concurrent monitoring on cognitive load and performance as a function of task complexity. Applied Cognitive Psychology, 25, 584–587.

Van Merriënboer, J. J., & Sluijsmans, D. M. (2009). Toward a synthesis of cognitive load theory, four-component instructional design, and self-directed learning. Educational Psychology Review, 21, 55–66.

Wang, C., You, X., & Lu, J. (2023). Reading ability and challenges in a project-based academic report writing course: A test of the threshold hypothesis. Language Teaching Research. https://doi.org/10.1177/13621688231212118

Winne, P. H., & Hadwin, A. F. (1998). Studying as self-regulated learning. Metacognition in educational theory and practice, 93, 27–30.

Wirth, J., Künsting, J., & Leutner, D. (2009). The impact of goal specificity and goal type on learning outcome and cognitive load. Computers in Human Behavior, 25, 299–305.

Yang, H., & Plakans, L. (2012). Second language writers' strategy use and performance on an integrated Reading-Listening-Writing task. TESOL Quarterly, 46(1), 80–103. https://doi.org/10.1002/tesq.6

Zheng, L. (2016). The effectiveness of self-regulated learning scaffolds on academic performance in computer-based learning environments:

A meta-analysis. Asia Pacific Education Review, 17, 187–202.

Zimmerman, B. J. (2005). Attaining self-regulation: A social cognitive perspective. In M. Boekaerts, P. R. Pintrich, & M. Zeidner (Eds.). Handbook of self-regulation (pp. 13–39). (2nd ed.). San Diego, CA: Academic Press.

**Appendix 1　Project-based Academic Writing Cognitive Load Scale (PBAW_CLS)**

Choose a number to show to what an extent did you feel the difficulty of the writing task, 1=very seldom, 6=very often

| | | | | | | |
|---|---|---|---|---|---|---|
| 1.  Understanding terminologies in English academic literature | 1 | 2 | 3 | 4 | 5 | 6 |
| 2.  Fast reading and judging the value of the literature in English | 1 | 2 | 3 | 4 | 5 | 6 |
| 3.  Fast reading and finding specific information in the literature in English | 1 | 2 | 3 | 4 | 5 | 6 |
| 4.  Detailed reading and understanding of the literature in English | 1 | 2 | 3 | 4 | 5 | 6 |
| 5.  Taking notes in your own language while reading English academic literature | 1 | 2 | 3 | 4 | 5 | 6 |
| 6.  Finding the topic worth of study | 1 | 2 | 3 | 4 | 5 | 6 |
| 7.  Finding the academic literature related to the topic | 1 | 2 | 3 | 4 | 5 | 6 |
| 8.  Clarifying the scope of knowledge involved in the topic | 1 | 2 | 3 | 4 | 5 | 6 |
| 9.  Designing research methods | 1 | 2 | 3 | 4 | 5 | 6 |
| 10.  Obtaining data | 1 | 2 | 3 | 4 | 5 | 6 |
| 11.  Analyzing data | 1 | 2 | 3 | 4 | 5 | 6 |
| 12.  Using appropriate academic language | 1 | 2 | 3 | 4 | 5 | 6 |
| 13.  Selecting the content of literature review | 1 | 2 | 3 | 4 | 5 | 6 |
| 14.  Comparing and synthesizing multiple articles | 1 | 2 | 3 | 4 | 5 | 6 |
| 15.  Writing in your own language | 1 | 2 | 3 | 4 | 5 | 6 |
| 16.  Writing in proper structure | 1 | 2 | 3 | 4 | 5 | 6 |

## Appendix 2　Reading/Writing Strategy Scale (RWSS)

Choose a number to show to what an extent did you use the following strategies in the process of writing. 1=very seldom, 6=very often

| | | | | | | | |
|---|---|---|---|---|---|---|---|
| Locating/ Reading strategies | Before writing, I searched for academic literature to obtain inspiration. | 1 | 2 | 3 | 4 | 5 | 6 |
| | When reading, I made written or electronic reading notes. | 1 | 2 | 3 | 4 | 5 | 6 |
| | When reading, I reflected on the advantages and disadvantages of the literature. | 1 | 2 | 3 | 4 | 5 | 6 |
| Proposing strategies | Before writing, I found a gap of the past literature. | 1 | 2 | 3 | 4 | 5 | 6 |
| | Before writing, I clearly identified the questions to be studied. | 1 | 2 | 3 | 4 | 5 | 6 |
| | Before writing, I had a clear understanding of the method to analyze research issue. | 1 | 2 | 3 | 4 | 5 | 6 |
| | Before writing, I worked hard to learn data analysis methods. | 1 | 2 | 3 | 4 | 5 | 6 |
| Translating strategies | When writing, I referred to the language patterns of samples. | 1 | 2 | 3 | 4 | 5 | 6 |
| | When writing, I used translation software to improve language quality. | 1 | 2 | 3 | 4 | 5 | 6 |
| | When writing, I followed the rhetorical devices learned in the course. | 1 | 2 | 3 | 4 | 5 | 6 |
| Revising strategies | When revising, I checked my writing against assessing rubric. | 1 | 2 | 3 | 4 | 5 | 6 |
| | When revising, I followed the feedback from the teacher or classmates. | 1 | 2 | 3 | 4 | 5 | 6 |
| | When revising, I checked if the language was concise and formal. | 1 | 2 | 3 | 4 | 5 | 6 |
| | When revising, I checked if the viewpoints were clearly expressed. | 1 | 2 | 3 | 4 | 5 | 6 |
| | When revising, I checked whether the writing had a focused idea. | 1 | 2 | 3 | 4 | 5 | 6 |

Appendix 3　Writing Assessment Rubric Template (Good, 2012)

| Writing dimensions | 1: Inadequate | 2: Marginal | 3: Acceptable | 4: Good | 5: Excellent |
|---|---|---|---|---|---|
| Focus: discipline-based written product | Student demonstrates a lack of awareness of purpose and audience; Unclear Focus; inappropriate tone. | Student demonstrates minimal awareness of purpose and audience; marginal ability to provide a clear focus; borderline ability to convey appropriate tone. | Student demonstrates acceptable awareness of purpose and audience; somewhat clear focus; indication of understanding of appropriate tone in writing. | Student demonstrates accurate awareness of purpose and audience; mostly clear focus; satisfactory use of tone in writing. | Student demonstrates perceptive awareness of purpose and audience; clarity of focus; deep understanding and ability to create appropriate tone. |
| Content: idea development | Student provides no explanation and illustration of key ideas; no attempt to incorporate primary concepts of the discipline or to analyze and weigh differing facts and ideas; no synthesis of content-area materials or facts. | Student provides vague explanation and illustration of key ideas; inconsistent incorporation of primary concepts of the discipline; weak effort to analyze and weigh differing facts and ideas; incomplete synthesis of material. | Student provides explanation and illustration of most key ideas; incorporation of some primary concepts of the discipline; analysis of differing facts and ideas and an effort to synthesize all materials, although possibly inconsistent | Student provides detailed explanation and illustration of key ideas; incorporation of several primary concepts of the discipline; accurate analysis of different facts and ideas and a clear synthesis of all material. | Student provides extensive explanations and illustrations of key ideas; thorough incorporation of primary concepts of the discipline; sophisticated ability to analyze and weigh different facts and ideas and synthesize all material. |
| Organization | Student does not use transitions or headings; student writing is absent of logical and clear arrangement of ideas; writing lacks unity and coherence of paragraphs. | Student minimally uses transitions or headings; provides inconsistent and sometimes unclear logic and arrangement of ideas; creates borderline unity and coherence of paragraphs. | Student uses some of transitions or headings; provides fairly logical and clear arrangement of ideas; creates adequate unity and coherence of paragraphs. | Student appropriately uses transitions or headings; provides mostly logical and clear arrangement of ideas; creates consistent unity and coherence of paragraphs. | Student efficiently uses transitions or headings; provides highly logical and clear arrangement of ideas; creates comprehensive unity and coherence of paragraphs. |

continue

| Writing dimensions | 1: Inadequate | 2: Marginal | 3: Acceptable | 4: Good | 5: Excellent |
|---|---|---|---|---|---|
| Style | Student's ability to use discourse and language appropriate to their academic discipline is weak with several redundancies; student does not use appropriate word choice and/or vocabulary of field; student does not demonstrate an understanding of specific style guide for documentation (i.e., APA, MLA, etc.). | Student uses minimal discourse and language appropriate to their academic discipline with some redundancy; inconsistently uses vocabulary of field and some inappropriate word choice; student makes several errors in using discipline-specific style guide for documentation (i.e., APA, MLA, etc.). | Student sometimes uses discourse and language appropriate to their academic discipline with some redundancy; attempts to use appropriate word choice that is specific to vocabulary of field; makes an effort at following discipline-specific style guide for documentation (i.e., APA, MLA, etc.), although some errors occur. | Student mostly uses discourse and language appropriate to academic discipline; avoids redundancy; demonstrates good use of appropriate word choice and vocabulary of field; demonstrates competence in following discipline-specific style guide for documentation (i.e., APA, MLA, etc.). | Student demonstrates an ease in using discourse and language appropriate to academic discipline; is not redundant; selects sophisticated word choice and masters accurate use of vocabulary in field; demonstrates accurate ability to use discipline-specific style guide for documentation (i.e., APA, MLA, etc.). |
| English language conventions | Student writes with many patterns of errors in grammar, and frequently includes comma splices, run-ons, and/or fragments; writing exhibits patterns of usage and grammatical errors; numerous misspellings. | Student writes several grammatically incorrect sentences, comma splices, run-ons, and/or fragments and a pattern of errors begins to emerge in any one error type; several misspellings. | Student writes some grammatically incorrect sentences, and has some comma splices, run-ons, and/or fragments but not a clear pattern in any error type; some misspellings. | Student writes mostly grammatically correct sentences, with few comma splices, run-ons, and/or fragments; writing has few to no misspellings. | Student writes grammatically correct sentences with an absence of comma splices, run-ons, fragments; writing is absent of usage and grammatical errors and maintains accurate spelling. |

**Appendix 4　Challenges of using reading/writing strategies summarized from learning journals**

| *Challenges met when using reading/writing strategies* | Lower reading ability students (n=6) | | Higher reading ability students (n=10) | |
| --- | --- | --- | --- | --- |
| | Frequency | percentage | Frequency | percentage |
| • Difficult to understand academic articles because of unknown terms or complicated disciplinary theory; | 9 | 18.8% | 4 | 5.1% |
| • Difficult to judge the value of the downloaded articles for lacking fast reading ability; time consuming, and repeating reading needed; | 11 | 23% | 6 | 7.5% |
| • Difficult to read sufficient articles in English needed for literature review or find research gap; | 6 | 12.5% | 4 | 5.1% |
| • Difficult to design research method for lack of ability to learn research method from reading; | 5 | 10.4% | 2 | 2.5% |
| • Difficult to find sample articles, do mine reading, and use mined expressions into writing; depending on dictionary and creation; unsure of the language quality | 8 | 16.7% | 2 | 2.5% |
| • Difficult to edit expressions after using translating software; unable to find proper academic phrases | 3 | 6.3% | 0 | 0 |

Note: The frequency of challenges listed in the table was summarized from the journals, and percentage of the challenges were calculated by dividing frequency with entry number of different groups.

**Appendix 5　Reading/writing strategies comparison between the learners of different reading abilities**

| | Reading/Writing strategies | Lower-reading ability (N=82) | | Higher-reading ability (N=83) | | t | p |
|---|---|---|---|---|---|---|---|
| | | M | SD | M | SD | | |
| Locating/ Reading strategies | Before writing, I searched for academic literature to obtain inspiration. | 5.14 | 1.27 | 5.47 | 1.27 | 1.630 | 0.105 |
| | When reading, I made written or electronic reading notes. | 4.58 | 1.34 | 5.12 | 1.44 | 2.466* | 0.015 |
| | When reading, I reflected on the advantages and disadvantages of the literature. | 4.43 | 1.42 | 5.02 | 1.38 | 2.673* | 0.008 |
| Proposing strategies | Before writing, I found a gap of the past literature. | 4.58 | 1.26 | 5.15 | 1.35 | 2.795* | 0.006 |
| | Before writing, I clearly identified the questions to be studied. | 5.06 | 1.31 | 5.51 | 1.04 | 2.475* | 0.004 |
| | Before writing, I had a clear understanding of the method to analyze research issue. | 4.62 | 1.28 | 4.89 | 1.26 | 1.357 | 0.177 |
| | Before writing, I worked hard to learn data analysis methods. | 4.75 | 1.36 | 5.08 | 1.56 | 1.436 | 0.153 |
| Translating strategies | When writing, I referred to the language patterns of samples. | 4.91 | 1.34 | 5.39 | 1.23 | 2.400* | 0.018 |
| | When writing, I used translation software to improve language quality. | 4.73 | 1.26 | 4.88 | 1.22 | 0.812 | 0.412 |
| | When writing, I followed the rhetorical devices learned in the course. | 4.62 | 1.21 | 5.03 | 1.41 | 2.015* | 0.046 |
| Revising strategies | When revising, I checked my writing against assessing rubric. | 4.59 | 1.44 | 4.89 | 1.53 | 1.268 | 0.217 |
| | When revising, I followed the feedback from the teacher or classmates. | 4.76 | 1.19 | 5.24 | 1.14 | 2.591* | 0.010 |
| | When revising, I checked if the language was concise and formal. | 5.02 | 1.11 | 5.28 | 1.11 | 1.531 | 0.128 |
| | When revising, I checked if the viewpoints were clearly expressed. | 5.01 | 1.16 | 5.38 | 1.11 | 2.109* | 0.036 |
| | When revising, I checked whether the writing had a focused idea. | 5.13 | 1.17 | 5.45 | 1.16 | 1.781 | 0.077 |

Note: * Correlation is significant at 0.05 level.

# 第十章　小组合作对认知负荷的影响
## Chapter 10　Influence of cognitive load from group work

**本章内容概要 Abstract of the chapter**

　　PBAW 常使用小组合作学习，通过与同班同学合作，加深对研究性课题的理解。本章关注 PBAW 课程的学习者形成小组学习的过程与相关认知负荷水平之间的关系。具体而言，研究分析了小组合作对内在学习动机与相关负荷之间关系的影响。研究提出两个假设：一、小组合作与相关认知负荷正相关；二、小组合作调节内在动机与相关认知负荷的关系。研究通过问卷调查收集数据。测量指标包括小组合作策略、相关认知负荷和内在动机。双变量相关性分析显示，小组合作与相关认知负荷、内在动机与相关认知负荷均呈显著正相关，且内在动机与小组合作也显著正相关。线性回归分析表明，小组合作和内在动机对相关认知负荷有较强的预测力。方差分析和交互效应检验进一步证实了小组合作对内在动机与相关认知负荷关系的调节作用。

　　结果表明，小组合作能调节内在学习动机与相关认知负荷之间的关系：虽然内在学习动机在所有的学生中均可以预测相关认知负荷，小组合作水平更高的学生获得了更多的相关负荷，也就是说产生了更多有效的学习。这项研究显示了小组合作在促进学习者学习上的细分作用。研究鼓励学习者充分参与小组的合作，进行有效的学习。最后，文章给出了提高学生团队合作技能的实用建议，包括确定团队领导、了解成员优势、确保良好沟通、及时处理问题、直接给予反馈、明确问题等，以避免冲突共同解决问题。

## 1. Introduction

There has been a growing emphasis on the importance of group work in higher education, highlighting its relevance in research focused on university students (Herrmann, 2013). This type of learning often arises when students need to navigate challenging aspects of a problem (Butson & Thomson, 2014). A common rationale for this perspective, and a reason for assigning tasks to groups, is the limitations individual students face in processing information (Davis, 1980). Specifically, individuals tend to retain information shared within groups more effectively than information learned in isolation (Tindale & Sheffey, 2002). While understanding of how group collaboration influences information processing has advanced, there are still limitations to the effectiveness of group work in enhancing teaching and learning (Kerr, MacCoun, & Kramer, 1996). For instance, while some individuals may retain more information shared in a group, others may experience cognitive overload due to the interaction (Wittenbaum & Stasser, 1996).

Existing research has examined ways to measure the progress of students working in groups, with germane cognitive load serving as a reliable metric for understanding the underlying learning processes. Germane load is one of three components of cognitive load theory, alongside intrinsic and extraneous load. Cognitive load theory pertains to how individuals retain information and the processes involved in transferring knowledge from working memory to long-term memory (Cierniak, Scheiter, & Gerjets, 2009; Kalyuga, 2011; Sweller, Van Merriënboer, & Paas, 1998). Given that working memory has a limited capacity for information retention, instruction that leads to excessive processing can result in heightened cognitive load (De Jong, 2010). The levels of information transfer that facilitate learning can be positively or negatively influenced by the type of information being processed (Chandler & Sweller, 1991; Mayer & Moreno, 1998; Mayer & Moreno, 2003; Moreno, Mayer, Spires & Lester, 2001). In terms of both intrinsic load (content complexity) and extraneous load (processing irrelevant information), higher levels are generally seen as detrimental to the learning process, unlike germane load, which actively contributes to learning through students' efforts to build schemas for better understanding (Sweller et al., 1998). Specifically, excessive intrinsic load can negatively impact germane load when combined with extraneous load (van Merriënboer & Sweller, 2010). Notably, high element interactivity associated with increased intrinsic load is crucial for linking new information to existing schemas, thereby enhancing germane load (Van Merriënboer & Sweller, 2010). However, if the disparity between a student's existing knowledge and the required learning leads to excessive cognitive processing related to element interactivity, it can hinder learning (Van Merriënboer & Sweller, 2010).

Students' motivation toward course content influences levels of germane load (Homer, Plass, & Blake, 2008). Intrinsic motivation, alongside effort, plays a significant role in learning (Martens, Gulikers, & Bastiaens, 2004). Intrinsic motivation encourages learners to engage in complex processing, as they seek to understand more sophisticated content for its own sake, rather than for external rewards (Pintrich, 1991). Intrinsically motivated students are more inclined to establish goals that shape how they approach the material (Meece, Blumenfeld, & Hoyle, 1988). Moreover, these students are more likely to adopt a mastery orientation, believing that knowledge can be cultivated through increased effort, and that tackling challenging situations enhances learning (Crippen, Biesinger, Muis, & Orgill, 2009). Students with a high intrinsic motivation often engage in the learning process out of a sense of challenge, curiosity, or desire for mastery (Pintrich, 1991). The observation that students with lower motivation tend to achieve less in certain contexts underscores the importance of group work, as it may assist less motivated individuals in increasing their levels of germane load (Puzziferro, 2008).

## 2.  Literature Review

### 2.1  Group Work and Germane Load

Group work enhances critical thinking, cognitive development, and socialization (Carss, 2007). Research indicates that students involved in group learning experience significant improvements in higher-order cognitive skills (Collier, 1980). Learning is optimized when individuals contribute to group goals through interactions (Johnson et al., 2014). Studies show that increased interaction during group work enhances the learning process (Tsay & Brady, 2010). In some cases, group work can be more effective than lectures, as students engage more deeply with concepts (Carlsmith & Cooper, 2002). The self-explanation principle suggests that explaining concepts to oneself enhances understanding (Van Merriënboer & Sweller, 2010). However, group work has potential drawbacks. Unequal participation can hinder knowledge construction (Lange et al., 2016), leading to "social loafing," where some members contribute less, burdening others (Kagan, 1989). Full interaction among all members is crucial for mutual understanding. Although group work is generally positive, they must consider learners' social and cognitive development (Costley & Lange, 2016).

## 2.2 Intrinsic Motivation and Germane Load

A meta-analysis by Payne, Youngcourt, and Beaubien (2007) indicates that students with mastery goal orientation excel in learning. High intrinsic motivation predicts a deeper understanding of tasks (Lyke & Kelaher Young, 2006) and fosters long-term learning persistence (Vansteenkiste, Lens, & Deci, 2006). Intrinsically motivated students process information effectively, enhancing germane load by utilizing working memory for goal-setting (Granger, 2012). Cognitive behavior modification incorporates goal-setting to improve cognitive processes

(Stipek, 1996). Moreover, specific goal orientations influence cognition, and achievement (Wolters, 2004). Pintrich and DeGroot (1990) demonstrated a link between intrinsic motivation and cognitive strategies that enhance learning. However, connecting intrinsic to cognitive processing remains underexplored, suggesting the need for further research on its impact on knowledge acquisition.

## 2.3  Group Work, Intrinsic Motivation, and Germane Load

Rienties et al. (2009) found that intrinsically motivated individuals contribute more to cognitive discussions and planning in group settings. It is important to explore whether group work can support less motivated learners. Järvelä, Volet, and Järvenoja (2010) noted that differing goals and motivations can lead to conflict in groups. When participating in group work, individuals must align their personal goals with group objectives (Wosnitza & Volet, 2009). This challenge can help less motivated students succeed by promoting knowledge sharing, as interdependent goals encourage collaboration (Pee et al., 2010). Intrinsically motivated learners facilitate this process by fostering positive interdependence, realizing their success depends on the group (Johnson & Johnson, 2003). Consequently, lower motivated students benefit from the contributions of their more motivated peers and may adopt learning goals to enhance their engagement (Johnson & Johnson, 2003). Research on these dynamics can inform e-learning strategies, particularly in offline group contexts that mirror online learning environments.

## 3. The Current Study

This research examined students participating in PBAW course at a university in Shanghai. Students working together in groups of 3—5 in class working on a reasearch-based academic writing task. As called on by researchers that it is important to understand if the benefits of group work can be transferred to gains in cognitive load as well (Van Merriënboer, & Sweller, 2010), the current study examines the following two hypotheses:

H1. Group work is positively correlated with germane load.

H2. Group work moderates the relationship between intrinsic motivation and germane load.

### 3.1 Participants

Participants were learners taking part in PBAW course provided by Shanghai University of International Business and Economics. All participants were informed by their teachers of the purpose of the study, their privilege to choose whether to take part in the survey voluntarily, and how their confidentiality would be protected. Written informed consent was obtained from a total of 274 students, 143 female (52%), and 131 male (48%) before the survey. They agreed to participate in the study and complete an online survey in the eighteenth week of the semester.

### 3.2 Research Procedures and Data Collection

The first step in this study was a development of a survey that focused on learners' self-regulated strategies of group cooperation. At the end of attending the PBAW course which lasted for 14 weeks, students were invited to fill in a survey on their group learning strategies, cognitive load experienced and motivation of learning PBAW course.

### 3.3  Instruments

- **Group cooperation strategies**

To generate the indicators for measuring the varying degree of group cooperation that the learners have taken part in, they were asked with the question "To what an extent do you take part in the whole group exploring work in the semester." They chose a number from 1 to 6, with 1 showing low degree of participation, and 6 showing high degree.

- **Germane Load**

The germane load measurement used in this study was made up of items from Leppink, Paas, Van der Vleuten, Van Gog, and Van Merriënboer's (2013) paper titled "The development of an instrument for measuring cognitive load", considering the influence of the paper. The Likert-type scale used for these items was set at a range from 1 to 6, with 1 representing "strongly disagree" and 6 representing "strongly agree". The current research uses the four items measuring germane load: 1) Group meeting really enhanced my understanding of the topic, 2) the teacher's lecture really enhanced my knowledge of the problem, 3) the peer review feedback really enhanced my understanding of writing quality. 4) writing samples really enhanced my writing knowledge.

Although the original cognitive load scale was designed to be set at a 0 to 10 Likert-type scale, the current study set it at 1 to 6 to ensure consistency with the range throughout the entire survey. Cronbach's alpha for the germane load construct was calculated to be .918.

- **Intrinsic Motivation**

The researchers asked students to endorse their agreement on three items addressing their interest in writing activities on a six-point scale (1=Strongly Disagree, 6=Strongly Agree). The descriptive statistics and reliability estimates of students' writing enjoyment are shown in Table 1. The three items were "I like academic writing" (M=3.98, SD=1.20), "I like attending academic writing class" (M=3.94, SD=1.15), and "I like to devote my time in academic writing" (M=3.76, SD=1.20). The Cronbach's Alpha for the three items was $\alpha$=0.86, which is acceptable for this type of research.

## 4. Results

To understand the two hypotheses of this research, Pearson's bivariate correlations were calculated. As can be seen in Table 1, there was a statistically significant positive relationship between group cooperation and germane load of .555. This shows that as group interaction increases, so does the student's levels of germane load. Furthermore, intrinsic motivation was statistically significantly correlated positively with germane load (.333). This shows that students with higher levels of intrinsic motivation will have higher levels of germane load. Also, intrinsic motivation was statistically significantly positively correlated with group work (.158), meaning that students with higher levels of intrinsic motivation were more likely to interact with other students.

Table 1    Descriptive Statistics and Correlations Between the Main Variables (n=227).

| | Mean | SD | 1 | 2 | 3 |
|---|---|---|---|---|---|
| **Group work** | 4.28 | 1.23 | 1 | | |
| **Intrinsic motivation** | 4.57 | 0.97 | .158** | 1 | |
| **Germane load** | 4.61 | 1.01 | .555** | .333** | 1 |

** $p<0.05$

We went on using linear regression to study how can group cooperation and intrinsic motivation predict germane load. Before conducting the regression analysis, we completed the following preliminary analyses: The independent variables did not have multicollinearity (for the two models, VIF values are smaller than 1.32). The data met the assumption of independent errors (for the two models, Durbin-Watson values are 2.05 and 2.18, respectively). All these tests indicated that multiple regression was appropriate for the present data. As shown by table 2, the overall model had strong predictive power in relation to germane load ($R^2$=.364; F=65.561; $p$=.000). Each one unit increase in the group cooperation scale led to 0.51 ($p$=.000) increase in germane load. For every one unit increase in intrinsic motivation there was a 0.25 ($p$=.001) increase in germane load.

**Table 2 Multiple linear regression of group cooperation and intrinsic motivation on germane load**

|  | SE | $\beta$ | $R^2$ | F | Sig |
|---|---|---|---|---|---|
| Model | .559 | / | .364 | 65.561 | .000 |
| Group cooperation | .413 | .51 | / | / | .000 |
| Intrinsic motivation | .346 | .25 | / | / | .001 |

To further establish the relationship between the main variables, ANOVA was used. Group cooperation variable was split into two groups at the mean score (4.28). The ANOVA results showed a total $R^2$ value of .25.

PROCESS macro (Hayes, 2013) was used to test the interaction effect of group work levels and intrinsic goal orientation on germane load as is shown in Figure 1. To show this, 10,000 bootstrap samples with a 95% confidence interval were used. Also, variables were mean centered to +/−1 standard deviation, to reduce multi-collinearity. The results showed strong evidence of an interaction effect based on a standardized coefficient. Group work positively moderated the effect of intrinsic goal orientation on germane load, or in other words, as levels of group work increase, the strength of relationship between intrinsic motivation and germane load increased.

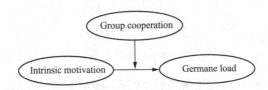

**Figure 1 The moderating effects of group cooperation on the relationship between intrinsic motivation and germane load.**

Table 3    Effects for intrinsic motivation on germane load at two levels of group cooperation

|  | $R^2$ | $b$ | $t$ | $p$ |
|---|---|---|---|---|
| Low group cooperation | .060 | .181 | .247 | .040 |
| High group cooperation | .110 | .340 | .459 | .000 |

To measure the effect of moderation, we use intrinsic motivation predicted germane load in high and low levels of group cooperation. As can be seen in Table 3 and Figure 2, in the high group cooperation condition the effect size (.340) is stronger than in the low group cooperation condition (.181). This shows that group cooperation strengthened the relationship between intrinsic goal orientation and germane load.

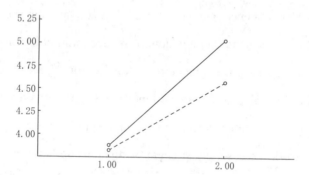

Figure 2    The relationships between intrinsic motivation and germane
load moderated by group corporation level.

(Note: 1=low group corporation level; 2=high group corporation level)

## 5. Discussion

Research has shown that PBAW course provides good environments for group corporation, and that students should have the ability to be a productive part of a learning group (Herrmann, 2013; Johnson et al., 2014). The levels of group work that have been found in this study are unsurprising, in view of the fact that many students find learning complex information difficult (Butson & Thomson, 2014). There is some research suggesting that group cooperation may not lead to gains in germane load (Kreijns et al., 2003). This may be because of transaction costs, lag in the cognitive benefits of interacting within a group, or off-task behavior (Gruenfeld, & Hollingshead, 1993; Kerr et al., 1996; Kirschner et al., 2009; Kreijns et al., 2003; Wittenbaum & Stasser, 1996). The results of the present study go some way to contradicting this point of view, and suggests that group work does benefit learners' levels of germane cognitive load. A possible reason for the cognitive benefits found in the current study is that the novelty and interest generated by this type of learning experience leads to a great deal of learning (Rogers & Price, 2008). Furthermore, the cognitive gains found from group work in this study may also be attributed to the variety of processes often inherent in group work. For example, tasks can become more engaging (Andriessen et al., 2003), the interaction can promote reflection (Baker & Lund, 1997), and more meaningful engagement with the contents of the class (Jonassen & Kwon, 2001).

The study has shown that students with high levels of intrinsic motivation are likely to learn more, and students with low levels of motivation are likely to learn less (Homer et al., 2008; Martens et al.,

2004). In the case of this research, students with low motivation may have felt less engaged with the contents and therefore less likely to get cognitive gains from the class contents. Students who were a part of this study who had high levels of intrinsic motivation likely valued deeper understanding of the topics, and tried to master the contents regardless of extrinsic motivating factors (Lyke & Kelaher Young, 2006; Vansteenkiste et al., 2006).

This research looked at how group work and intrinsic motivation interact to affect germane cognitive load. It was shown that as group corporation increased, the relationship between intrinsic motivation and germane load increased. Although motivation was generally found to have a positive relationship with germane load, the relationship was shown to be stronger in the high group work condition, showing that there is more of a benefit to having high levels of group cooperation than it is to have low level. With more group work, the link between motivation and germane load is stronger, which means intrinsic motivation and group work are integrative in creating more effective learning. In PBAW tasks, less entering group work with pre-formed ideas means less chance to acquire knowledge, and less chance to trigger cognitive processing of new knowledge for the students with the same motivation. Furthermore, students may be more likely to form a set of goals within a group work setting than if they work alone (Johnson & Johnson, 2003), allowing them to better take advantage of the group work setting.

## 6. Conclusion

The study shows group work not only directly facilitates germane load in PBAW tasks, it also enhances the association between intrinsic motivation and germane load. The higher group work participation, the higher chance for intrinsic motivation to influence germane. We conclude that it is beneficial for students to participate in group work so that they can share information in a way that is helpful to learn PBAW tasks. Based on the results of this study, group work should be encouraged as a means of enhancing the learning experience, and gain better learning effects.

## 7. Implication tips

Although the book is research based, we aim to give practical suggestions at the end of the study to teachers on helping students improve team work skills. During academic study, just like in workplace, professional sports, team building requires a keen understanding of people, their strengths and what gets them excited to work with others. It also requires the management of egos and their constant demands for attention and recognition. Student need to, therefore, practice it instead of avoiding it because a group could do much bigger things than a single person, no matter how powerful he is. Here are several rules about what student can do to make sure team is as strong as possible.

- Student need a team leader to make things go efficiently, allocating work, making decisions and urging the poor performers. Get to know the rest of the team. If the team leader has not chosen the team members he wants, it is still a good opportunity to work with someone new.

- Try to gather intelligence from each member and find out their respective strengths and capabilities — the real assets that each member brings to the table, those they leave behind and those yet to be developed.

- Flawless communication is vital to successful team work. Please ensure smooth communication during each phase of students' team work. Whenever someone has a question or gets an idea, he/she should be able to communicate it. For instance, during task division, each member should express freely their opinions on it: their doubts, different ideas, etc. Only by doing so can students work be done effectively.

- Have the talk immediately. When student spot any unsatisfactory things happening, please remember to point it out immediately, rather than wait till a bigger problem arise. If student point out the problem immediately on the spot, students target is the problem, not the person who causes it. If student try to avoid the conflicts to achieve the temporary harmony and bear it until student couldn't, the talk then becomes blame instead. Students' relations will be tense.

- Get down to the point directly. If student want to give negative feedback to someone, do it directly. Don't use "praise sandwich" (start with a positive comment on performance, then provide negative feedback which is the key and finally close the sandwich by offering a final positive comment). Although popularly used, it is misleading, making the listener get lost in students real purpose. Get down to it directly instead. For instance: "I want to talk with student about students share of work because student have delayed for two days." Don't talk through the phone or type through We chat or QQ. Have a face-to-face talk would be much better and more effective.

- Get things clear. After the opening sentence mentioned above, ask the question: "What's going on?" Then listen carefully to the description of the fact from his/her perspective. The facts from different angles could be different. Maybe student think it is due to poor attitude but it is actually because of lack of information which he/she didn't get. Maybe student think the reason is lack of information but it is actually misunderstanding.

- Get back on track. Ask the question: "If student want to finish students share and meet our partial goals, what help do student need?" This could redirect the talk to students goal and the settlement of the problem. The key is not why it is wrong, but how it could be corrected.

- Set the further feedback point. After student reach agreement on how to settle the problem, readjust the schedule and plan. For example,

"Student will get three more days to finish students share of work."

- All in all, when tackling conflicts, please remember don't throw anyone under the bus or turn a damage-control discussion into a blame game. This never helps anybody. Instead, give students team equal responsibility to put students heads together and figure out the next steps or pivots.

## 8. References

Andriessen, J., Baker, M., & Suthers, D. (2003). Arguing to learn. Confronting cognitions in computer-supported collaborative learning environments. Dordrecht: Kluwer

Baker, M., & Lund, K. (1997). Promoting reflective interactions in a CSCL environment. Journal of Computer Assisted Learning, 13(3), 175–193.

Butson, R., & Thomson, C. (2014). Challenges of effective collaboration in a virtual learning environment among undergraduate students. Creative Education, 5, 1449–1459.

Carss, W.D. (2007). The effects of using think-pair-share during guided reading lessons (Doctoral dissertation, The University of Waikato, Diterbitkan) Retrieved from https://researchcommons.waikato.ac.nz/handle/10289/2233

Carlsmith, K. M., & Cooper, J. (2002). A persuasive example of collaborative learning. Teaching of Psychology, 29, 132–135.

Cierniak, G., Scheiter, K., & Gerjets, P. (2009). Explaining the split-attention effect: Is the reduction of extraneous cognitive load accompanied by an increase in germane cognitive load? Computers in Human Behavior, 25, 315–324.

Chandler, P., & Sweller J. (1991). Cognitive load theory and the format of instruction. Cognition and Instruction, 8(4), 293–332.

Collier, K. G. (1980). Peer-group learning in higher education: The development of higher order skills. Studies in Higher Education, 5(1), 55–62.

Davis, J. H. (1980). Group decision and procedural justice. In M. Fishbein (Ed.), Progress in social psychology (Vol. 1, pp. 157–230). Hillsdale, NJ: Erlbaum.

De Jong, T. (2010). Cognitive load theory, educational research, and instructional design: Some food for thought. Instructional Science, 38(2), 105–134.

Hayes, A. F. (2013). Introduction to mediation, moderation, and conditional process analysis. New York: The Guilford Press.

Herrmann, K. J. (2013). The impact of cooperative learning on student engagement: Results from an intervention. Active Learning in Higher Education, 14(3), 175–187.

Homer, B. D., Plass, J. L., & Blake, L. (2008). The effects of video on cognitive load and social presence in multimedia-learning. Computers in Human Behavior, 24(3), 786–797.

Jonassen, D. H., & Kwon, H. I. (2001). Communication patterns in computer mediated and face-to-face group problem solving. Educational Technology Research and Development, 49(1), 35–51.

Johnson, D. W., Johnson, R. T., & Smith, K. A. (2014). Cooperative learning: Improving university instruction by basing practice on validated theory. Journal on Excellence in University Teaching, 25(4).

Kagan, S. (1989). The structural approach to cooperative learning. Educational Leadership, 47(4), 12–15.

Kalyuga, S. (2011). Cognitive load theory: How many types of load does it really need? Educational Psychology Review, 23(1), 1–19.

Kirschner, F., Paas, F., & Kirschner, P. A. (2009). A cognitive load approach to collaborative learning: United brains for complex tasks. Educational Psychology Review, 21, 31–42.

Kreijns, K., Kirschner, P. A., & Jochems, W. (2003). Identifying the pitfalls for social interaction in computer-supported collaborative learning environments. A review of the research. Computers in Human Behavior, 19(3), 335–353.

Kerr, N. L., MacCoun, R. J., & Kramer, G. P. (1996). Bias in judgment: Comparing individuals and groups. Psychological Review, 103, 687–719.

Lange, C., Costley J., & Han, S. (2016). Informal cooperative learning in small groups: The effect of scaffolding on participation. Issues in Educational Research, 26(2), 260–279.

Leppink, J., Paas, F., Van der Vleuten, C. P., Van Gog, T., & Van Merriënboer, J. J. (2013). Development of an instrument for measuring different types of cognitive load. Behavior research methods, 45(4), 1058–1072.

Martens, R. L., Gulikers, J., & Bastiaens, T. (2004). The impact of intrinsic motivation on e-learning in authentic computer tasks. Journal of Computer Assisted Learning, 20(5), 368–376.

Mayer, R. E., & Moreno, R. (1998). A split-attention effect in multimedia learning: Evidence for dual processing systems in working memory. Journal of Educational Psychology, 90(2), 312–320. http://doi. org/10.1037//0022–0663.90.2.0focinstruction. Cognition and Instruction, 8(4), 293–332.

Mayer, R. E., & Moreno, R. (2003). Nine ways to reduce cognitive load in multimedia learning. Educational Psychologist, 38(1), 43–52.

Meece, J. L., Blumenfeld, P. C., & Hoyle, R. H. (1998). Students' goal orientations and cognitive engagement in classroom activities. Journal of Educational Psychology, 80(4), 514.

Moreno, R., Mayer, R. E., Spires & Lester, 2001. The case for social agency in computer-based teaching: Do students learn more deeply when they interact with animated pedagogical agents? Cognition and instruction, 19(2), 177–213.

Pintrich, P. R., Smith, D. A. F., Garcia, T., & McKeachie, W (1991). A manual for the use of the motivated strategies for learning questionnaire (MSLQ). Ann Arbor, MI: The University of Michigan. Retrieved from https://eric.ed.gov/?id=ED338122.

Puzziferro, M. (2008). Online technologies self-efficacy and self-regulated learning as predictors of final grade and satisfaction in college-level online courses. The American Journal of Distance Education, 22(2), 72–89.

Rogers, Y., & Price, S. (2008). The role of mobile devices in facilitating collaborative inquiry in situ. Research and Practice in Technology Enhanced Learning, 3(3), 209–229.

Sweller, J., Van Merriënboer, J. J. G., & Paas, F. (1998). Cognitive architecture and instructional design. Educational Psychology Review, 10, 251–296.

Tindale, R. S., & Sheffey, S. (2002). Shared information, cognitive load, and group memory. Group Processes & Intergroup Relations, 5(1), 5–18.

Tsay, M., & Brady, M. (2008). A case study of cooperative learning and communication pedagogy: Does working inteams make a difference? Journal of the Scholarship of Teaching and Learning, 10(2), 78–89.

van Merriënboer, J. J. G., & Sweller, J. (2005). Cognitive load theory and complex learning: Recent developments and future directions. Educational Psychology Review, 17(2), 147–177.

Wittenbaum, G. M., & Stasser, G. (1996). Management of information in small groups. In J. L. Nye & A. M. Brower (Eds.), What's social about social cognition (pp. 3–28). Thousand Oaks, CA: Sage.

# 第十一章 AI 工具的使用对认知负荷的影响
## Chapter 11 Influence of cognitive load from AI tools

**本章内容概要 Abstract of the chapter**

学习环境对学习者的认知负荷会产生影响。生成式人工智能 (AI) 工具的出现对学术英语写作的冲击是颠覆性的。AI 工具的开发者与语言教师认为，对二语写作者而言，AI 工具可以降低他们遇到的认知负荷，提高写作的效率。但我们在研究生班级进行的研究表明并非如此。

本章报告了一项 AI 工具使用与写作认知负荷关系的研究。研究者调查了 AI 对 PBAW 中不同外语水平学习者的认知负荷产生的影响。研究数据来自作者与同事为研究生开设的写作课程。课程采用 PBAW 模式，允许学习者使用 Quillbot、Kimi 和 小绿鲸等 AI 工具，教师鼓励使用 AI 工具，但要求学生不能用其生成的内容替代自己的工作。共有 327 名研究生参与问卷调查，8 名学生参与了后续的半结构化访谈。结果显示，AI 使用中出现了"专家反转效应"：不同外语水平的学习者在 AI 使用后，效果有差异：对于英语水平较低的学习者，AI 使用与认知负荷无显著关系，但 AI 使用与写作自我效能感呈正相关，主要在阅读文献和学习研究方法方面提高了学习者的效能感。对于高英语水平的研究生，AI 使用与认知负荷呈显著正相关，与自我效能感无显著关系。研究还发现 AI 工具没有显著降低研究生的写作认知负荷，且未能提高他们在语言使用方面的自我效能感。

这项研究表明教师与研究人员应理解如何利用 AI 技术提高学术写作的能力，降低写作过程中的认知负荷。AI 技术人员和教育者需要合作设计专门用于写作的 AI 工具，减少无用信息增加学习者外在认知负荷。教师应根据学生二语水平，调整 AI 工具的使用方式。语言水平低的学生可将其作为支持手段，但语言水平高的学生应使用 AI 完成更复杂任务，并学习与 AI 有效互动的能力。教师还应规范 AI 使用范围，避免学习者过多使用 AI，从而阻碍语言能力发展的可能性。

## 1. Introduction

The academic community appears to concur with the promising effects brought about by AI tools such as Grammarly, Quillbot, Google Translator, ChatGPT, and similar chatbots, suggesting that the Sisyphean ordeal of academic research and writing will be alleviated. These tools exhibit remarkable capabilities in summarizing, proofreading, translating, and generating contextually relevant text (Kurniati & Fithriani, 2022; Cancino & Panes, 2021; Koltovskaia, 2020). It has been claimed that AI tools have the potential to reduce the cognitive challenges faced by academic writers (Warschauer et al., 2023) and to enhance their writing confidence or self-efficacy (Kim et al., 2024).

However, when it comes to the complex academic writing tasks faced by L2 postgraduates, the legendary capacity mentioned above remains questionable. Only a small amount of research has examined the perceptions of L2 postgraduates when AI tools are incorporated into their writing process. Postgraduates have to produce academic writing that demands a higher level of quality and complexity compared to their undergraduate counterparts (Hyland, 2016). The significant challenges encountered by postgraduates in L2 academic writing have been extensively documented (Lin & Morrison, 2021; Hyland, 2016). There is an apprehension that open AI tools, such as ChatGPT, may not be sufficiently equipped to meet the specialized needs and address the sophisticated and intricate issues required by postgraduates (Gao et al., 2022; Malik et al., 2023).

Moreover, according to cognitive load (CL) theory, the effectiveness of learning or instructional methods is contingent upon the pre-existing knowledge of the learners. Although AI tools have garnered widespread acceptance, their utility may be perceived differently among students with varying degrees of L2 literacy. Notably, in Xu and Zhang (2021), students with advanced English proficiency found the feedback from automatic writing evaluation tools to be of limited utility, whereas students with less developed English skills derived greater satisfaction from such feedback.

Our study seeks to delve into the nuanced perspectives of AI tools used in academic writing tasks by postgraduates with different L2 literacies. Exploring this topic is meaningful for English L2 learners, who may have the most to gain or lose when higher education faces unprecedented changes and opportunities brought about by new technology (Warschauer et al., 2023). The study has practical significance in that writing teachers may better understand how students perceive the effects of AI tools on influencing learners' writing efficacy and cognitive load, so that they can effectively and efficiently integrate AI tools into the academic writing curriculum.

In the study, postgraduates at a Chinese business university in Shanghai were investigated regarding their perceptions of writing self-efficacy and cognitive load after using AI tools to write academic proposals. Both qualitative and quantitative research methods were employed. The study found that AI tools did not have the expected effects of lowering cognitive load and increasing writing self-efficacy for all learners. The positive psychological effects were only found among lower L2 learners.

## 2. Literature Review

### 2.1 AI using in academic writing

AI is a technological paradigm that emulates human cognitive and intellectual processes in solving problems (Cope et al., 2020; Kohnke et al., 2023). In the realm of L2 writing, Google Translate, Quillbot, Turnitin, and Grammarly, have become useful AI tools facilitating broader research access and various writing endeavors (Kurniati &

Fithriani, 2022). Generative AI tools like ChatGPT and Kimi (an AI tool popular in China), exhibit an enhanced capacity to process extensive inputs, offering support for a range of writing challenges, from fundamental language issues to the more complex demands of argument structure and persuasive strength (Su et al., 2023; Guo, Wang, & Chu, 2022).

Khalifa and Albadawy (2024) summarized the main AI utilizing strategies in academic writing process, including supporting idea generation, bolstering the literature review and synthesis processes, augmenting data management and analytical capabilities, providing advanced vocabulary options, and even enriching the content's depth and offering stylistic insights. Empirically, using AI tools to enhance translation (Dwivedi et al. 2023), improve the use of advanced vocabulary (H. Chen et al., 2020), create coherent and well-structured paragraphs (Tang et al., 2023) were all reported. AI's benefits of facilitating critical thinking (Yan, 2023), enhancing learning motivation, and reducing the cognitive load (Nguyen et al., 2024; Hartwell & Aull, 2023) have also been observed.

Despite their potential, AI tools face criticism. For instance, AI tools have been criticized for their limited ability to generate authentic text and provide real academic literature (Gao et al., 2023; Barrot, 2023). They require precise prompts to function effectively, and as a result, refining AI-generated content can be time-consuming (Malik et al., 2023;). Pedagogically, the use of AI tools in academic writing may lead to plagiarism or superficial engagement with the material, where students do not fully understand the underlying processes (Ismael et al., 2022). Some teachers criticize the problems brought about by AI in educational settings. For example, Ranalli (2021) found that AI writing tools failed to enhance writing skills or contribute to second language development because students used them with minimal cognitive processing.

## 2.2  Cognitive load and AI using in academic writing

Cognitive load (CL) refers to the mental effort required to process and understand information, particularly within the context of learning and instruction (Sweller, 1988). The CL that a task may place on learners' working memory can be divided into three kinds: intrinsic load, extraneous load, and germane load (Plass & Kalyuga, 2019). Intrinsic load concerns the burden imposed by the internal complexity of information (Sweller, 1988). Extraneous load is introduced by the cognitive processes unnecessary for learning (Kalyuga, 2011; Sweller, 1988). Germane cognitive load refers to the mental resources that learners deploy to deal with the intrinsic cognitive load of the learning tasks (Sweller, 2010). Given their high overlap, germane and intrinsic loads are usually not distinguished (Kalyuga, 2011). CL is an indispensable theoretical foundation for evaluating the effectiveness of technological advances in education (van Gog et al., 2010). Sweller et al.

(2019) proposed that when designing instruction, information should be organized and presented in a way that reduces cognitive load on working memory.

The CL of academic writing is demanding for all student writers, particularly for L2 postgraduates (Hyland, 2016; Morrison & Evans, 2018). AI tools like ChatGPT are promising in reducing the cognitive load experienced by L2 student writers by providing scaffolding throughout the entire writing process. For example, AI-powered writing assistants help students focus on content and structure, rather than getting bogged down by mechanical errors, thus optimizing their cognitive resources for higher-order writing skills (Shadiev & Huang, 2020). AI tools also enhance motivation and engagement through interactive and immersive feedback mechanisms, potentially transforming the writing process into a more dynamic and less daunting task (Brom et al., 2018). Furthermore, AI tools help manage the cognitive load associated with complex writing tasks by breaking them down into manageable chunks and providing scaffolding for learners at various stages (Kalyuga, 2007).

However, AI tools are not specifically designed for academic writing courses, and using them effectively requires expertise or trying different prompts, which may introduce an increase of cognitive load (Lin Z., 2024). Malik et al. (2023) reported that Indonesian college students were reluctant to use AI partly due to the cognitive effort required to correct misinformation and inaccuracies, difficulties with handling complex subjects, and the time-consuming nature of adjustments and fixes to the results provided.

## 2.3 AI utilization and writing self-efficacy

Self-efficacy is a person's perception of their capability to perform a particular task (Bandura, 1997). Writing self-efficacy refers to learners' confidence in being able to handle writing tasks at hand (Christensen & Knezek, 2016; Teng et al., 2017). Many studies (e.g., Song & Song, 2023; Kim et al., 2024) have found that one of the psychological effects of AI assistance on writers is the bolstering of writing self-efficacy. AI-driven writing assistance can empower writers throughout the entire writing process with idea-generating tools, grammar and style correction tools, and personalized feedback tools (Liang et al., 2023). By engaging with these technologies, students can perceive themselves as capable of attaining their objectives. As Kim et al. (2024) stated, AI emerges as a catalyst for fostering students' belief in their writing ability. Furthermore, AI applications can tailor content according to students' comprehension levels and subject backgrounds, thereby creating a personalized learning environment that fosters easier access to and understanding of complex knowledge (Mollick, 2023; Peres et al., 2023).

However, the integration of AI tools also raises concerns about potential harm to a writer's self-efficacy. On one hand, over-reliance on AI tools may hinder a writer's development of essential writing skills. For instance, L2 writers might complete their work by translating from their first language or by having AI tools create entire paragraphs; these activities do not contribute to their acquisition of the target language or writing skills (Gayed et al., 2022). The efficiency of AI in grammar correction and style refinement might inadvertently discourage writers from actively learning from their mistakes and improving their skills (Malik et al., 2023). Writers may also experience a loss of authenticity and their unique voice, which could negatively affect their self-efficacy beliefs (Nilson, 2023).

## 2.4  The expert reversal effect (ERE)

Recent CL studies have demonstrated significant interactions between levels of learner expertise and learning or instructional methods. Learners' expertise levels can determine whether information is essential or extraneous for a learning task (Kalyuga, 2007, 2008; Sweller, 2010). High-expertise learners might find previously learned information redundant and potentially detrimental to their learning, whereas low-expertise learners still need to acquire this information and can benefit from it (Kalyuga, 2007). This is called the expertise reversal effect (ERE) (Kalyuga, 2007, 2008; Sweller, 2010; O. Chen et al., 2016). For instance, Xu and Zhang (2021) show that automatic writing evaluation tools offer "superficial" feedback for advanced students' English writing, whereas students with lower English writing proficiency often find feedback from these tools "useful".

The ERE can be understood by considering processing limitations of our working memory and the role of organized knowledge base (Kalyuga, 2007). Human working memory is severely limited in duration and capacity (Baddeley, 1997). With little relevant prior knowledge, novice learners have to deal with much new information that may soon overwhelm their working memory capacity. These learners may experience significant cognitive overload unless external support can be provided. The external support helps solving problem and alleviates the intrinsic cognitive load. However, if the same support is provided for learners with more previous knowledge, the process of integrating their available knowledge and externally provided guidance would be unnecessary. The instructional implication of the ERE is the need to adjust the instructional methods to changing levels of learner expertise.

If the ERE exists in the context of open AI-integrated academic writing process, while AI-integrated learning is generally beneficial, the perceived effectiveness of these tools can vary among students with different L2 proficiency levels. Consequently, processing the same information provided by AI tools may introduce extraneous (useless) or germane (useful) load depending on the learners' expertise and needs (Sweller, 2010). This suggests that for optimal development of writing ability, assistance provided to learners by AI tools should be tailored to their specific needs; otherwise, it may have unintended negative consequences.

## 2.5 Research gaps

The literature review indicates that while some previous studies highlighted the psychological benefits of using AI tools in enhancing learners' writing self-efficacy and reducing cognitive load, some studies have cautioned against the potential ineffectiveness of AI tools in these areas (Malik et al., 2023; Barrot, 2023), and especially when complex researched-based-writing tasks required by L2 postgraduates are concerned. Moreover, previous studies have predominantly sampled students with mixed L2 proficiency levels, despite warnings about the ERE related to L2 proficiency in AI-integrated academic writing instruction (Gao et al., 2023; Xu & Zhang, 2021). Empirical studies that examine the relative effectiveness of AI use in research-based academic writing, moderated by L2 literacy, are still scarce. This study aims to bridge this gap and the following two questions will be addressed:

1. Can the use of AI predict an increase in writing self-efficacy and a decrease in cognitive load for postgraduates with lower English literacy?

2. Can the use of AI predict an increase in writing self-efficacy and a decrease in cognitive load for postgraduates with higher English literacy?

## 3. Method

### 3.1 Settings

The research data came from an academic writing course of 14 weeks provided for postgraduates. The writing course was based on research projects. Students engaged in do research on problematic issues related to their disciplines and wrote research proposals. AI tools were allowed to be used when learning the course. Free versions of Quillbot, Kimi, and Xiao Lvjing were introduced as main intervention instruments. Of the tools, Quillbot is a product that uses AI to paraphrase, summarize, translate and check grammar (Dale, 2020). Kimi is a multilingual AI assistant developed by Moonshot AI (https://kimi.moonshot.cn/), with similar functionality to ChatGPT. With Kimi, users can attach multiple documents and ask for help with summarizing, synthesizing, or creating texts. It can check grammar and improve language quality. But as ChatGPT, Kimi cannot get access to the latest internet resources. It creates faked academic information. Xiao Lvjing (https://www.xljsci.com) is a tool for academic reading and translating. It helps reading and explaining long academic articles. Although ChatGPT is not available to most users in China, postgraduates working in international companies can use ChatGPT in their office.

Course instructors encouraged the use of AI as a learning aid in the writing process, from searching for academic resources, creating outline of the proposal to create text. But students were instructed not to use AI-generated content as a replacement for their own work. If AI tools were utilized, they must illustrate how AI has been used. To discourage over-reliance on AI, throughout the course, students were required to give two oral presentations on their progress—covering literature review and research methodology—as part of their research project design. After they wrote the first draft, a peer review process was implemented. These strategies aimed to enable students to effectively use AI support while maintaining academic integrity.

## 3.2 Participants

A total of 327 postgraduates from a business university in Shanghai were invited to participate in this study. They came from various schools related to business, economics, or finance studies. Among these students, there were 135 male participants (41.3%) and 192 female participants (58.7%). Their English proficiency levels ranged from B2 to C1 according to the Common European Framework of Reference for Languages (CEFR), as judged by the College English Test (CET) Band 6 scores reported at the beginning of the course (Jin et al., 2022). Although the participants were taught by three different teachers, they all followed the same teaching syllabus. The university does not have a specific organization responsible for supervising research ethics; however, we respected participants' rights by informing them of the research purpose and clarifying that they could withdraw from the survey at any time. The researchers obtained signed written consent from participants before they took part in the survey.

Eight participants took part in follow-up semi-structured interviews to provide qualitative insights into the quantitative findings (See Table

1). Of the eight participants, five were male and three were female, and they were from different disciplines. Four of them were from the lower English literacy group, and the remaining four from the higher group, based on their self-reported L2 reading and writing levels at the end of the course.

**Table 1    Participants characteristics**

| Participant | Gender | Major | CET 6 score | English Literacy |
|:---:|:---:|:---:|:---:|:---:|
| Xu | F | Business Management | 582 | High |
| Du | M | Accounting | 575 | High |
| Li | M | International Trade | 580 | High |
| Zhang | M | Digital Economics | 492 | Low |
| Xiao | M | Event | 487 | Low |
| Zhao | F | International Investment | 501 | Low |
| Shang | M | International Investment | 536 | Low |
| Zhong | F | Finance | 620 | High |

### 3.3  Measures

- AI Using Strategy Scale (AUSS)

A 13-item questionnaire about the use of AI strategies in the academic proposal writing process was used in the survey. Items were prepared with reference to the utilization of AI in helping academic writing (Khalifa & Albadawy, 2024). One of the researchers prepared the items and asked six students to participate in telephone interviews to provide feedback on the content and wording. Based on this feedback, two researchers made the necessary adjustments to the items. The AUSS primarily measured how AI tools are used in the research proposal writing process. It was designed with a six-point Likert scale ranging from 1 (not true of me at all) to 6 (very true of me). Appendix 1 shows the 13 items.

We validated the constructs through exploratory factor analysis (EFA) and found that all necessary assumptions were met: Bartlett's test indicated significance ($p<0.05$), and the Kaiser-Meyer-Olkin Measure of Sampling Adequacy (KMO) was 0.96. The scree plot suggested the presence of three factors with clear meaning: AI utilization for literature reading (AULR), AI utilization for proposal planning (AUPP), and AI utilization for proposal writing (AUPW). The high reliability of these three factors was shown by Cronbach's alpha values, which were 0.876, 0.901 and 0.890. These results demonstrate that the questionnaire was psychometrically reliable.

● Research Proposal Writing Cognitive Load Scale (RPWCLS)

Cognitive load refers to the load imposed by task demands. The cognitive load of the research proposal writing task was measured by a subjective self-reporting instrument of 13 items with reference to Li and Wang (2024). We adjusted the questionnaire according to the writing process of research proposal. Students were asked to evaluate the extent of difficulty they encountered during the academic writing process using a 6-point scale (1=little difficult, 6=extremely difficult). The questionnaire primarily measured the difficulties across three stages of writing: information search and interpretation before writing, generation of writing ideas, and academic writing. The overall internal consistency of the scale was assessed with Cronbach's alpha=0.921. Appendix 2 shows the 13 items.

- Research Proposal Writing Self-Efficacy Scale (RPWSS)

Among the academic writing self-efficacy measuring tools, we adopted the 9-item scale developed by Kong and Wang (2022) because the writing task in our study is similar to project-based academic writing tasks, involving complicated research methods and disciplinary knowledge. This 6-point scale, ranging from 1 (not true of me) to 6 (very true of me), assessed students' confidence in their academic writing abilities. The scale's reliability was supported by a Cronbach's alpha value of 0.897, indicating good internal consistency. Appendix 3 shows the 9 items.

- Semi-structured interviews

We conducted semi-structured interviews to gather information from students regarding their strategies for using AI, as well as the potential factors influencing their strategy adoption. The interviews were conducted during students' leisure time after the conclusion of the writing course, in Chinese, and each participant was interviewed for 25–30 minutes to collect rich and reliable data. In the interview, we focused on two questions: what are the most useful and least useful AI utilization strategies? The interviews were conducted in Chinese to allow participants to provide detailed responses (Aizawa et al., 2020).

### 3.4 Procedures

This study consisted of three stages. In the first stage, during the 14-week academic writing course, the teachers introduced how to use AI tools and other academic writing strategies from locating academic resources, reading, note-taking, summarizing, synthesizing to research proposal genre knowledge. Every student searched for academic literature, chose a research topic, and wrote a proposal. Two meeting times were allocated to learn AI tools. In the first one (week 3 and 4) teachers showed how to use Kimi, Xiao Lvjing and Quillbot for reading and writing. In the second meeting students exercised on using these tools in searching for academic literature and read literatures. In the rest of the semester they finished writing the first draft, revised and handed in their paper.

In the second stage, after completing the writing course, participants were asked to voluntarily fill out a questionnaire. The questionnaire included their strategies for using AI, the cognitive load felt during the writing process, and self-efficacy for academic writing. It also incorporated students' self-evaluations of their English reading and writing literacy. Based on their self-reported L2 reading and writing literacy, 327 students were categorized into two levels. 163

was on the lower side out of the scale, and 164 of them were on the higher side.

In the third stage, we invited 8 students from different L2 literacy groups and organized semi-structured interviews to add contextualized and qualitative data to our interpretation of the quantitative results.

## 3.5 Data analysis

We conducted a three-stage statistical analysis to determine the association between the use of AI tools, perceived cognitive load, and writing self-efficacy:

Firstly, we did descriptive analysis to assess normality in distributions and bivariate correlation analysis of the key variables.

Secondly, we employed structural equation modeling (SEM) using AMOS version 26.0 to investigate the predictive effects of AI utilization strategies (AUS) on cognitive load and self-efficacy separately within the high and low literacy groups. The fit of the confirmatory factor analysis model was evaluated using the comparative fit index (CFI), Tucker-Lewis index (TLI), root mean square error of approximation (RMSEA), and standardized root mean square residual (SRMR). Specifically, model fit was considered acceptable when RMSEA and SRMR were below 0.08 and CFI and TLI were above 0.90. An excellent fit was indicated when RMSEA and SRMR were below 0.05 and CFI and TLI were above 0.95 (Kline, 2015).

For the analysis of the interview, the thematic analysis strictly followed the procedures suggested by Braun and Clarke (2021). Two additional lecturers were recruited to assist the researchers in coding and theme extraction. A joint discussion was convened to settle disagreements among coders. When the data analyses were finalized, all findings were converged and triangulated for the major findings of the study.

## 4. Results

### 4.1 Preliminary analysis

Descriptive statistical analyses, as shown in Table 2, revealed that the mean scores of the main variables ranged from 3.41 to 4.05 with standard derivations ranging from 0.75 to 1.33. All items exhibited skewness and kurtosis values falling within the range of ±2, indicating reasonably normal distributions (Hogg, et al., 2015).

The AI using strategy (AUS) displays a positive correlation with both the cognitive load ($r=0.24$, $p<0.01$) and the self-efficacy ($r=0.13$, $p<0.05$). More specifically, the AI using for literature reading strategy (AULRS), proposal planning strategy (AUPPS), and proposal writing strategy (AUPWS) are positively correlated with cognitive load with all the $p$ values$<0.01$. Regarding self-efficacy, the AUPPS and the AUPWS both exhibit significant positive correlations with self-efficacy. However, the AULRS does not show a significant relationship with self-efficacy ($r=0.10$, $p=0.8$).

**Table 2    Descriptive statistics and correlations among target variables**

| | Mean | SD | Skewness | Kurtosis | 1 | 2 | 3 | 4 | 5 | 6 |
|---|---|---|---|---|---|---|---|---|---|---|
| 1. AUS | 3.48 | 1.12 | −0.15 | −0.49 | 1 | | | | | |
| 2. AULRS | 3.46 | 1.33 | −0.14 | −0.68 | 0.86** | 1 | | | | |
| 3. AUPPS | 3.56 | 1.30 | −0.21 | −0.74 | 0.91** | 0.75** | 1 | | | |
| 4. AUPWS | 3.44 | 1.17 | −0.03 | −0.56 | 0.92** | 0.67** | 0.73** | 1 | | |
| 5. CL | 3.41 | 0.79 | −0.13 | 0.55 | 0.24** | 0.19** | 0.21** | 0.24** | 1 | |
| 6. SE | 4.05 | 0.75 | 0.26 | −0.04 | 0.13* | 0.10 | 0.13* | 0.12* | −0.12* | 1 |

Note. **p<0.01, *p<0.05. AUS=AI using strategy; AULRS=AI using for literature reading strategy; AUPPS=AI using for proposal planning strategy; AUPWS=AI using for proposal writing strategy; CL=cognitive load; SE= self-efficacy.

## 4.2  Results of model fit

Next, we utilized confirmatory factor analysis (CFA) to assess the model fit of the measurement and structural equation models in the higher and lower L2 groups respectively. We evaluated the model fit for three correlated measurement models in the two groups: Model 1 for the measurement of cognitive load with 13 items; Model 2 for self-efficacy with 9 items; Model 3 for AI using strategies with 13 items categorized into three types: AULRS, AUPPS, and AUPWS. Then we evaluated the data fit of Model 4: cognitive load and self-efficacy were predicted with AI using strategies. Both Model 4a and 4b had good data fit (RMSEA=0.06, CFI=0.92, TLI=0.90, and SRMR=0.07 for Model 4a; and RMSEA=0.05, CFI=0.95, TLI=0.94, and SRMR=0.07 for Model 4b); Table 3 presents the results of model fit in lower and higher literacy groups respectively, indicating that all models demonstrated excellent fit with the data.

Table 3　Results of model fit in low and high literacy group

| | $x^2$ | $df$ | $P$ | RMSEA | SRMR | CFI | TLI |
|---|---|---|---|---|---|---|---|
| Model 1. a. CL in Group 1 | 94.95 | 55 | <0.001 | 0.08 | 0.06 | 0.93 | 0.90 |
| b. CL in Group 2 | 103.42 | 55 | <0.001 | 0.06 | 0.03 | 0.97 | 0.96 |
| Model 2. a. SE in Group 1 | 36.36 | 21 | <0.02 | 0.08 | 0.06 | 0.95 | 0.92 |
| b. SE in Group 2 | 41.48 | 19 | <0.01 | 0.07 | 0.03 | 0.98 | 0.96 |
| Model 3. a. AUS in Group 1 | 88.36 | 55 | <0.01 | 0.08 | 0.05 | 0.96 | 0.95 |
| b. AUS in Group 2 | 98.59 | 48 | <0.001 | 0.07 | 0.03 | 0.98 | 0.96 |
| Model 4. a. SEM in Group 1 | 895.77 | 516 | <0.001 | 0.06 | 0.07 | 0.92 | 0.90 |
| b. SEM in Group 2 | 779.56 | 516 | <0.001 | 0.05 | 0.07 | 0.95 | 0.94 |

Note: CL=cognitive load; SE= self-efficacy; AUS= AI using strategy; Group 1= lower L2 literacy group; Group2= higher L2 literacy group.

## 4.3 Quantitative analysis for RQ1

Can the use of AI predict an increase in writing self-efficacy and a decrease in cognitive load for postgraduates with lower English literacy?

To address the first research question, we conducted bivariate correlation analyses on relevant variables within the lower English literacy group. Within the group with lower English literacy, the correlation between AI using and cognitive load was not significant ($r$=0.14, $p$=0.16). However, there was a significant positive relationship between AI using and writing self-efficacy ($r$=0.24, $p$=0.01). In the AMOS structural equation model, as shown by Figure 1, AI using strategies significantly predicted an increase of self-efficacy ($\beta$=0.36, $p$<0.01), without showing significant relationship with cognitive load

($\beta$=0.11, $p$=0.20).

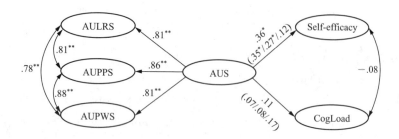

**Figure 1　The relationship between AI using, writing self-efficacy and cognitive load (lower literacy group)**

Note: AUS=AI using strategy; AULRS=the AI using for literature reading strategy; AUPPS=the AI using for proposal planning strategy; AUPWS=the AI using for proposal writing strategy; CogLoad=cognitive load. *$p$<0.05, **$p$<0.01.

To further explore the predictive effects of AI using on self-efficacy during the writing process, we divided writing self-efficacy into three parts according to Kong and Wang (2020): literature reading, method searching, and idea translating self-efficacy. We predicted them with AI using strategy. All the measurement and structure models fit well. AI using significantly predict self-efficacy in literature reading ($\beta$=0.35, $p$<0.001), method searching ($\beta$=0.27, $p$<0.01), but not in idea translating ($\beta$=0.12, $p$=0.33). Similarly, cognitive load was subdivided into literature reading, method searching, and translating stages. We predicted them with AI using strategy. It is shown that AI using did not predict cognitive load, whether in literature reading, method searching, or idea translating (see Figure 1 for reference). To summarize, for the lower L2 learners, AI tools enhanced their self-efficacy mainly in the aspects of reading literature and searching for research method. AI using did not significantly influence cognitive load.

## 4.4 Quantitative analysis results for RQ2

Can the use of AI predict an increase in writing self-efficacy and a decrease in cognitive load for postgraduates with higher English literacy?

Figure 2 illustrates the structural equation modeling results depicting the predictive effects of AI using strategies on self-efficacy and cognitive load in the higher English literacy group. In contrast to the findings in the lower literacy group, AI using showed a significant positive effect on cognitive load ($\beta$=0.26, $p$<0.001), whereas no significant relationship was observed with self-efficacy ($\beta$=0.10, $p$=0.10).

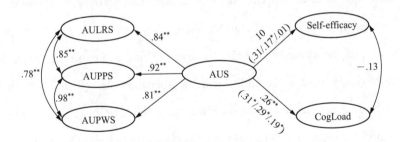

**Figure 2　The relationship between AI using, writing self-efficacy and cognitive load (higher literacy group)**

Note: AUS=AI using strategy; AULRS=the AI using for literature reading strategy; AUPPS=the AI using for proposal planning strategy; AUPWS=the AI using for proposal writing strategy; CogLoad=cognitive load. *$p$<0.05, **$p$<0.01.

We went on using AI using strategies to predict self-efficacy and cognitive load during the literature reading, method searching, and idea translating processes within the high literacy group. All the measurements and structure models were checked and found with good fit. It turned out that AI using had no significant effects on self-efficacy in the aspects of literature reading and idea translating, but it significantly predicted self-efficacy in method searching ($\beta$=0.17, $p$=0.03). Moreover, AI using positively influenced cognitive load during the whole writing stages. To summarize, for the higher L2 literacy learners, unfortunately, AI using positively predicted cognitive load, but on the whole did not generally influence self-efficacy except for the aspect of searching for research method.

## 4.5  Quantitative analysis results

Students with lower literacy explained that the benefits of AI tools exist in three aspects: AI tools helped them search for literature, read multiple articles, and read in detail. They used *"links provided by Kimi"*, as mentioned by Student Zhang, to find academic literature. Moreover, Kimi has the ability to remember multiple articles and can write literature reviews based on the uploaded articles. This is quite helpful for them to understand topic knowledge efficiently. Another tool that is good at aiding reading is Xiao Lvjing's AI tool. *"[It] provides accurate academic translations and [is] very useful when reading long academic articles"*, as stated by Student Zhao. Students in the lower L2 group also frequently used AI tools for patch translation. Student Zhao said, *"I sometimes gave Kimi the Chinese version, asking it to translate a whole paragraph into English.*" However, he clearly expressed that this function did not contribute to the improvement of his own writing ability. To summarize, the function of AI tools in aiding extensive and intensive reading helped compensate for the lower reading abilities in the lower L2 group, assisting them in learning the topic knowledge and research methods required by proposal writing tasks. These lower L2 learners experienced an enhanced sense of self-efficacy in these areas.

Compared with lower-literate students, students who possess higher literacy found using AI tools less helpful and time-consuming. In their eyes, AI functions of information seeking, literature summarizing, idea creating, and text translating were less satisfactory and involved much extra work. For seeking information, AI tools *"provide general, rather than research needed knowledge"* (Student Xu). Higher-literate students would rather search academic information provided by university library, such as using Science Direct or EBSCO datasets. Summarizing and synthesizing done by AI tools were criticized as of low quality and have to be revised. For example, Student Zhong in the higher group stated, *"Summary provided by Kimi cannot grasp the important information. It evaluates literature from writing skill, which is not what I need"*. Even the translating function provided by AI tools was not relied on, because the higher L2 learners worried about the loss of their voice, as Student Li mentioned, *"It [AI tool] uses strange expressions. I don't use it"*. Among the four higher L2 learners being interviewed, two mentioned that they seldom use AI tools except for checking grammars. For higher L2 students, using AI tools is closely associated with extra work, which involves adjusting prompts, checking output quality, and revising. However, AI tools brough limited benefit in solving research-based writing problems faced by them in assisting with disciplinary knowledge or translating complex disciplinary thoughts.

The interview also explained to some extent why AI using could not predict the idea translating efficacy. Both students in the lower and higher groups expressed concerns about the authenticity of using AI tools in creating text and the potential harm to their own language output abilities. One of them mentioned that the language outputted by ChatGPT was not his own. Student Zhang in the lower L2 literate group said, "*It is too good to be mine. I feel this is AI's writing, not my own language.*" He thought that the AI's writing did not represent his true writing proficiency. His ability to output English was not enhanced with AI's help.

## 5. Discussion

This study aimed to explore the nuanced impacts of open AI tool using on writing self-efficacy and cognitive load, considering the effect of L2 literacy.

Findings support the existence of expert reversal effect considering different effects of AI tools on learners' writing self-efficacy between higher and lower L2 groups. It was shown that AI tools significantly enhanced the self-efficacy for the lower L2 literate learners, in the aspects of understanding academic articles and learning research methods. The supportive role of AI tools suggests that these tools act as beneficial scaffoldings, providing assistance that complements the learner's level of L2 expertise (Kalyuga, 2007). The qualitative data from interviews further enriched our understanding of these dynamics. Students with lower L2 literacy perceived AI tools as instrumental in overcoming reading barriers, providing them with the confidence to engage with academic reading, researching and writing tasks. These findings resonated with the observations made by Liu et al. (2021) and Yan (2023), who underscored the profound contributions of AI-assisted language learning tools in advancing EFL learners' writing abilities. However, for students with higher L2 literacy, AI using, on the whole, could not predict their writing self-efficacy ($\beta$=0.10, $p$=0.10). Interview showed that students with higher L2 literacy were concerned about the depth of AI-generated content, which did not align with the needs of writing research proposals. Besides, they already possessed high reading skills, making the support provided by AI tools (such as the fast reading and intensive reading functions provided by Kimi and Xiao Lvjing) redundant.

Findings also support the existence of expert reversal effect considering the different effects of AI tools on learners' cognitive load. For the lower L2 learners, the use of AI was not associated with significant increase in cognitive load. AI tools may have reduced the task complexity and, therefore, reduced the intrinsic load of research-based proposal writing, by providing learners with effective supports in reading of long articles, summarizing main ideas, or translating ideas into texts, although at the same time, the use of AI may have introduced similar amount of extraneous (unproductive, irrelevant) cognitive load by diverting cognitive resources to activities irrelevant to learning goals (such as reading unreliable resources provided by AI tools). But generally, the perceived cognitive load was not increased. However, for the higher L2 learners, the significantly increased cognitive load indicated that the use of AI tools may have introduced more irrelevant information that may add extraneous load than relevant support that may reduce task complexity and intrinsic load. For learners with higher L2 literacy, the reading scaffoldings, needed by the lower L2 learners, may have turned out to be unnecessary because of their higher reading ability; texts created by AI tools, acceptable for the lower L2 learners, may be regarded as unacceptable because, with higher language proficiency, critical analysis ability is usually higher (Dong & Chang, 2023; Shen & Teng, 2024).

Besides the unproductive scaffolding that may have raised extraneous load for the higher L2 literate learners, critical analysis might have added an additional layer of cognitive load. The process for students to engage in verification and refinement of the output of AI tools can increase their cognitive load rather than decrease it (Malik et al., 2023). However, the extra cognitive load related to critical analysis might have been heavier for students with higher L2 literacy. According to researchers, learners with higher L2 literacy are more likely to exert cognitive effort in filtering essential information and assessing the reliability of provided content (Dong & Chang, 2023; Shen & Teng, 2024, Hartwell & Aull, 2023). Unfortunately, the detailed observation of cognitive load related to critical analysis could not be observed by the study.

Except for the expert reversal effects in both writing self-efficacy and cognitive load, we noticed two interesting findings: Firstly, AI tools did not significantly reduce cognitive load of writing for either the higher or the lower L2 literate postgraduates. This finding may be related to the inherent complexity of the task. Research-based academic writing is a multifaceted task requiring the integration of academic reading, content understanding, researching, linguistic expressing and rhetorical structuring (Hyland 2016; Sweller et al., 2019). This complexity imposes a significant intrinsic cognitive load, which may not be significantly mitigated by AI tools. The complexity of the task may have exceeded AI tools' capabilities (Gao et al., 2022).

Secondly, we noticed AI using failed to enhance idea translating self-efficacy for either the lower or the higher L2 literate learners. This could be related to their over reliance on these tools for convenience, which might have undermined the important goals of learning in order to enhance the ability to articulate ideas with clarity and precision. As one student mentioned in the interview that he felt the outputted language was not his own. The writing performance with the help of AI tools did not reflect learner's writing ability and their perceived idea translating efficacy failed to be enhanced.

To summarize, AI tools benefited the lower L2 learners more by introducing higher writing self-efficacy and no-significantly-increased cognitive load. For the higher L2 postgraduates, on the whole no higher writing efficacy or alleviated cognitive load were felt by using AI tools.

## 6. Implications

Two major findings emerge out of the study: Firstly, AI using brings out inevitable cognitive load increase to various degrees for all the learners, and especially so for the higher ones. Secondly, only the lower L2 literate learners improved writing efficacy in the process of AI using. Besides, the study indicated that AI using did not enhance idea translating efficacy for all the learners.

Regarding the fact that AI tools did not reduce cognitive load, a potential collaboration between AI technicians and L2 educators on a locally designed AI program is needed. This collaboration could decrease extraneous cognitive load related to irrelevant literature and non-specialized knowledge provided by open AI tools nowadays. This program should be crafted to support research-based academic writing, providing the latest disciplinary insights, delivering authentic and credible academic resources, and even offering insightful research recommendations, thus serving effectively as an academic mentor.

Considering the varying effects of AI tools on students with different levels of L2 literacy, educators should consider tailoring the integration of AI tools to match the proficiency levels of their students. For students with lower L2 literacy, AI can serve as a valuable scaffold, assisting with reading and researching. For students with higher L2 literacy, the focus should be on using AI to support more complex tasks. For these students, the perceived low usefulness of AI output may be related to a lack of prompting skills, and therefore, there is a need to train them to interact effectively with AI systems to produce more productive output (Kohnke et al., 2023; Walter, 2024).

Given the finding that AI using did not enhance idea translating efficacy, it is essential for instructors to make sure that students strike a balance between leveraging these tools and honing their writing skills (Kasneci et al., 2023). Writing teachers can position AI as a collaborative tool rather than a sole solution. Students should be encouraged to use AI to generate ideas, draft sections, or find resources, but the final output should be a result of human-AI collaboration, ensuring that the student's voice and critical engagement are preserved. Teachers should maintain a dialogue with students about the ethical use of AI. Clear guidelines on academic integrity should be provided, and students should be made aware of the importance of original thought and the potential consequences of relying too heavily on AI-generated content.

## 7. Conclusion

The study explores the moderating effects of L2 literacy on the effectiveness of AI usage in academic writing. The findings support the existence of the expert reversal effect in cognitive load theory, suggesting that AI use benefits learners with lower L2 literacy more. Postgraduates with higher L2 literacy did not benefit as much, considering the increased cognitive load and the insignificant change in writing efficacy. Practically, the study offers insights for educators and AI developers, emphasizing the importance of tailoring AI tools to L2 learners with different needs and striking a balance between leveraging AI tools and honing their writing skills.

There are several limitations to the study, and the conclusions should be viewed with caution. Firstly, the study does not account for potential developments in AI tool design and functionality, which are among the most dynamic areas in various fields around the world. Additionally, the study's cross-sectional design does not allow for the examination of the long-term effects of AI tool usage on writing self-efficacy and cognitive load. The study leaves unaddressed questions about the sustained impact of AI assistance on a writer's self-efficacy and cognitive load over time. Lastly, the study did not measure critical thinking skills, which could be an important variable affecting how students interact with AI tools. Future research should address these limitations by exploring the impact of different AI tools and employing longitudinal research designs.

## 8. References

Aizawa, I., Rose, H., Thompson, G., & Curle, S. (2020). Beyond the threshold: Exploring English language proficiency, linguistic challenges, and academic language skills of Japanese students in an English medium instruction programme. *Language Teaching Research*, 27(4), 136216882096551. https://doi.org/10.1177/1362168820965510.

Baddeley, A. (1997). *Human memory: Theory and practice*. Psychology Press.

Bandura, A. (1997). *Self-efficacy: The exercise of control*. W. H. Freeman.

Barrot, J. S. (2023). Using ChatGPT for second language writing: Pitfalls and potentials. *Assessing Writing, 57*, 100745. https://doi.org/10.1016/j.asw.2023.100745.

Braun, V., & Clarke, V. (2021). *Thematic analysis: A Practical Guide*. SAGE.

Brom, C., Stárková, T., Bromová, E., & Děchtěrenko, F. (2018).

Gamifying a simulation: Do a game goal, choice, points, and praise enhance learning? *Journal of Educational Computing Research*, 57(6), 1575–1613. https://doi.org/10.1177/0735633118797330.

Cancino, M., & Panes, J. (2021). The impact of Google Translate on L2 writing quality measures: Evidence from Chilean EFL high school learners. *System, 98*, 102464. https://doi.org/10.1016/j.system.2021.102464.

Chen, H. H., Yang, C. T., & Lai, K. K. (2020). Investigating college EFL learners' perceptions toward the use of Google Assistant for foreign language learning. *Interactive Learning Environments*, 31(3), 1335–1350. https://doi.org/10.1080/10494820.2020.1833043.

Chen, O., Kalyuga, S., & Sweller, J. (2016). The Expertise Reversal Effect is a Variant of the More General Element Interactivity Effect. *Educational Psychology Review*, 29(2), 393–405. https://doi.org/10.1007/s10648-016-9359-1.

Christensen, R., & Knezek, G. (2016). Validating the Technology Proficiency Self-Assessment Questionnaire for 21st Century Learning (TPSA C-21). *Journal of Digital Learning in Teacher Education*, 33(1), 20–31. https://doi.org/10.1080/21532974.2016.1242391.

Cope, B., Kalantzis, M., & Searsmith, D. (2020). Artificial intelligence for education: Knowledge and its assessment in AI-enabled learning ecologies. *Educational Philosophy and Theory*, 53(12), 1229–1245. https://doi.org/10.1080/00131857.2020.1728732.

Dale, R. (2020). Natural language generation: The commercial state of the art in 2020. *Natural Language Engineering*, 26(4), 481–487. https://doi.org/10.1017/s135132492000025x.

Dong, Y., & Chang, X. (2023). Investigating EFL Writers' Critical Thinking Performance across *Languages. Thinking Skills and Creativity, 47*, 101232. https://doi.org/10.1016/j.tsc.2023.101232.

Dwivedi, Y. K., Sharma, A., Rana, N. P., Giannakis, M., Goel, P., & Dutot, V. (2023). Evolution of artificial intelligence research in Technological Forecasting and Social Change: Research topics, trends, and future directions. *Technological Forecasting and Social Change*, 192, 122579. https://doi.org/10.1016/j.techfore.2023.122579.

Gao, C. A., Howard, F. M., Markov, N. S., Dyer, E. C., Ramesh, S., Luo, Y., & Pearson, A. T. (2023). Comparing scientific abstracts generated by ChatGPT to real abstracts with detectors and blinded human reviewers. *Npj Digital Medicine*, 6(1), 1–5. https://doi.org/10.1038/s41746-023-00819-6.

Gayed, J. M., Carlon, M. K. J., Oriola, A. M., & Cross, J. S. (2022). Exploring an AI-based writing Assistant's impact on English language learners. *Computers and Education Artificial Intelligence*, 3, 100055. https://doi.org/10.1016/j.caeai.2022.100055.

Van Gog, T., Kester, L., & Paas, F. (2010). Effects of concurrent monitoring on cognitive load and performance as a function of task complexity. *Applied Cognitive Psychology*, 25(4), 584–587. https://

doi.org/10.1002/acp.1726.

Guo, K., Wang, J., & Chu, S. K. W. (2022). Using chatbots to scaffold EFL students' argumentative writing. *Assessing Writing, 54*, 100666. https://doi.org/10.1016/j.asw.2022.100666.

Hartwell, K., & Aull, L. (2023). Editorial Introduction — AI, corpora, and future directions for writing assessment. *Assessing Writing, 57*, 100769. https://doi.org/10.1016/j.asw.2023.100769.

Hogg, R. V., Tanis, E. A., & Zimmerman, D. L. (2015). *Probability and Statistical Inference (9th ed.)*. Pearson Educational Limited.

Hyland, F. (2016). Challenges faced by second language doctoral student writers in Hong Kong and their writing strategies. *Australian Review of Applied Linguistics*, 39(2), 158–180. https://doi.org/10.1075/aral.39.2.04hyl.

Ismael, K. O., Saeed, K. A., Ibrahim, A. S., & Fatah, D. S. (2022). Effects of Auto-Correction on Students Writing Skill at Three Different Universities in Sulaimaneyah City. *Arab World English Journal*, 8(8), 231–245. https://doi.org/10.24093/awej/call8.16.

Jin, Y. Jie, W. & Wang, W. (2022). An Alignment Study of College English Tests Band 4 & 6 and Standard Language Competence, *Foreign Language World (Waiyu Jie)* (02), 24–32. https://kns.cnki.net/kcms2/article/abstract?v=3uoqIhG8C44YLTlOAiTRKibYlV5Vjs7iJTKGjg9uTdeTsOI_ra5_XU8T4AGvM8I2DVmuF1zB5hHyHJqgwrSkJs9a0SkFvJaI&uniplatform=NZKPT.

Kalyuga, S. (2007). Expertise Reversal Effect and its Implications for Learner-Tailored Instruction. *Educational Psychology Review*, 19(4), 509–539. https://doi.org/10.1007/s10648-007-9054-3.

Kalyuga, S. (2008). Relative effectiveness of animated and static diagrams: An effect of learner prior knowledge. *Computers in Human Behavior*, 24(3), 852–861. https://doi.org/10.1016/j.chb.2007.02.018.

Kalyuga, S. (2011). Cognitive load theory: How many types of load does it really need? *Educational Psychology Review*, 23(1), 1–19. https://doi.org/10.1007/s10648-010-9150-7.

Kasneci, E., Sessler, K., Küchemann, S., Bannert, M., Dementieva, D., Fischer, F., Gasser, U., Groh, G., Günnemann, S., Hüllermeier, E., Krusche, S., Kutyniok, G., Michaeli, T., Nerdel, C., Pfeffer, J., Poquet, O., Sailer, M., Schmidt, A., Seidel, T., ... Kasneci, G. (2023). ChatGPT for good? On opportunities and challenges of large language models for education. *Learning and Individual Differences*, 103, 102274. https://doi.org/10.1016/j.lindif.2023.102274.

Khalifa, M., & Albadawy, M. (2024). Using Artificial Intelligence in Academic Writing and Research: An Essential Productivity Tool. *Computer Methods and Programs in Biomedicine Update, 5*, 100145–100145. https://doi.org/10.1016/j.cmpbup.2024.100145.

Kim, J., Yu, S., Detrick, R., & Li, N. (2024). Exploring students' perspectives on Generative AI-assisted academic writing. *Education and Information Technologies*. https://doi.org/10.1007/s10639-024-

12878-7

Kline, R. B. (2015). *Principles and Practice of Structural Equation Modeling.* Guilford Press

Kohnke, L., Moorhouse, B. L., & Zou, D. (2023). Exploring generative artificial intelligence preparedness among university language instructors: A case study. *Computers and Education Artificial Intelligence,* 5, 100156. https://doi.org/10.1016/j.caeai.2023.100156

Koltovskaia, S. (2020). Student engagement with automated written corrective feedback (AWCF) provided by Grammarly: A multiple case study. *Assessing Writing, 44,* 100450. https://doi.org/10.1016/j.asw.2020.100450

Kong, Y., & Wang, C. (2022). The effects of self-efficacy on the use of self-regulated learning strategies and project-based writing performance. *International Journal of English for Academic Purposes: Research and Practice: Volume 2022, Issue Spring, 2022*(Spring), 21–39. https://doi.org/10.3828/ijeap.2022.3

Kurniati, E. Y., & Fithriani, R. (2022). Post-Graduate students' perceptions of Quillbot utilization in English Academic Writing class. *Journal of English Language Teaching and Linguistics, 7*(3), 437. https://doi.org/10.21462/jeltl.v7i3.852

Li, J., & Wang, J. (2024). A measure of EFL argumentative writing cognitive load: Scale development and validation. *Journal of Second Language Writing,* 63, 101095. https://doi.org/10.1016/

j.jslw.2024.101095

Liang, J., Wang, L., Luo, J., Yan, Y., & Fan, C. (2023). The relationship between student interaction with generative artificial intelligence and learning achievement: serial mediating roles of self-efficacy and cognitive engagement. *Frontiers in Psychology, 14*. https://doi.org/10.3389/fpsyg.2023.1285392

Lin, L. H., & Morrison, B. (2021). Challenges in academic writing: Perspectives of Engineering faculty and L2 postgraduate research students. *English for Specific Purposes, 63*, 59–70. https://doi.org/10.1016/j.esp.2021.03.004

Lin, Z. (2024). Techniques for supercharging academic writing with generative AI. *Nature Biomedical Engineering.* https://doi.org/10.1038/s41551-024-01185-8

Liu, C., Hou, J., Tu, Y.-F., Wang, Y., & Hwang, G.-J. (2021). Incorporating a reflective thinking promoting mechanism into artificial intelligence-supported English writing environments. *Interactive Learning Environments, 31*(9), 1–19. https://doi.org/10.1080/10494820.2021.2012812

Malik, A. R., Pratiwi, Y., Andajani, K., Numertayasa, I. W., Suharti, S., Darwis, A., & Marzuki Marzuki. (2023). Exploring artificial intelligence in academic essay: Higher education student's perspective. *International Journal of Educational Research Open, 5*, 100296, https://doi.org/10.1016/j.ijedro.2023.100296

Mollick, E. R., & Mollick, L. (2023). Using AI to Implement Effective Teaching Strategies in Classrooms: Five Strategies, Including Prompts. *SSRN Electronic Journal.* https://doi.org/10.2139/ssrn.4391243

Morrison, B., & Evans, S. (2018). Supporting non-native speaker student writers making the transition from school to an English-medium university. *Language Learning in Higher Education, 8*(1), 1–20. https://doi.org/10.1515/cercles-2018-0001

Nguyen, A., Hong, Y., Dang, B., & Huang, X. (2024). Human-AI collaboration patterns in AI-assisted academic writing. *Studies in Higher Education*, 1–18. https://doi.org/10.1080/03075079.2024.2323593

Nilson, L. B. (2023). *Creating Self-Regulated Learners*: Strategies to Strengthen Students' Self-Awareness and Learning Skills. http://ci.nii.ac.jp/ncid/BB1645321X

Peres, R., Schreier, M., Schweidel, D., & Sorescu, A. (2023). On ChatGPT and Beyond: How Generative Artificial Intelligence May Affect Research, Teaching, and Practice. *International Journal of Research in Marketing, 40*(2). https://doi.org/10.1016/j.ijresmar.2023.03.001

Plass, J. L., & Kalyuga, S. (2019). Four ways of considering emotion in cognitive load theory. *Educational Psychology Review*, 31(2), 339–359. https://doi.org/10.1007/s10648-019-09473-5

Ranalli, J. (2021). L2 student engagement with automated feedback on writing: Potential for learning and issues of trust. *Journal of*

*Second Language Writing, 52*, 100816. https://doi.org/10.1016/j.jslw.2021.100816

Shen, X., & Teng, M. F. (2024). Three-Wave Cross-Lagged Model on the Correlations Between Critical Thinking Skills, Self-Directed Learning Competency and AI-Assisted Writing. *Thinking Skills and Creativity, 52*, 101524. https://doi.org/10.1016/j.tsc.2024.101524

Shadiev, R., & Huang, Y. (2020). Exploring the influence of technological support, cultural constructs, and social networks on online cross-cultural learning. *Australasian Journal of Educational Technology, 36*(3), 104–118. https://doi.org/10.14742/ajet.6038

Song, C., & Song, Y. (2023). Enhancing academic writing skills and motivation: assessing the efficacy of ChatGPT in AI-assisted language learning for EFL students. *Frontiers in Psychology, 14*, 1260843. https://doi.org/10.3389/fpsyg.2023.1260843

Su, Y., Lin, Y., & Lai, C. (2023). Collaborating with ChatGPT in argumentative writing classrooms. *Assessing Writing, 57*, 100752. https://doi.org/10.1016/j.asw.2023.100752

Sweller, J. (1988). Cognitive load during problem solving: Effects on learning. *Cognitive Science*, 12(2), 257–285. https://doi.org/10.1016/0364-0213(88)90023-7

Sweller, J. (2010). Element interactivity and intrinsic, extraneous, and germane cognitive load. Educational Psychology Review, 22(2), 123–138. https://doi.org/10.1007/s10648-010-9128-5

Sweller, J., van Merriënboer, J. J. G., & Paas, F. (2019). Cognitive Architecture and Instructional Design: 20 Years Later. *Educational Psychology Review*, 31(2), 261–292. https://doi.org/10.1007/s10648-019-09465-5

Tang, A., Li, K., Kwok, K. O., Cao, L., Luong, S., & Tam, W. (2023). The importance of transparency: Declaring the use of generative artificial intelligence (AI) in academic writing. *Journal of Nursing Scholarship*, 56(2), 314–318. https://doi.org/10.1111/jnu.12938

Teng, L. S., Sun, P. P., & Xu, L. (2017). Conceptualizing Writing Self-Efficacy in English as a Foreign Language Contexts: scale validation through structural equation modeling. *TESOL Quarterly, 52*(4), 911–942. https://doi.org/10.1002/tesq.432

Walter, Y. (2024). Embracing the future of Artificial Intelligence in the classroom: the relevance of AI literacy, prompt engineering, and critical thinking in modern education. *International Journal of Educational Technology in Higher Education, 21*(1). https://doi.org/10.1186/s41239-024-00448-3

Warschauer, M., Tseng, W., Yim Soobin, Webster, T. J., Jacob, S., Du, Q., & Tate, T. (2023). The affordances and contradictions of AI-generated text for writers of English as a second or foreign language. *Journal of Second Language Writing, 62*, 101071. https://doi.org/10.1016/j.jslw.2023.101071

Xu, J., & Zhang, S. (2021). Understanding AWE Feedback and English

Writing of Learners with Different Proficiency Levels in an EFL Classroom: A Sociocultural Perspective. *The Asia-Pacific Education Researcher, 31*, 357–367. https://doi.org/10.1007/s40299-021-00577-7

Yan, D. (2023). Impact of ChatGPT on learners in a L2 writing practicum: An exploratory investigation. *Education and Information Technologies, 28*, 13943–13967. https://doi.org/10.1007/s10639-023-11742-4

## Appendix 1　AI Using Strategy Scale (AUSS)

*Prompt: Please choose one number that most properly suits the strategies taken by you to use AI tools when writing the research proposal: 1 means it is not at all true of you; 6 means it is very true of you.*

| AI Using for Literature Reading | | | | | | |
|---|---|---|---|---|---|---|
| 1. Using AI to search for literature | 1 | 2 | 3 | 4 | 5 | 6 |
| 2. Using AI to read literature | 1 | 2 | 3 | 4 | 5 | 6 |
| 3. Using AI to evaluate literature | 1 | 2 | 3 | 4 | 5 | 6 |
| AI Using for Proposal Planning | | | | | | |
| 1. Using AI to acquire disciplinary knowledge | 1 | 2 | 3 | 4 | 5 | 6 |
| 2. Using AI to understand disciplinary hot topics | 1 | 2 | 3 | 4 | 5 | 6 |
| 3. Using AI to determine research topics | 1 | 2 | 3 | 4 | 5 | 6 |
| 4. Using AI to provide research methods | 1 | 2 | 3 | 4 | 5 | 6 |
| AI Using for Proposal Writing | | | | | | |
| 1. Using AI to draft outlines for literature reviews | 1 | 2 | 3 | 4 | 5 | 6 |
| 2. Using AI to write paragraphs | 1 | 2 | 3 | 4 | 5 | 6 |
| 3. Using AI to replace expressions | 1 | 2 | 3 | 4 | 5 | 6 |
| 4. Using AI to correct grammar errors | 1 | 2 | 3 | 4 | 5 | 6 |
| 5. Using AI to edit reference lists | 1 | 2 | 3 | 4 | 5 | 6 |
| 6. Using AI to check for plagiarism | 1 | 2 | 3 | 4 | 5 | 6 |

## Appendix 2  Research Proposal Writing Cognitive Load Scale (RPWCLS)

*Prompt: Please choose one number that most properly suits the degree of difficulty you perceived when writing research proposal: 1 means little difficult; 6 means extremely difficult.*

| | | | | | | |
|---|---|---|---|---|---|---|
| 14. Look for academic literature | 1 | 2 | 3 | 4 | 5 | 6 |
| 15. Take notes while reading | 1 | 2 | 3 | 4 | 5 | 6 |
| 16. Summarize while reading | 1 | 2 | 3 | 4 | 5 | 6 |
| 17. Synthesize while reading | 1 | 2 | 3 | 4 | 5 | 6 |
| 18. Decide a research topic to write on | 1 | 2 | 3 | 4 | 5 | 6 |
| 19. Understand the knowledge related to the topic | 1 | 2 | 3 | 4 | 5 | 6 |
| 20. Design research method | 1 | 2 | 3 | 4 | 5 | 6 |
| 21. List the outline of research proposal | 1 | 2 | 3 | 4 | 5 | 6 |
| 22. Translate ideas into texts | 1 | 2 | 3 | 4 | 5 | 6 |
| 23. Write with focus | 1 | 2 | 3 | 4 | 5 | 6 |
| 24. Write with clear structure | 1 | 2 | 3 | 4 | 5 | 6 |
| 25. Write with good convention | 1 | 2 | 3 | 4 | 5 | 6 |
| 26. Write with good academic style | 1 | 2 | 3 | 4 | 5 | 6 |

## Appendix 3  Research Proposal Writing Self-Efficacy Scale (RPWSS)

*Prompt: Please choose one number that most properly describes the confidence that you felt when conducting research proposal writing: 1 means it is not at all true of you; 6 means it is very true of you.*

| | | | | | | |
|---|---|---|---|---|---|---|
| 1. I can write with clear structure. | 1 | 2 | 3 | 4 | 5 | 6 |
| 2. I can avoid grammatic errors. | 1 | 2 | 3 | 4 | 5 | 6 |
| 3. I can use appropriate academic language. | 1 | 2 | 3 | 4 | 5 | 6 |
| 4. I can cite properly. | 1 | 2 | 3 | 4 | 5 | 6 |
| 5. I can find academic literature. | 1 | 2 | 3 | 4 | 5 | 6 |
| 6. I can understand the academic literature in English. | 1 | 2 | 3 | 4 | 5 | 6 |
| 7. I can synthesize academic resources in English. | 1 | 2 | 3 | 4 | 5 | 6 |
| 8. I can find valuable research topics. | 1 | 2 | 3 | 4 | 5 | 6 |
| 9. I can design proper research methods. | 1 | 2 | 3 | 4 | 5 | 6 |

# 第十二章 写作任务类型对认知负荷的影响
## Chapter 12 Influence of cognitive load from task types

**本章内容概要 Abstract of the chapter**

认知负荷理论的研究者针对口语和写作任务的复杂性做了广泛的研究，这些研究为教学中安排口语或者写作任务的顺序给出参考。Robinson 考虑了任务复杂性的认知因素、环境因素和学习者因素对口语表现的影响，但该模型针对口语活动的复杂性，因此在写作活动中不适用。本章写作体裁作为任务复杂性变量的研究。这类研究大多比较议论文和记叙文写作任务对学习者产生的认知负荷影响。这些研究表明体裁作为任务变量确实引发了学习者不同的语言使用。比如：议论文比记叙文更能促使学习者使用复杂的句法结构。但是体裁之间的复杂性比较很少在其他类型的任务中进行过讨论。议论文和研究报告是两种常见的学术体裁，议论文需要逻辑推理、反驳和说服，认知复杂性高；研究报告需要处理一手信息资料、综合分析得出结果，也有很高的认知负荷，但很少有研究观察过这两种体裁带来的认知负荷。

本章分析了研究性报告与议论文产生的认知负荷差异。参与者分别为来自研究性报告写作课程的 240 名本科生以及来自议论文写作课程的 177 名本科生。参与者均为商科院校非英语专业学生。这些课程旨在培养学生的学术写作技能，帮助他们提高学术写作中的读者意识、语篇结构和学术语言能力。这两个班级的学习者分别在一个学期中完成自选题目的写作，写作长度为 2000 字。学习者自己收集有价值的文献信息，完成观点性的议论文写作，或者是研究性的报告写作。在一个学期学习之后，教师使用问卷测量学生对写作任务认知负荷的感知。研究结果表明，两种体裁都对学习者产生很高的认知负荷，但比起议论文写作，报告写作任务产生的认知负荷更高，因为报告写作需要更多的子步骤（收集分析一手数据）和新知识（统计分析）。议论文依靠二手研究资料，相对步骤少，且为学习者熟悉的体裁。步骤少与经验知识多结合，降低了学习者感知的认知负荷。

本章中的研究案例证明体裁与认知负荷之间存在紧密联系。研究表明教学中教师需要了解学生对不同体裁的写作知识和学习需求，帮助学习者在 PBAW 课程中选择适合的写作任务类型。此外，二语写作教学往往侧重于提高学习者的议论文写作技能，而对其他体裁的关注相对较少。建立基于任务复杂度评估的 PBAW 任务类型，将使二语学习者更有效地发展写作能力。比如：如果在报告写作中希望减少内在认知负荷，可以考虑减少写作步骤，通过直接提供样本数据，省略收集信息和分析信息的步骤，把能力培养范围集中在狭义的学术写作概念下。

## 1. Introduction

In writing, genres often dictate the structure, tone, and narrative style. Some common literary genres include narrative genres such as stories or novels aiming to entertain or inform, expository genres aiming to explaining or describing, argumentative or persuasive genres aiming to convince readers to adopt a certain viewpoint, etc. Genres have identifiable structural elements. For example, a mystery novel typically has a crime, investigation, and resolution, while a scientific paper follows a structure of introduction, literature review, methodology, results, and discussion. In educational contexts, different genres can impose varying cognitive loads on learners. Argumentative writing, for instance, may require more complex reasoning and logical structuring, leading to higher cognitive demands compared to descriptive writing.

Understanding genre is crucial for educators and learners. It helps teachers design appropriate writing tasks and provides learners with a framework to understand and produce texts effectively. As learners navigate the complexities of academic writing, the genre they encounter can significantly influence the cognitive resources they must allocate to complete their tasks effectively. This chapter delves into the intricate relationship between writing task types and the cognitive load they impose on L2 learners, offering insights into how different genres can shape the writing process and its outcomes.

The chapter discusses the operationalization of genre as a task variable and the implications of genre on L2 writing performance. The study presented in this chapter aims to fill a gap in the literature by comparing the cognitive load perceived by L2 learners when engaging in argumentative writing versus report writing tasks. Through a self-rating questionnaire, the study explores how learners perceive the cognitive demands of these two distinct genres and whether these perceptions align with theoretical predictions of task complexity.

## 2. Literature Review

### 2.1 Task complexity in L2 writing

It has been argued that task complexity, defined as the attentional, memory, reasoning, and other information processing demands imposed by the structure of the task on the language learner (Robinson, 2001), influences the amount of attentional and cognitive resources available for language structures during task performance. Thus, manipulations of task complexity are expected to generate different levels of cognitive demands in the conceptualization stage, which in turn lead to changes in the complexity of linguistic forms (Robinson, 2005; Skehan, 1998). Several task variables are hypothesized to affect the allocation of attentional resources for linguistic complexity (e.g., here-and-now, number of elements, and conceptual demands).

In the context of L2 writing, much attention has been given to the effect of conceptual demands on language use (e.g., Kormos, 2011; Kormos & Trebits, 2012; Ong & Zhang, 2010; Tavakoli, 2014), with the prediction that a task with greater complexity at the level of idea conceptualization would allow writers to formulate more complex language (see Robinson, 2001, 2005). Studies have employed picture-based writing tasks for conceptualization-level manipulations (e.g., Kormos, 2011; Kormos & Trebits, 2012; Tavakoli, 2014). Additionally, the degree of conceptual demands has been operationalized as the provision of supporting ideas for argumentation (e.g., Ong, 2014; Ong & Zhang, 2010). For example, Ong and Zhang (2010) explored the effect of idea support on language, and their findings showed significant effects of idea support on lexical diversity (more complex tasks eliciting increased lexical diversity).

## 2.2  Genre as a task variable in L2 writing research

Writers are expected to communicate different functions in different genres. For example, narrative essays entail accounts of connected events or people's actions in a specific time frame, while non-narrative essays involve the argumentation or explanation of general ideas (Berman & Slobin, 1994). Genre studies have examined patterns of language variation across genres and explained writers' use of different linguistic features as an attempt to fulfill different rhetorical functions (e.g., Lu, 2011; Qin & Uccelli, 2016; Staples & Reppen, 2016; Yoon & Polio, 2017).

Genre has been operationalized as a task complexity variable (e.g., Alexopoulou et al., 2017; Ruiz-Funes, 2015; Yang, 2014). This line of research is based on the assumption that argumentative tasks that involve logical causal reasoning would be more cognitively demanding to L2 learners than narrative tasks. Ruiz-Funes (2015) reported on two studies, each of which involved two writing genres. Her first study examined L2 learner performance on analytic and argumentative tasks, and the second study on personal narrative and expository tasks. In these studies, Ruiz-Funes operationalized the argumentative and expository tasks as more cognitively demanding than the analytic and narrative tasks.

Task-based studies have mainly focused on exploring whether their results correspond to the predictions of the task complexity frameworks. That is, a researcher manipulates a task variable based on the assumption of how it will affect the cognitive demands of the task imposed on learners and, as a result, their language use. Since learner perceptions of language tasks may not always match the intention of the researcher because of their different learning experiences, some researchers (Qin & Karabacak, 2010; Wolfe, 2011) called for the use of an independent measure for task perceptions. Returning to the discussion of genre as a task complexity variable, we can argue that L2 learners may not find it more cognitively demanding to compose argumentative than other writing tasks because of their extensive experience with argumentative writing as a typical genre for standardized testing and higher education (Qin & Karabacak, 2010; Wolfe, 2011).

Many studies such as Yoon (2021), Lu (2011), Qin & Uccelli (2016) indicated that genre indeed functions as a task variable eliciting different language use from L2 learners; argumentative tasks encourage learners to use more syntactically complex language than narrative tasks. Additionally, the result showed that the argumentative essays tended to contain more adverbial and adjectival clauses than the narrative essays did, but nominal clauses were more frequent in the narrative than the argumentative essays.

## 2.3 Factors influencing task complexity by Robinson

In his Triadic Componential Framework (also called the Cognition Hypothesis), Robinson (2001, 2005, 2007) predicted that increasing task complexity along the so-called resources-directing variables may lead to higher structural complexity. Table 1 shows the three different types of task factors related to different levels of task complexity in his Cognition Hypothesis model. *Task complexity* refers to the intrinsic cognitive demands of the task. It distinguishes task characteristics on the basis of the conceptual demands (Robinson, 2007). They are supposed to have differential effects on learning and performance.

Table 1　Robinson's model of task complexity

| Cognitive factors | Interactive factors | Difficulty factors |
|---|---|---|
| Task complexity<br>a) Resource directing e.g.,<br>　+/− few elements<br>　+/− Here-and-Now<br>　+/− no reasoning demands<br>　+/− spatial location<br>　+/− first person perspective<br>b) Resources dispersing e.g.,<br>　+/− planning<br>　+/− single task<br>　+/− prior knowledge<br>　+/− clear structure<br>　+/− few steps<br>　+/− sequence | Task conditions<br>a) participation variables e.g.,<br>　one way/two way<br>　convergent/divergent<br>　open/closed<br>b) participant variables e.g.,<br>　gender<br>　familiarity<br>　power/solidarity | Task difficulty<br>a) affective variables e.g.,<br>　motivation<br>　anxiety<br>　confi-dence<br>b) ability variables e.g.,<br>　working memory<br>　aptitude<br>　proficiency<br>　intelligence |

Robinson's task sequence considered the context of speaking task, which is different from writing task in many aspects. For example, speaking is an online activity, with little space for consideration or planning, while writing is recursive in that the writer can use wide resources to do profound preparation. Few studies have done on the consequence of academic type tasks on cognitive load. Although much research has been done describing the challenge of academic writings faced by college students, the comparison of different academic genres between each other is seldom done.

Argumentation and report are two frequently deployed genres. Argumentative writing often requires the writer to engage in logical reasoning, counter-argumentation, and persuasion, which can be cognitively demanding. Research-based reports, on the other hand, may require extensive information processing, synthesis, and critical analysis of sources, which also imposes a high cognitive load but of a different nature.

As far as resource directing is concerned in Robinson's model, argumentative tasks might have fewer elements to consider but require more reasoning and spatial location (organizing arguments). Reports might have more elements (data, sources) and less immediate reasoning demands but require a broader perspective and integration of information. Both report and argumentative writing benefit from planning and clear structures, which are resource dispersing factors that can help manage cognitive load. Rhetorical moves and steps in empirical studies are helpful (less cognitive loaded) for novice writers to organize their thoughts. But report may involve more steps and complexity in getting first-hand data, doing statistical analysis, and integrating information from various sources.

When participant variables are concerned, familiarity with the genre of argumentation may affect the perceived sense of cognitive load to be lower in favor of argumentation. Affective variables like motivation and confidence could play a role in how writers perceive the difficulty of the task. If learners are more confident in their argumentative skills, they might perceive argumentative tasks as less cognitively demanding than reports. Learners' ability variables such as working memory, aptitude, and proficiency are crucial as well. Argumentative writing might tax working memory with the need to juggle multiple arguments and counterarguments, while research reports might tax memory with the need to recall and synthesize information from various sources.

As few study has addressed the cognitive load comparison of the two genres, this study aims to study the two and explicate distinct roles of genre in influencing cognitive load. It examines argumentative and report writing, two functionally distinct genres widely employed in academic writing. A self-rating questionnaire is used to measure L2 learner perceptions of the writing tasks to explore the connection between cognitive load and writing genres. This study addresses the following question:

- How do the genres of argumentation and report influence L2 learners' perceptions of cognitive load?

## 3. Method

### 3.1　Participants and settings

We invited 417 students writing two different PBAW tasks: 240 from report writing course, 177 from argumentation writing course. Report writing course was provided to one third of the entire undergraduate students who had the best English proficiency in the university. Argumentation writing course was provided to students who selected academic writing course for aiming to improve logic thinking and writing abilities required for further development after graduation. The two courses provided writing instruction in the same semester composing of 14 teaching times. The academic teachers were all experienced in teaching academic English with more than 10 years' experience.

The common objectives of the two courses were to prepare students for university-level academic writing skills and to help them understand the importance of sense of audience in academic writing, academic style, structure and conventions. The specific goals included developing students' academic reading, summarizing, paragraphing, rhetorical and revising skills of research-based argumentation and report, as well as guiding them in completing several multi-draft research-based writing tasks. The difference of the two genres lies in that argumentation writing is to pervade readers on taking a side in a disputable issue, while report is to find a problem, analyze it and provide solutions to the problem. As research method is concerned, argumentation writing is based on second hand resources, while report is mainly based on first hand data.

## 3.2 Instruments

These PBAW tasks gave learners full freedom to choose research topics, and write their own papers. We controlled the length of their writings to be 1000 words for every learner. Self-rating results using a questionnaire (PBAW_CLS) have been used to reflect the cognitive effects of task manipulations on learners' cognitive load (more complex tasks rated as cognitively more demanding). We also asked their confidence of writing these academic papers after learning the course.

## 4. Results

The descriptive results of the cognitive load perception data were presented in Table 2. Test showed that the students perceived different genres as imposing significantly different levels of cognitive load ($t=3.00$, $p=.001$). They felt argumentation writing was less cognitively loaded than report writing. The manipulation of genre actually led to significant changes in the students' perceptions of confidence of writing ($t=-2.92$, $p=.003$). Their confidence of writing was significantly higher for argumentation than for academic report. These results might confirm the role of genre as a variable affecting cognitive load in writing and support the general assumption that argumentative tasks would be cognitively less demanding to L2 writers than report tasks.

**Table 2    Descriptive Statistics for students' perceptions of writing tasks**

| Item | Argument | | Report | | $t$ | $p$ |
|---|---|---|---|---|---|---|
| | M(SD) | 95% CI | M(SD) | 95% CI | | |
| **Cognitive load** | 4.84 (1.86) | [4.42,5.27] | 5.20(1.74) | [4.80,5.59] | −2.92 | .003 |
| **Confidence** | 4.95 (2.00) | [4.49,5.40] | 4.64(2.04) | [4.18,5.11] | 3.00 | .001 |

## 5. Discussion

The results of this study indicated that L2 learners view both genres as imposing high cognitive demands (higher than 4.8 out of the range of 1 to 6), and this can possibly be explained by the prediction of cognitive models of L2 writing (Hayes, 2012; Hyland, 2016) that cognitive pressures are influenced by genre schemas, and previous experiences related to the task. The finding can be explained by lacking learning experiences by L2 learners who have few research-based writing experience for educational and testing purposes, and do not possess well-established genre schemas for it. On the other hand, argumentative tasks would be perceived less cognitively demanding than report tasks because argumentation necessitates learners to use less reasoning and interpretations compared with report. Report writing goes beyond experience and knowledge telling for argumentation based on second hand data (Bereiter & Scardamalia, 1987).

For research based academic report, the multiple steps of doing the task, complex disciplinary conceptions, statistic knowledge, and the difficulty of collecting first hand data, all contributed to the intrinsic cognitive loads of this genre. In the whole writing process, students' working memory is under high challenge weather in learning new disciplinary knowledge or establishing new connections with the previous knowledge. The lower writing confidence shown by learners when doing the task support the finding that they are less prepared to do report writing, compared with the learners who do argumentative writing tasks.

## 6. Conclusion

As evidenced by the result of this study, the cognitive complexity of report writing tasks does have an effect on perceived cognitive load compared with argumentation. The strong connection between genre and cognitive load was proved by the study.

Pedagogical implications of this study involve how teachers need to understand and implement different genres for L2 writing instruction. Teachers are advised to have a clear awareness of their students' difficulties, needs, or preferences for different genres. Based on this understanding, writing tasks appropriate for the students can be designed, selected, and sequenced.

Moreover, L2 writing instruction tends to focus on learners' improvement in argumentative writing skills and pay relatively less attention to other genres. Report writing tasks are more frequently used by graduates, but it is not well trained for most undergraduates in Chinese universities. Building a writing curriculum including various genres would enable L2 learners to develop genre awareness and improve linguistic competence more effectively.

Taking these findings as a starting point, further studies can be conducted to explore how to minimize the unintended high cognitive load of report writing tasks and test the applicability of providing more scaffolding into teaching, by prolonging project doing time, or strictly preventing from using too complicated research methods. Unless research ability is aimed to be cultivated in the PBAW course, narrowly defined academic writing syllabus can even be considered if focusing learners' attention on writing knowledge is a practical choice to lower down cognitive load. By doing so, learners' cognitive resources would convergent on idea translating stage instead of on both idea planning and idea translating stages.

# 7. References

Alexopoulou, E., Patsala, M., & Tsangaridou, N. (2017). Task complexity and genre in L2 writing: An investigation of Greek EFL learners. Journal of Second Language Writing, 36, 47–60.

Berman, R. A., & Slobin, D. I. (1994). Relating events in narrative: A cross-linguistic study. Hillsdale, NJ: Lawrence Erlbaum Associates.

Bereiter, C., & Scardamalia, M. (1987). The Psychology of Written

Composition. Hillsdale, NJ: Lawrence Erlbaum Associate.

Hayes, J. R. (2012). A New Framework for Understanding Cognition and Affect in Writing. In C. M. Levy & S. Ransdell (Eds.), The Science of writing: Theories, Methods, Individual Differences, and Applications (pp. 1–28). Mahwah, NJ: Lawrence Erlbaum Associates.

Hyland, K. (2016). Genre analysis for academic writing. In C. A. MacArthur, S. Graham, & J. Fitzgerald (Eds.) Handbook of writing research (pp. 41–53). New York: The Guilford Press.

Kormos, J. (2011). Task complexity and the development of L2 writing skills. In G. Rijlaarsdam, H. van den Bergh, M. C2. Revista Internacional de Didáctica de las Ciencias Socialesouzijn, & L. Janssen (Eds.), Handbook of writing research (pp. 499–517). New York: Guilford Press.

Kormos, J., & Trebits, A. (2012). Task complexity and the development of L2 writing skills: The case of Hungarian EFL learners. System, 40 (1), 116–127.

Lu, X. (2011). Genre and syntactic complexity in L2 writing: A study of Chinese EFL learners. Journal of Second Language Writing, 20 (3), 161–178.

Ong, C. M., & Zhang, L. J. (2009). Idea support and L2 writing complexity: An exploratory study. TESOL Quarterly, 44 (4), 657–686.

Qin, J., & Karabacak, E. (2010). Genre knowledge and L2 writing performance: A study of Turkish EFL learners. Journal of Second Language Writing, 19 (4), 293–304.

Qin, J., & Uccelli, P. (2016). Genre and L2 writing: The relationship between genre knowledge and syntactic complexity. Journal of Second Language Writing, 29, 36–49.

Revesz, A., Michel, M. C., & Navarro, E. (2017). The impact of task complexity on L2 writing performance: A comparison of three types of tasks. Journal of Second Language Writing, 34, 22–34.

Robinson, P. (2001). Task complexity, cognitive resources, and syllabus design: A triadic framework for examining task influences on SLA. In P. Robinson (Ed.), Cognition and Second Language Instruction (pp. 287–318). Cambridge: Cambridge University Press.

Robinson, P. (2005). Cognitive complexity and task sequencing: Studies in a componential framework for second language task design. International Review of Applied Linguistics 43: 1–32.

Robinson, P. (2007). Criteria for classifying and sequencing pedagogic tasks. In Maria del Pilar García Mayo (Ed.) Investigating Tasks in Formal Language Learning (pp. 7–26). Clevedon: Multilingual Matters.

Ruiz-Funes, R. (2015). Task complexity and genre in L2 writing: A study of Spanish EFL learners. Journal of Second Language Writing, 24 (1), 1–13.

Skehan, P. (1998). A cognitive approach to language learning. Oxford:

Oxford University Press.

Staples, S., & Reppen, R. (2016). Genre and language variation in L2 writing: A corpus-based study. Journal of Second Language Writing, 31, 37. Revista Internacional de Didáctica de las Ciencias Socialesouzijn, & L. Janssen (Eds.), Handbook of writing research (pp. 499–517). New York: Guilford Press.

Tavakoli, P. (2014). Task complexity and L2 writing performance: A longitudinal study. Language Learning, 64 (2), 381–41 constatívulos. prepub; Quelques remarques sur les deuteronomistes devant la loi mosaïque comme loi morale contemporaine. Revue Internationale de Didáctica de las Ciencias Socialesouzijn, & L. Janssen (Eds.), Handbook of writing research (pp. 499–517). New York: Guilford Press.

Wolfe, D. E. (2011). Genre and the L2 writing process: A case study of Chinese EFL learners. Journal of Second Language Writing, 20(2), 117–133.

Yoon, H., & Polio, C. (2017). Genre and syntactic complexity in L2 writing: A comparison of narrative and argumentative essays. Journal of Second Language Writing, 33, 127–140.

# 第三部分
## 认知负荷理论下的课程设置

# Part III
## Cognitive theory guided curriculum

# 第十三章　任务型学术英语写作课程的认知负荷层级设置

## Chapter 13　PBAW curriculum with cognitive load layers

### 本章内容概要 Abstract of the chapter

　　基于前面章节认知负荷影响因素的分析，PBAW 课程设计可以利用认知负荷理论，从三个方面调节课程的复杂性：首先是学习者因素。学习者的二语阅读 / 写作能力、项目有关专业知识和学术研究知识，以及学习者对研究性学习的动机是否足够积极是调节认知负荷的主观层面；其次是任务本身的复杂性：研究项目中概念的复杂性、问题和解决方案所涉及的认知过程的复杂性、数据获取和分析步骤的多少、写作时间和写作长短是影响认知负荷的客观层面；最后是任务执行的环境因素：教师的支持、学习小组的支持、数据的可用性以及技术手段（如，人工智能工具）的可获得性是影响认知负荷的环境因素。基于认知负荷理论的课程设计应将这三方面的要素整合到不同复杂度层级的 PBAW 课程中，从低复杂性学习任务和高教学支持开始，辅助不同能力的学习者，一直到自主完成高复杂性任务。本章给出基于认知负荷理论的课程设置指导原则。这 8 个课程设置原则分别是：1. 确定课程任务所需的前行知识和能力；2. 确定课程任务复杂度的层级；3. 了解学习者写作能力的发展；4. 确定支持水平的高低；5. 训练合作学习能力；6. 监控认知负荷；7. 明确教师的重要性；8. 控制学术

资源。接着作者用一个任务复杂度层级设置案例说明了该理论的
应用。

## 1. Introduction

As illustrated in the previous chapters, cognitive load of PBAW is related to the complexity of the task itself, such as the genre of argumentation or report which decides the perceived sense of cognitive load. It can be related to learning environment, such as the scaffolding of knowledge or motivation provided by teacher and team members, the use of AI tools etc. It can also be related to learners' previous knowledge related to disciplinary knowledge, L2 reading ability, and research knowledge. Based on the findings of the factors that affect cognitive load, PBAW curriculum informed by cognitive load theory could be worked out to help teachers in making decisions on how to structure their course in order to support student learning academic writing with proper cognitive load. Using the concepts and principles from cognitive load theory (Young et al. 2014; Leppink et al. 2015), this chapter attempts to bridge theory into the practice of curriculum development.

In essence, cognitive load theory can be used to deal with the potential problem that the processing demands evoked by learning tasks as complex as those in PBAW may exceed the processing capacity of the learner's cognitive system (i.e. they cause overload) or that the learner's cognitive resources are allocated in a suboptimal manner. This is a challenge for both teachers and students, as meaningful learning often requires substantial cognitive processing using a cognitive system that is inherently limited (namely, the human brain). In cognitive load theory, learning and instruction are structured in such a way that we take into account the mental effort being used in the working memory when dealing with a particular task.

## 2. Factors to be considered when designing PBAW curriculum based on CLT

In the PBAW course context, as shown in Table 1, there are three factors to consider when evaluating the perceived sense of cognitive load for a project. The first factor, task complexity, pertains to the difficulty of a learning task or activity. For PBAW tasks, the extent of complexity of the problem being studied involves complexity of genre, the interaction of concepts, steps needed to obtain data, steps of analyzing data, and interactive factors involved in reasoning. For example, if a problem (e.g., "How is economic condition of China in the past 10 years") involves descriptive information, instead of comparing and contrasting information (e.g., "Compare economic condition of China with Japan in the past 10 years"), the problem is less complex. If the problem can be solved with second-hand resources available from library (e.g., GDP of China in the past 10 years), instead of first-hand research (e.g., GDP of a city in Shanghai in the past 10 years), the problem is easier to be solved; The problem of reasoning with less interactive factors (e.g., why Chinese economic development is fast in the past 10 years) is easier compared with reasoning with more interactive factors (e.g., Comparing with the past 10 years, will China develop with the same speed in the coming 10 years). Genre theories are insightful in considering the difference of cognitive complexity. Broadly speaking, as argumentation writing is mainly based on second-hand data, it is less loaded compared with report writing which involves first hand data investigation, as far as steps of collecting and analyzing data are concerned. However, establishing logic connections between various elements are complicated of another kind when doing argumentation task.

According to Sweller (1988) task complexity cannot be reduced, by chunking or segmentation, if the variables interact. This is a generalization of the point that dimensions cannot be chunked if relations between them must be used in making the current decision. It is analogous to say that an interaction cannot be decomposed into the constituent variables. Because each variable influences the effect of the others, they must be interpreted jointly. Complexity of a cognitive process can only be reduced if decisions can be made about a subset of variables without taking the remaining variables into account. If task complexity is to be lowered, cutting down the number of interactive factors can be considered. For example, in English mediated instructions

(EMI), learners can learn related disciplinary knowledge with L1 before attending to EMI class, so that establishing some of related schema and eliminating interactive factors in learning new knowledge. In PBAW course, academic papers written in Chinese language is helpful in establishing disciplinary knowledge efficiently.

**Table 1　PBAW cognitive load factors**

| Task Complexity factors | Learner factors | Environmental factors |
|---|---|---|
| a. | a. Knowledge/ability variables e.g., | a. Tutor e.g., |
| +/− complexity of genre | +/− Reading/writing proficiency | +/− Content lecture/ |
| +/− complexity of concept | +/− Research knowledge | +/− example illustration/ |
| +/− steps of obtaining data | +/− Topic knowledge | +/− group tutorial/ |
| +/− steps of analyzing data | +/− aptitude | +/− writing feed back |
| +/− interactive factors | +/− intelligence | b. Learning group e.g. |
| b. Conditions | b. affective variables e.g., | +/− Brain storm for |
| +/− time | +/− motivation | planning/ |
| +/− writing length | +/− anxiety | +/− data sharing/ |
| | +/− confidence | +/− cooperate when writing |
| | c. learning skills/experience e.g., | c. source availability e.g., |
| | +/− self-regulation learning | +/− AI tools/ |
| | strategies | +/− reliable data/ |
| | | +/− topic related resources |

The second factor, learners' previous knowledge or ability, includes reading, writing and researching knowledge or ability. As shown in our studies, PBAW task is reading and writing integrated task, which prerequires high reading ability at least at the level of higher B2 or C1 according to CEFR. Topic knowledge and self-regulation skills are, similarly, important factors in influencing the effects of lowing cognitive load and contributing to writing performance as shown in the two studies in the book. Previous knowledge of how to use statistic tools is also required before starting PBAW tasks. The individual baffling effects of these elements and their interaction effects would make cognitive load multiply if left uncontrolled.

Finally, the third or environmental issue includes teaching support, team cooperation, and the use of technology. Teaching support extends all the way from fully worked examples, detailed instruction on researching and writing knowledge, team writing, using AI tools help ideation, to autonomous task performance. Teaching support plays a pivotal role in guiding students through the complex process of academic research and writing. Experienced tutors can provide valuable feedback, clarify concepts, and offer strategies for managing the research and writing process, thereby enhancing the quality and coherence of the final output. Team cooperation is another critical factor that can significantly impact academic writing. Collaborative efforts can lead to the sharing of ideas, division of labor, and peer review, all of which contribute to a more robust and comprehensive research project. Working in teams can also help students develop essential communication and interpersonal skills that are invaluable in academic and professional settings. The use of technology, particularly AI tools, has revolutionized the way research and writing are conducted. AI can assist in various stages of the research process, from literature reviews to data analysis. Tools like natural language processing can help in summarizing large volumes of text, while AI-powered writing assistants can offer suggestions for grammar, style, and even content. They can also help in organizing references and citations, which is a common challenge in academic writing.

PBAW curricula comprise the following elements: (a) Students are assembled in small groups; (b) these groups receive training in group collaboration skills prior to the instruction; (c) they do this by initially discussing the problem at hand, activating whatever prior knowledge is available to each of them; (d) a tutor is present to facilitate the learning; (e) (s)he does this by using class lectures, group conference, sample writing, scoring rubric, writing feedback, mock academic conference etc.; and (f) resources for self-directed study by the students such as text books, sample articles, academic data, team to work with, disciplinary tutor and AI tools. Although the exact implementation of these elements may differ between curricula (Lloyd-Jones et al., 1998), which, as Dochy et al. (2015) point out, is the case with every instructional approach, these elements can be and are being used to provide guidance in alignment with students' cognitive architecture. In terms of CLT, these elements of PBAW are used to optimize the relationships between the intrinsic load imposed by the task and the extrinsic load imposed by the instruction.

When using cognitive load theory as the principal model, curriculum planners ought to consider factors in three aspects: learners'

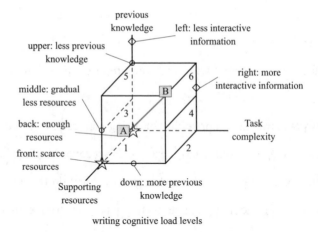

**Figure 1    CLT based PBAW course design cube**

previous knowledge, task complexity, and instructional support (Leppink et al. 2015). These issues can be conceived as three dimensions of a cube, as depicted in Figure 1. The purpose of teaching is to help a learner with low competence (Point A) to improve his/her competence gradually to arrive at Point B with high competence. In designing courses, task complexity (on the right side) is increased, while supporting resources are decreased. The starting point of learning is decided by judging previous knowledge owned by the learner. Detailed analysis of the factors for the three sides of the cube will be given in the following part in the context of PBAW course.

## 3. Curriculum designing guidelines

The above PBAW cognitive load model illustrates the factors adjustable to the overall PBAW load. In designing a project these factors should be considered by the designers. Working memory load may be affected by the intrinsic nature of the learning tasks (intrinsic load), by the manner in which the tasks are presented (extraneous load), and by the learning that actually occurs (germane load) when dealing with intrinsic load. Cognitive load theory assumes that intrinsic and extraneous cognitive loads are additive. For teaching complex tasks (i.e. involving high element-interactive materials), the sum of the intrinsic and extraneous loads may easily surpass working memory capacity and yield overload. Then, extraneous load and, if the reduction of extraneous load is still insufficient, intrinsic load must be lowered to free up processing resources necessary for learning. We discuss ways to integrate learning tasks and activities that facilitate an individual student's journey through a multi-level curriculum. The following guidelines should be considered when designing PBAW course.

• Guideline 1: Determine the prerequisite knowledge for PBAW course

Cognitive load depended on students' prior knowledge. It is important to decide the competences needed for PBAW tasks. We have found the necessity for learners to gain basic reading skills before the possibility to use reading and writing strategies effectively. For the relationship between effective learning and the preparedness of topic knowledge, research ability, motivation and affection, more exploration should be carried out. After the understanding of prerequired knowledge and ability, elf-evaluation of competence can be provided for the learners intending to choose the course. For those students who are less competent, for example, academic reading training or research knowledge training should be provided before the course.

Prerequisite knowledge is needed because higher demanding on working memory would easily be over taxed. Intrinsic load depends on the number of elements that must be processed simultaneously in working memory, a number which, in turn, depends on the extent of element interactivity of the materials or tasks that must be learned. Tasks with high element interactivity are difficult to understand and yield a high cognitive load because learners must deal with several elements simultaneously. The only way to foster understanding and to reduce intrinsic cognitive load is to develop schemas that incorporate the interacting elements. It follows that a large number of interacting elements for one person with less previous knowledge might be included within a single element for another more experienced person who already has a schema that incorporates the elements.

- Guideline 2: Determine the number of complexity levels

Failing to differentiate in complexity, we may under-load some students (Young & Stanton 2002) and overload others (Kalyuga & Hanham 2011). The more a student advances, the more complexity — in terms of for instance factors to consider in a diagnosis or in terms of the elaborateness of a sequence of moves — this student can handle. To neither under-load nor overload the student, we should strive for a gradual increase in task complexity (Leppink & Van den Heuvel 2015). An example of this gradual increase could be from tasks requiring less cognitive processing, such as summary, literature review, comparison and contrast, to genres involving more processing steps or more complex reasoning such as argumentation or report.

- Guideline 3: Move to higher complexity

As for task complexity, we must keep students' zone of proximal development in mind. To avoid overload, starting at or moving to a higher level of complexity should be accompanied by sufficient instructional support. The use of worked examples, completion tasks, non-specific goals, and presentations that avoid learners having to split their attention between multiple sources constitute well-known tools to reduce redundant cognitive load among novice learners (Sweller et al. 1998). These tools can be applied at any level of complexity.

- Guideline 4: Determine the number of support levels

Choices regarding the extent of variation in support depend on students' prior knowledge, the competency under consideration, choices with regard to competency end terms, and logistic factors. It is of crucial importance to consider which tools are needed to what extent for which complexity and which competence levels to avoid increases in redundant cognitive load. That is, tools aimed at reducing redundant cognitive load among novices tend to contribute to redundant cognitive load among learners who are able to find their way without that guidance (Kalyuga et al. 2001). From the robust finding that the need for instructional support on a type of learning task of a given complexity decreases as learners advance (Kalyuga et al. 2015), it follows that one should start with relatively high support and gradually fade that support for that type of learning task with time.

For instance, if one cannot yet get beyond low-complexity fast reading and summarizing task, one is unlikely to be successful in dealing with synthesizing of several literatures. If one is still struggling with simple word completion tasks in a textbook, one cannot expect a more solid understanding of sentence patterns that is needed to have a somewhat meaningful communication in that language with a teacher in class let alone for some meaningful communication in an everyday environment of native speakers. Likewise, if one does not understand what a standard deviation is, one cannot understand statistical tools including that concept, and consequently, one cannot expect to be able to appropriately apply these tools to real cases. One appears to need a sufficient proficiency at lower layers to continue the journey at a subsequent layer.

- Guideline 5: Train Group Collaboration Skills

To mitigate the extraneous cognitive load when unfamiliar instructional techniques or technologies are introduced, students should be trained beforehand. This training is crucial for effective group collaboration, focusing on translating problems into individual study issues and structuring group communication. At Shanghai University of International Business and Economics, students are trained in a systematic step-by-step procedure that involves clarifying terms, defining problems, brainstorming, systematizing ideas, identifying learning issues, guiding individual study, and sharing and discussing findings. This procedure simplifies the learning process and reduces unnecessary cognitive load. Additionally, students are trained to play various roles, such as the chairperson and scribe, to facilitate group dynamics and ensure adherence to the seven-step procedure, further minimizing extraneous cognitive load. This comprehensive training enables students to engage effectively with the curriculum and manage cognitive demands efficiently.

- Guideline 6: Keep track of cognitive load

Apart from qualitative and quantitative indicators of performance in formative assessments, teachers and curriculum developers should consider keeping track of cognitive load experienced by their students along the way (Leppink & Van den Heuvel 2015; Leppink et al. 2015). When timed carefully, these measures can help teachers and curriculum developers to understand to what extent specific choices made on the dimensions of the cube may stimulate or hamper learning on the part of individual learners. This may result in specific adjustments in terms of personalized learning trajectories, the design of specific coursework or training or perhaps adjustments in the end terms or assessment thereof.

Simultaneously, questions on cognitive load may help students to reflect on their learning experiences and stimulate self-regulated learning.

- Guideline 7: Tutorial is important

When a learning task is too complex or if crucial knowledge isn't activated in group discussions, tutors are advised to share this knowledge to reduce intrinsic cognitive load. Research aligns with Cognitive Load Theory (CLT), suggesting that the effectiveness of tutors is contingent on their subject-matter expertise, students' prior knowledge, and the instruction's structure. For instance, Schmidt (1994) discovered that tutors' expertise was critical in courses with low student prior knowledge or poor instruction structure. Tutors are also instructed to minimize extraneous load by preventing students from focusing on irrelevant details. When appropriate, tutors can encourage a germane load by prompting students to engage in cognitive activities that enhance learning, such as self-explanation or reflection on their group contributions. Tutors are equipped with an instructional guide to align learning objectives with the group's problem-solving process.

- Guideline 8: Limiting resources is needed

Searching for literature and other resources is considered an important constituent skill that is mastered by successful professionals. However, successfully searching for literature is highly dependent on domain knowledge. Hence, novice learners are likely to engage in irrelevant literature search activities, which impose a high extraneous load. Therefore, novice students in PBAW are provided with a restricted set of resources (e.g., book chapters, articles) to choose from for individual study. With increasing expertise students are provided with fewer and fewer specified resources to stimulate them to search for relevant literature themselves.

## 4. A model curriculum

The model is designed to carefully titrate cognitive load: Learners progress through a series of whole tasks of increasing difficulty, with each task appropriately scaffolded to maintain learners in their zone of proximal development. The four components of instructional design are 1) learning tasks, 2) supportive information, 3) just-in-time information, and 4) part-task practice. The model will be briefly recapped here.

*Learning tasks* form the backbone of the curriculum. Learning tasks are based on authentic examples of the whole task (e.g. writing a case presentation). The learning tasks are organized into "task classes," deliberately sequenced from simple-to-complex. All the tasks within a given task class are relatively equivalent in complexity. More advanced task classes increase in complexity as the learner demonstrates mastery of a class and moves on to the next. Throughout the curriculum, learning tasks are deliberately varied to provide a wide array of practice opportunities, representative of the variety encountered in real life.

A high level of support is provided early on, and progressively diminishes over time, both within and across task classes. This support is labelled as *supportive* or *just-in-time information* depending on whether it supports all of the activities in a given task class or only a specific task support to a specific student group. Supportive information is provided at the beginning of a task class and is always available to aid learning. Supportive information can explain how to approach a problem (e.g. offer a reading strategy); suggest how the concepts are related (e.g. provide a mental model); or offer foundational knowledge. *Just-in-time information*, in contrast, is only relevant to a specific learning project and not others in the task class. The information is provided right when the learner needs it (e.g. in group conference time). The final component in the instructional design model is *part-task practice*. It is only needed when a routine aspect of the complex skill requires a degree of automation, such as fast reading for main idea.

- Approach to develop the curriculum

We used a case of curriculum developed in 2023 to show here. This is an academic writing course provided to undergraduates. Students had no academic writing learning experience, and their discipline-related knowledge is limited. Before designing PBAW course, we defined teaching objectives.

We took a broad definition of academic writing competence point of view, and included the abilities needed in the whole writing process into training scope. As most students learned the course to prepare for business courses taught in English, we decided that the course aimed to cultivate PBAW competence of three levels based on their previous knowledge: Level one course aimed at training students with limited business knowledge and low reading ability. We aimed to train their habit of reading economic news about the economy they are researching on, using different news sources. We chose synthesis as the genre of writing; Level two aimed to train learners' ability to analyzing economic facts. We chose essay as the genre of writing; Level three train their abilities to use statistical analyzing methods and the ability to create tables and graphs to support their point of view, we chose empirical research report as the genre of writing. After deciding the aim of the course, teachers set out to identify the constituent components of skills in a project that must be integrated by the learner. Following an initial brainstorm on what made the project, teachers organized sub-skills into three broad categories: information reading and synthesis, economical analyzing essay, and report writing. With each category detailed skills were clearly listed in the curriculum, and were allocated to lectures in the course.

Using the themes and categories as a guide, we developed *project descriptions* for three classes of increasing task complexity. All conditions that simplified the whole task of writing a report were applied to Level one class (e.g. the context was casual with ample time;

392    任务型学术英语写作认知负荷的调节策略研究

information was easy to get hand on; the reasoning was straightforward.) Similar descriptions were developed for the remaining classes, with attention given to how complexity increased in each category from class to class. The process of developing the curriculum began once the task class descriptions had been developed.

- Curricular content

Learning projects were developed and then sequenced across classes from simple to complex. Within each class, support for learners was designed to be high initially, then faded over time. In level one class, the project was on less challenging reading and writing skills, including judging the value of information, summarizing, synthesizing, and understanding key economic concepts. In level two class, the training focused on basic macroeconomic condition of the country being chosen, helping students develop some economic knowledge and more complicated disciplinary knowledge. In level three class, the task focused on full research-based report writing.

Supportive information was designed to scaffold students' learning across in every task class. Supportive information took many forms, including brief lectures on reading and writing strategies, genre knowledge, and data analysis exercise. How to find reliable economic information, fast reading to judge the quality of information, summarizing, report structure, and genre knowledge were provided. For more advanced task classes, supportive information increased in complexity. For example, the Level three class focused more on the development of complex researching method and with critical reasoning ability.

Each individual learning task was evaluated to determine if just-in-time information was valuable to support learning. This was done based on what the average learner at that level would require based on faculty input during the workshop. Not every learning task required this type of scaffolding, but to keep learners in their zone of proximal development, careful attention was paid to titrating intrinsic cognitive load. Intrinsic load was estimated by considering the interaction between the nature of the learning task and the expertise of the learner. One type of just-in-time information provided in early task classes was targeted information about important macroeconomic indexes, and news sources. This allowed novice learners to focus on the process and content of case country. Another common type of just-in-time information was formative feedback. In different classes, we utilized feedback that shifted emphasis on different learning objectives. In level one class the feedback was focused on information reliability. In level two class the feedback was focused on information organizing quality with the consideration of interactive of concepts. For level three, the feedback was focused on research method, logic and creativity of the research. This technique avoided overwhelming the student with too much simultaneous feedback, which can impede learning.

Part-task practice was used several times, and especially when a high level of automaticity was desired to improve performance on routine aspects of the whole task. In the PBAW course for undergraduates, we used *part-task practice* to teach students how to do fast reading and how to use statistic software in making tables and figures. These two skills are needed for preparing their writing. In level one task class, students practiced reporting "valuable" news (e.g. income of citizens, unemployed rate, foreign direct investment of the country that they choose to study.) We encouraged wide reading to familiarize learners with important economic news sources and familiar with normal terminology. In higher task complex classes, learners needed to insert their own analyzing, such as determining if the country they were studying is suitable for doing business or investment.

- Implementation

The curriculum is intended for longitudinal implementation over one or two semesters. Each class outline contains multiple sessions, and typically aligns with a phase in the curriculum. Tasks are spaced out to provide variable practice over a significant time frame. This curriculum may be horizontally integrated with instruction of other complex skills in a longitudinal reading and writing skills course.

A faculty development session on cognitive load and the curriculum model can help make the curriculum more learner-centered. Supportive information, learning tasks and just-in-time information in the outlines are targeted toward the *average* anticipated learner level. Skilled faculty can further adjust the curriculum based on individual learners' abilities. For instance, a student who is excelling may be given more challenging cases early on, and a learner who is struggling may be offered additional scaffolding. Variations of the curriculum have been implemented at various student levels in my university. The following is the description of the three projects:

- Projects description:

*Choose a country to study with your team. This country should not be your home country. To avoid overlap between students, please share your country choice with the teacher (first come first serve). Get into the habit of following the economic news about the economy you are researching, using different news sources. You are advised to show trends in macro performance over the last decade (latest). Use data, tables and graphs to present the research.*

*Necessary for a good score. You will need to provide a bibliography of at least 6 references in your essay. You will need to use Harvard referencing. Your report needs to show proof that you have researched and analyzed information. You have used critical thinking and analysis. Hopefully economic theory, a high-quality written English and a logical flow can be found out.*

*Extra guide*

*You may use the following databases to find data: Trading Economics,*

*World Bank Databank, United Nations Database, International Labor Organization (ILO) Statistics and Database, and other sources advised by your tutor.*

*You must not reference any user-generated sources of information such as Wikipedia or forums. You could read these to get a general overview for your own understanding, but they should not be used in your references as they are not always reliable sources of information. If you are unsure of what is expected of you, please speak to your tutor.*

*Structure is important. The idea of setting essays is to offer you the chance to make a longer, more complex argument. Nonetheless, in the model we recommend, the fundamentals remain the same. In each paragraph, a flow of the main idea (thesis) —explanation/reasoning (justification) — evidence/example (support) is an excellent structure to use. An essay has conventional sections that it is wise to follow. These are an introduction, the main body and a conclusion. The "LSE" essay structure can be described as say what you're going to say (intro), say it in detail (main body), and say what you've said (conclusion). Although this may appear repetitive, it offers the reader great clarity. Also, if you think about the executive summary, background, analysis and conclusions/recommendations sections of a business report, you can see that a similar structure holds.*

*The following tasks were based on different complexity levels. For level one class, task 1 was required. For level two class, task 1 and task 2 was required. For level three class, task 1 and 3 was required.*

**Task 1:** *Synthesizing*

*Research and synthesize economic condition of a chosen economy in the past 10 years from the following aspects: 1) the GDP / GDP per capita of the chosen economy. 2) the main reasons for the economic growth/decline over the last decade. 3) the business/economic cycle in the context of your chosen economy. 4) the levels of unemployment in the economy researched, and 5) policies that were taken by the government to reduce unemployment in the economy.*

*(Note: Only task 1, information description, is required for Level one students. This writing aims to improve reading ability and accumulate their knowledge of vocabulary and disciplinary concepts. Genre of writing is summarizing and synthesizing with less complexity compared with reasoning required for students in Level two. Students have a semester to do the project, with teacher and team member to support. When they are familiar with the economic condition of the chosen country, and they have improved their reading ability, they are ready to proceed with task 2. Teachers should keep record of the difficulties met by learners in the process, provide in time support. Teachers should keep record of cognitive load felt by learners when doing the task, the effort made, and their performance.)*

***Task 2:*** *Essay writing*

*Based on your understanding of the economic conditions of the chosen economy, explain the main reasons for the economic growth/ decline over the last decade. Describe the business/economic cycle in the context of your chosen economy, and comment on the policies taken by the Government to deal with the business/economic cycle. Use data to explain the impacts of inflation and the balance of payment (deficit or surplus) on the economic agents.*

*(Note: Level 2 students do both task 1(information description) and task 2(information evaluation). Commenting is cognitively more complex than summarizing. The two writing tasks required for Level two students are more complex compared with Level one. In the learning process more scaffolding is needed for research knowledge and genre knowledge. Sample paper with similar topic or research method would be helpful. Writing knowledge of how to describe and report tables and figures is included. Students with good statistic knowledge can use analyzing skills in supporting their analysis. Teachers should keep record of cognitive load, effort of learning, and achievement before deciding if learners are ready to proceed to the next level.)*

***Task 3:*** *Report Writing based on first-hand research*

*Based on your understanding of the chosen economy, discuss the possibilities for doing international investment or international trade with it. You need to consider a detailed line of trade to do analysis.*

*Use economic and social development data analysis to support your view.*

*(Note: For Level 3 students, task 3 requires to find valuable information, consider multiple interactive factors in analyzing. They also need to create statistic data with tables or figures to establish logic relationship between economic variables. Writing knowledge of how to write empirical research paper is included, focused on method and result parts. Level 3 suits students with good disciplinary, research and writing ability. Linguistic and business teachers are encouraged to work together guiding students learning.)*

The following assessment criteria can also serve as a writing guide, or a checklist for essay writing.

**Table 2　Assessment criteria for PBAW essay writing**

| *Dimensions* | *Descriptors* |
| --- | --- |
| *Focus* | ***Purpose and Audience***<br>• *Demonstrates good **awareness of purpose**—to summarize or to analyze, to inform or to persuade*<br>• *Demonstrates good **awareness of audience**—supporters or opponents, specialists or non-specialists*<br>• *Creates an appropriate **tone** for the purpose and the audience **Introduction (like an inverted triangle)***<br>• *Has an engaging **hook***<br>• *Gives general/**background** information that connects the hook to the thesis, . **basic concepts** explained if necessary*<br>• *Contains a **thesis**, including a claim and reasons, being assertive and sophisticated **Conclusion (like a regular triangle)***<br>• ***Links back** to the thesis*<br>• *Leaves a **lasting impression** to the audience by posing a question and proposing a solution, providing advice, expressing hope, or calling for action* |

continue

| Dimensions | Descriptors |
|---|---|
| Content | **Essay Development (Coherence)**<br>• The thesis statement is **supported fully** by supporting points<br>• The **controlling idea** is developed fully, **supported** with effective evidence: examples, statistics, expert opinions, etc., followed by explanations<br>• Credible **sources** are integrated |
| Organization | **Logic and Cohesion**<br>• Arranges supporting points **logically** to persuade<br>• Creates cohesion (sense of **flow**) between and within paragraphs, using cohesive devices naturally |
| Style | **Language and Vocabulary**<br>• Demonstrates sentence **fluency**, the readability for ears<br>• Uses appropriate **vocabulary** to create **persuasive devices** (ethos, logos, pathos, stylistic techniques, etc.) to serve the purpose and the audience<br>• Uses **clear** and **concise** language, cutting off unnecessary words |
| Citation | **Citations and References**<br>• Uses **APA** style for documentation<br>• Cites all information sources properly (without plagiarism)<br>• Uses no more than 1 long quotation; if used, it is formatted correctly<br>• In-text citations include **snippet quotations** in " " and author names and page numbers in ( )<br>• The works-cited list is formatted correct and complete, **matching** the intext citations |
| Conventions | **Grammar and Mechanics**<br>• Grammar and sentence structures are correct<br>• There are no comma splices, run-ons, or fragments<br>• Punctuations, capitalizations, and spellings are correct |

The following assessment criteria can also serve as a writing guide, or a checklist for report writing.

**Table 3　Assessment criteria for PBAW report writing.**

| | Incomplete 0–1 | Unsatisfactory 2–3 marks | Satisfactory 4–5 marks | Strong 6–7 marks | Exceptional 8–10 marks |
|---|---|---|---|---|---|
| Literature review & introduction | Work is incomplete and / or bears no /little resemblance to the task. | • Limited evidence of a literature review / having taken place / literature review was inappropriate or ineffectual.<br>• The introduction fails to describe the previous research in appropriate detail / it is unclear how the previous research relates to the topic under investigation. | • There is some evidence of a literature review having taken place.<br>• The introduction adequately describes the previous research which is related to the topic under investigation.<br>• Reference is made to at least one piece of appropriate research which may be from a reliable / unreliable source. | • Clear evidence of a literature review having taken place.<br>• The introduction effectively describes the previous research which is clearly and directly linked to the topic under investigation.<br>• Previous research is clearly explained and mentioned throughout the introduction.<br>• Reference is made to one or more relevant pieces of research which are from reliable sources. | • Evidence of an in-depth and highly relevant literature review having taken place.<br>• The introduction flows showing a high level of understanding of previous research in the area under investigation.<br>• Detailed reference is made to one major piece of research, although others may be mentioned alongside.<br>• All research mentioned comes from highly reliable sources. |

continue

| | Incomplete 0–1 | Unsatisfactory 2–3 marks | Satisfactory 4–5 marks | Strong 6–7 marks | Exceptional 8–10 marks |
|---|---|---|---|---|---|
| Research aim (If required) | • Work is incomplete and / or bears no /little resemblance to the task. | • The aim is absent / inappropriate/ does not relate to the prior research contained in the introduction. | • The aim of the study is clearly stated and linked to the previous research contained in the introduction.<br>• Questions devised are appropriate in number, style, and relevance. | • The aim of the study is clear. It is obviously linked to the previous research and relevant for the topic under investigation.<br>• Questions are sufficient in number to address the task in hand and are very pertinent. | • The aim of the study is highly relevant to the research contained in the introduction and is very succinctly stated.<br>• Questions are well-conceived to specifically address the aim of the study which is exceptionally relevant to the topic under investigation.<br>• An appropriate number of open and closed questions are used competently to gather very specific data to address the aim. |

continue

|  |  | Incomplete | Unsatisfactory | Satisfactory | Strong | Exceptional |
|  |  | 0–1 | 2–3 marks | 4–5 marks | 6–7 marks | 8–10 marks |
|---|---|---|---|---|---|---|
| research method (if required) |  | • No evidence of research having taken place. <br> • Work is incomplete/ bears no resemblance to the task. | • Research may be ineffectual (e.g., inappropriate number of participants / did not manage to collect majority of questionnaires /do not have enough time to conduct sufficient number of interviews). <br> • Method section is absent / severely lacking in detail with parts missing completely (e.g., participants / method / materials, etc). | • There is evidence that some research has taken place (small number of participants / small number of completed questionnaires / interviews). <br> • Method section is adequate with all individual sections being addressed. | • Research has clearly taken place with sufficient reading and critical thinking. <br> • Method section is completed in its entirety with enough detail for the study to be replicated. | • Research has obviously taken place as evidence by a good summary and clear presentation. <br> • Method section is completed with a high level of detail that would easily allow for replication. |

continue

| | Incomplete | Unsatisfactory | Satisfactory | Strong | Exceptional |
| | 0-1 | 2-3 marks | 4-5 marks | 6-7 marks | 8-10 marks |
|---|---|---|---|---|---|
| Results (if required) | Work is incomplete/ bears no resemblance to the task. | • Results are partially incomplete / inappropriately presented.<br>• No graphical representation. | • Results section is complete. An attempt has been made at providing some descriptive statistics but may contain errors.<br>• A graphical representation of the data is provided and clearly labelled.<br>• There is a basic level of description of the statistics presented, but not necessarily comprehensive. | • Descriptive statistics are well presented in a table with an appropriate title.<br>• Graphical representation of the data is appropriate for the data collected and is clearly labelled and titled.<br>• There is a clear description of what the data shows. | • Results are extremely well presented with attention to detail in the presentation including appropriate labels and thoughtful titles.<br>• Descriptive statistics are appropriately chosen to highlight the aim of the study.<br>• The description demonstrates clear understanding of what the data shows. |

continue

| | Incomplete 0–1 | Unsatisfactory 2–3 marks | Satisfactory 4–5 marks | Strong 6–7 marks | Exceptional 8–10 marks |
|---|---|---|---|---|---|
| Discussion | • Work is incomplete/ bears no resemblance to the task. | • Discussion of results is extremely limited or incomplete. <br> • There may be an attempt to link the results of this study to that mentioned in the introduction although the link may not be clear. <br> • There is no attempt to identify strengths and/or limitations / suggestions are inappropriate. | • Discussion of results is limited but appropriate. <br> • There is an attempt to link the results of this study to the study/ studies mentioned in the introduction. <br> • Identification of strengths and/or limitations of this study are tentative/limited. | • Discussion of results is appropriate and clearly linked to the research mentioned in the introduction. <br> • Identification of strengths and limitations of this study are appropriate and demonstrate reasonable understanding of how research progresses knowledge. | • Discussion of results is highly relevant. <br> • The discussion flows, with clear links made between the results of the current study to studies mentioned in the introduction. <br> • Identification of strengths and limitations of this study are highly appropriate and show an excellent level of understanding of research and how it progresses knowledge. |
| Citation | • Work is incomplete/ bears no resemblance to the task. | • References are incomplete / do not follow required format. | • References appear in standard format for all the studies mentioned in the introduction. | • References appear in a reference list at the end of the report in standard format. <br> • All references contained within the introduction appear in the reference list. <br> • There may be occasional referencing error. | • All references in the introduction are referenced in correct standard format. They also all appear correctly in the reference list at the end of the document. |

## 5.  Suggestions for future research

This chapter provides researchers and education designers with factors to consider when designing curriculum, and these factors should be used along with performance indicators to judge the suitability of the course designed. Preferably, these variables should be measured repeatedly in the whole process of PBAW course. It has been demonstrated that a one-time measurement of cognitive load using single items at the end of a series of tasks yields higher ratings than the average of multiple repeated measurements. Add to this the notion that cognitive load can vary substantially throughout and between learning activities, and one realizes the importance of administering cognitive load and performance measures repeatedly. Finally, one should not aggregate these measurements to one average score but treat them as they are in multilevel analysis or path analysis for accurate outcomes and interpretations. In the case that a larger series of repeated measurements is considered, for instance eight tasks, one could seek a combination of administering single-item ratings—such as the mental effort rating scale or single items after each task, and a multiple-item rating scale after each block of tasks. In any case, the repeated administration of cognitive load measures can help to study the guidelines provided in the previous section, which are based on more than two decades of CLT and research inspired by that theory. Further, it can help to facilitate research that seeks to expand the CLT framework for education purposes.

In the future CLT based PBAW research could be extended further in a model considering the required competence of learning PBAW course. In the book only reading ability, learning strategy, and topic knowledge are considered in deciding the effect of doing PBAW. We need a whole competence model to assess the starting and ending abilities from the dimension of cognitive ability, affection orientation and others. Take motivation as an example, how motivation can influence our ability to process information in a variety of cognitive load circumstances is one worthy of answering. To date, this factor has received minor thought. Recent findings such as intrinsic motivation (for example, writing enjoyment) could inhibit learning and decision-making should serve as a point of departure for more in-depth research. Also, how cognitive load is related to the effort of learning and performance across levels of task complexity deserves to be learned.

Another factor which has been equally under-researched is assessment. While CLT's emphasis has been essentially on learning and instruction, it has been less concerned with addressing how end terms and assessment criteria can affect the extent to which we actually engage in learning. The experiment by Lafleur and colleagues demonstrates that slightly more challenging end terms and assessment criteria can stimulate learners to invest more effort in learning. In the context of the model in Fig. 1, more challenging end terms and assessment criteria may result in a larger cube that comprises more levels of complexity and/or fidelity. This may undermine learning when the combination of intrinsic and extraneous cognitive load is taken to the limits of working memory but may stimulate learning when extraneous cognitive load is kept to a minimum and intrinsic cognitive load is around an optimum. The aforementioned experiment should be replicated in a variety of settings, with different kinds of courses, at different stages of a curriculum, and in different contexts of learning at the workplace to further assess this statement.

To conclude, this chapter has provided a model for education design along with guidelines for future research. Given the excellent context education delivers for extending CLT further, by incorporating factors hardly considered thus far, both L2 writing education *and* CLT could thrive on an increased application of CLT principles. Given that the sum of intrinsic and extraneous cognitive load should respect the limits of working memory and learning is about dealing with intrinsic cognitive load, extraneous cognitive load should be minimized while intrinsic cognitive load should be optimized. Instructional support that reduces extraneous cognitive load among novice learners may contribute to extraneous cognitive load among more proficient learners; this instructional support should therefore fade gradually as learners become more proficient. More proficient learners have more elaborate cognitive schemas of a type of learning task and therefore experience a lower intrinsic cognitive load than their less proficient peers when dealing with a task of that type; learning task complexity should gradually increase as learners become more proficient. Measures of intrinsic and extraneous cognitive load should be used along with performance indicators to facilitate further study and the progress of individual learners in a course, curriculum or individual learning trajectory. CLT would lead PBAW educators understand clearly the efficiency of teaching and learning, and therefore improve the arrangement of curriculum to be more scientific.

**References**:

Dochy, F., Segers, M., Van den Bossche, P., & Gijbels, D. (2015). Effects of problem-based learning: A meta-analysis. Learning and Instruction, 13, 533–568.

Kalyuga, S., & Hanham, J. (2011). Instructing in generalized knowledge structures to develop flexible problem-solving skills. Contemporary Educational Psychology, 27, 63–68. https://doi.org/10.1016/j.cedpsych.2015.03.003.

Kalyuga, S., Ayres, P., Chandler, P., & Sweller, J. (2015). The expertise reversal effect. Educational Psychologist, 38(1), 23–31. https://doi.org/10.1207/S15326985EP3801_4.

Kalyuga, S., Chandler, P., & Sweller, J. (2001). When problem-solving is superior to studying worked examples. Journal of Educational Psychology, 93(3), 579–588. https://doi.org/10.1037/0022-0663.93.3.579.

Lafleur, A., Côté, L., & Leppink, J. (2015). Influences of OSCE design on students' diagnostic reasoning. Medical Education, 49(2), 203–214. https://doi.org/10.1111/medu.12628.

Leppink, J., & Duvivier, R. (2015). Twelve tips for medical curriculum design from a cognitive load theory perspective. Medical Teacher. Advance online publication. https://doi.org/10.3109/0142159X.2015.1132829.

Leppink, J., & Van den Heuvel, M. P. (2015). Measuring cognitive load in educational settings: A review of the literature. Educational Psychology Review, 27(4), 599–622.

Leppink, J., Paas, F., Van der Vleuten, C. P. M., Van Gog, T., & Van Merriënboer, J. J. G. (2015). Development of an instrument for measuring different types of cognitive load. Behavioral Research Methods, 45(2), 1058–1072. https://doi.org/10.3758/s13428-013-0409-5.

Lloyd-Jones, G., Margetson, D., & Bligh, J. G. (1998). Problem-based learning: A coat of many colours. Medical Education, 32, 492–494.

Sweller, J., Van Merrienboer, J. J. G., & Paas, F. G. W. C. (1998). Cognitive architecture and instructional design. Educational Psychology Review, 10(3), 251–296. https://doi.org/10.1023/A:1022885921375.

Young, M. F., & Stanton, J. M. (2002). Designing effective e-learning environments for complex tasks. Educational Technology Research and Development, 50(4), 29–43.

**图书在版编目(CIP)数据**

任务型学术英语写作认知负荷的调节策略研究 / 王
春岩著. -- 上海 : 上海三联书店, 2024. 12. -- ISBN
978-7-5426-8779-1

Ⅰ. H319.36

中国国家版本馆 CIP 数据核字第 2024CG0511 号

---

任务型学术英语写作认知负荷的调节策略研究

著　　者 / 王春岩

责任编辑 / 殷亚平
装帧设计 / 徐　徐
监　　制 / 姚　军
责任校对 / 王凌霄

出版发行 / 上海三联书店
　　　　　(200041)中国上海市静安区威海路 755 号 30 楼
邮　　箱 / sdxsanlian@sina.com
联系电话 / 编辑部: 021-22895517
　　　　　发行部: 021-22895559
印　　刷 / 上海惠敦印务科技有限公司

版　　次 / 2024 年 12 月第 1 版
印　　次 / 2024 年 12 月第 1 次印刷
开　　本 / 890 mm × 1240 mm　1/32
字　　数 / 280 千字
印　　张 / 13.25
书　　号 / ISBN 978-7-5426-8779-1/H·149
定　　价 / 88.00 元

敬启读者,如发现本书有印装质量问题,请与印刷厂联系 13917066329